KEYNES AND THE MODERN WORLD

T0312226

KEYNES AND THE MODERN WORLD

*Proceedings of the
Keynes Centenary Conference,
King's College, Cambridge*

Edited by
DAVID WORSWICK
and
JAMES TREVITHICK

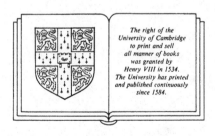

The right of the
University of Cambridge
to print and sell
all manner of books
was granted by
Henry VIII in 1534.
The University has printed
and published continuously
since 1584.

CAMBRIDGE UNIVERSITY PRESS

Cambridge
London   New York   New Rochelle
Melbourne   Sydney

CAMBRIDGE UNIVERSITY PRESS
Cambridge, New York, Melbourne, Madrid, Cape Town, Singapore, São Paulo, Delhi

Cambridge University Press
The Edinburgh Building, Cambridge CB2 8RU, UK

Published in the United States of America by Cambridge University Press, New York

www.cambridge.org
Information on this title: www.cambridge.org/9780521108027

First published 1983
Reprinted 1984
This digitally printed version 2009

A catalogue record for this publication is available from the British Library

Library of Congress Catalogue Card Number: 83-18944

ISBN 978-0-521-25853-1 hardback
ISBN 978-0-521-10802-7 paperback

CONTENTS

PREFACE

John Maynard Keynes was born in 1883 and died in 1946. He gave a large share of his working life to the Royal Economic Society, as Secretary and as Editor of the *Economic Journal*. As a memorial to him the Society planned an edition of his collected works. Under the direction of Sir Austin Robinson, with the help of Elizabeth Johnson, Donald Moggridge and many others, the magnificent edition of the *Collected Writings of John Maynard Keynes* reached its concluding volume this year, the centenary of his birth, with only the complete index still to come. The extraordinary range of Keynes's interests and the brilliance of his intellect are now readily accessible to scholars throughout the world, and it was decided to celebrate the centenary year by calling an international conference of economists to draw some of the lessons of his revolutionary contribution to economic ideas. Of possible locations for such a conference Cambridge was thought most appropriate, and if in Cambridge it should be held in King's College of which Keynes was both Fellow and Bursar. The Cambridge Faculty of Economics and King's College both welcomed the Society's proposal and joined in the preparations of the conference, which was held on 15 and 16 July 1983.

The theme chosen for the conference was the relevance of the ideas of Keynes for the world today. Had such a conference been held twenty five years ago its outlook would almost certainly have been congratulatory and optimistic. In strong contrast with the Great Depression of the 1930s, the two decades after the Second World War saw the world enjoying rapid growth of output and exceptionally high employment. The Bretton Woods monetary system was working well enough to permit the removal of trade controls and the reduction of tariffs, and international trade was growing at a rate without precedent in world history. Many economists would have attributed a good part of this success to the absorption into policy making of the analysis of Keynes. There might well have been many detailed matters of concern about the way the real world was developing and about the state of economics – when would there not? – but the general tone of a conference on the ideas of Keynes would have been complacent. No such complacency is possible today.

The world economy is now experiencing the worst set-back since the Depression of the 1930s. The *General Theory* was published at a time when unemployment in Britain had already fallen from around three millions to below two millions and was still falling. Today unemployment is over three millons and still rising. The international order of Bretton Woods has crumbled, not to be replaced by some superior system, but to give way to no system at all. Turbulence in the real world is matched by turbulence in economic theory. The Keynesian consensus was challenged in the late 1960s by the first wave of monetarism and in the 1970s the idea of rational expectations raised doubts about the validity of Keynesian econometric models, whether as descriptions of the economy or as guides to economic policy. Far from being aids to full employment, fiscal and monetary instruments, argue some, can have no lasting effect on real output and employment.

Keynes's most famous book, the *General Theory of Employment, Interest and Money*, was 'chiefly addressed to my fellow economists. I hope that it will be intelligible to others'. The essays in this collection were commissioned in the same spirit from professional economists who knew they would be addressing their fellows. Inevitably, therefore, some of the arguments presented here are technical and may be inaccessible to the general public. But the issues are of great importance and the layman who listens in to these debates will find much to interest him.

The *General Theory* has been criticized for simplifying its arguments by assuming a 'closed economy'. How, in particular, could a British economist make such an assumption, when every schoolboy knows that Britain is an open economy, heavily involved in trade with the rest of the world? But the device can be defended. Just because the book is not about any specific national economy, it can focus more sharply on certain fundamental theoretical issues. Three of these essays, by Kaldor, Meltzer and Leijonhufvud, are concerned with these theoretical questions as well as others which have been raised since. In the light of new experience and new knowledge, how much of Keynes's edifice still stands, and how much must be modified or replaced? Kaldor asks why the ideas of the *General Theory* generated so much controversy which has lasted so long. He argues that had Keynes shown a full awareness of increasing returns and imperfect competition, much of the controversy about the nature of Keynesian theory might have been avoided. He also thinks that the stir caused by monetarism would have been less if Keynes had explicitly recognized the quantity of money as an endogenous variable, and not uniquely fixed by the monetary authority. Meltzer compares his own interpretation of Keynes's theory with some specific monetarist theories, notably that of Friedman and the more recent version incorporating rational expectations. Monetarists build on the micro-foundations of Walrasian general equilibrium, but Keynes was not a Walrasian. The missing links are a valid theory of the risk premium, and of the liquidity premium. Leijonhufvud asserts that the younger generation of economists consider Keynesian economics to belong to the history of economic thought and that they adhere to the New Classical Economics. In his opinion, however, there is something profoundly unsatisfactory about the handling of the relationship between nominal and real magnitudes. To help sort things out he provides a taxonomy of three types of monetarism, real and nominal, and well- and ill-behaved expectations and a spectrum of monetary regimes. Godley's paper is also theoretical, but of a different kind, in which he develops a particular model designed to remedy a specific deficiency which he finds in Keynes.

Though undoubtedly his finest intellectual achievement, as well as his most influential book, the *General Theory* was not the whole of what Keynes had to give to economics and to the welfare of his fellow citizens. Nowadays the typical professional economist is an academic, writing highly technical papers addressed to other academics. Keynes was an academic, but he was a great many other things as well. In particular he was a man of action, an economic statesman, deeply involved in developments in Britain and in the wider world. His criticism of the restoration of the gold standard at the pre-war parity was powerful and prophetic. During the Second World War he strove to secure a post-war international order which would prevent the spread of depression which had dislocated the world economy in the 1930s. His views on these matters are surveyed in Williamson's paper. In the Great Depression there was mass unemployment but little fear of inflation, whereas in recent times the simultaneous appearance of high inflation with high unemployment has seemed to put in question conventional Keynesian policies. Scitovsky's paper examines the nature of inflation.

Each of the six main papers was sent in advance to two discussants, with an eye on the need to secure wide representation of conflicting views. The papers and comments were posted to the participants and were taken as read at the conference, so giving maximum opportunity for open discussion. The proceedings were recorded, and Geoff Harcourt, assisted by Jayati Ghosh and Terry O'Shaughnessy, have prepared a summary, which includes also introductory remarks which extended beyond the written papers, and a summary of the principal authors' replies.

On 16 July King's College gave a dinner to mark the centenary, at which three close colleagues of Keynes, Professors Sir Austin Robinson, Richard

Braithwaite and James Meade, gave their personal impressions of Keynes the man. These speeches were recorded and it is with great pleasure that we include them in this volume.

Throughout the book the symbol J. M. K. followed by the appropriate Roman numeral has been used for references to the Royal Economic Society edition of *The Collected Writings of John Maynard Keynes*.

August 1983   G.D.N.W.
                                                                J.A.T.

LIST OF PARTICIPANTS

Christopher Allsopp   *University of Oxford*
M.J. Artis   *University of Manchester*
Lord Balogh   *University of Oxford*
Andrew Britton   *National Institute of Economic and Social Research*
A.J. Brown   *University of Leeds*
Sir Terence Burns   *H.M. Treasury*
Sir Alec Cairncross   *University of Oxford*
D.G. Champernowne   *University of Cambridge*
Victoria Chick   *University College, London*
R.W. Clower   *U.C.L.A.*
Francis Cripps   *University of Cambridge*
David Currie   *Q.M.C., London*
Paul Davidson   *Rutgers University*
Phyllis Deane   *University of Cambridge*
Sidney Dell   *U.N., New York*
Rudiger Dornbusch   *M.I.T.*
J.C.R. Dow   *Bank of England*
C.H. Feinstein   *University of York*
John Flemming   *Bank of England*
W.A.H. Godley   *University of Cambridge*
C.A.E. Goodhart   *Bank of England*
R.M. Goodwin   *University of Cambridge*
F.H. Hahn   *University of Cambridge*
G. Harcourt   *University of Cambridge*
Susan Howson   *University of Toronto*
Sir Bryan Hopkin   *University College, Cardiff*
Elizabeth Johnson   *University of Chicago*
Lord Kaldor   *University of Cambridge*
Lord Kahn   *University of Cambridge*
Axel Leijonhufvud   *U.C.L.A.*

List of participants

Edmond Malinvaud *Institut National de la Statistique et des Etudes Economiques, Paris*
R.C.O. Matthews *University of Cambridge*
James Meade *University of Cambridge*
A.H. Meltzer *Carnegie-Mellon University*
Marcus Miller *University of Warwick*
Franco Modigliani *M.I.T.*
Donald Moggridge *University of Toronto*
R.R. Neild *University of Cambridge*
Luigi Pasinetti *Università Cattolica del Sacro Cuore, Milan*
Don Patinkin *Hebrew University of Jerusalem*
Jukka Pekkarinen *University of Helsinki*
M.H. Pesaran *University of Cambridge*
Michael Posner *Social Science Research Council*
W.B. Reddaway *University of Cambridge*
Sir Austin Robinson *University of Cambridge*
Lord Roll *University of Southampton*
Tibor Rybczynski *Royal Economic Society*
P.A. Samuelson *M.I.T.*
W.S. Salant *Brookings Institution, Washington*
Tibor Scitovsky *Stanford University*
Maurice Scott *University of Oxford*
A.K. Sen *University of Oxford*
G.L.S. Shackle *University of Liverpool*
Z.A. Silberston *Imperial College, London*
R.J.A. Skidelsky *University of Warwick*
R.M. Solow *M.I.T.*
L. Tarshis *University of Toronto*
A.P. Thirlwall *University of Kent*
James Tobin *Yale University*
J.A. Trevithick *University of Cambridge*
John Williamson *Institute for International Economics, Washington*
Thomas Wilson *University of Glasgow*
Donald Winch *University of Sussex*
G.D.N. Worswick *University of Oxford*

1

Keynesian Economics after Fifty Years

NICHOLAS KALDOR

INTRODUCTION

Keynes's *General Theory of Employment, Interest and Money* is undoubtedly regarded as the most important book on economics in the
twentieth century, and this view would be shared, I think, by those who are
wholly opposed to its teaching as well as by its adherents. Nearly 50 years
after its appearance controversy still rages around its basic ideas and
prescriptions, and I do not think that any major economist in the West
would regard the issues raised by Keynes as finally settled. In this respect
Keynes's *General Theory* is in sharp contrast to all the previous pathbreak-
ing books on economics – such as Adam Smith's *Wealth of Nations* or
Ricardo's *Principles* or Marshall's *Principles* – whose main tenets have not
given rise to violent controversies in the same way as Keynes's. The possible
exception is Karl Marx's *Capital*, but then Marx was a revolutionary which
Keynes was certainly not – Keynes's avowed purpose was to save the
capitalist system, not to destroy it.

Why then all this turbulence? We have authors who have written several
fat books on Keynes (and I presume still keep on writing them) the main
message of which is that Keynes said nothing new, and others who spent
the better part of their life-time in demonstrating (unsuccessfully in my
view) that Keynes was entirely wrong.

I cannot point to any single dominant reason for this – I believe there
must be several.

The first and perhaps the most important is that Keynes's main message
ran counter to the basic tenet of respectable practitioners of the art which
always has been that production in general was confined by the scarcity of
human and material resources; that human welfare can be improved only
by 'economizing' in the use of scarce resources (whether of land, labour or
capital) which means securing the best allocation of what is available. This
meant that an 'economy' – a term which implied a community who satisfy

1

their wants by mutual cooperation between their members – was necessarily constrained in its activities by its resource endowment: it was the poverty (or insufficiency) of resources which limited the satisfaction of wants. Since the endowment of resources available to a 'community' was supposed to be determined exogenously, the welfare of the community could be maximised (or its misery minimised) only by the free play of market forces under a free enterprise system, with the minimum of government interference and regulation.

Keynes asserted the contrary. His main proposition was that in normal circumstances, production in general was limited by effective demand which determined *how much* of potential resources were effectively utilised. Hence there was scope (in normal circumstances) for securing greater material welfare through the purposeful direction of the economy by a combination of fiscal and monetary policies which could secure full employment whilst avoiding inflation.

In order to explain how this could be done Keynes put forward a model of the interaction of a limited number of strategic variables operating on the economy which serve to explain how, in given circumstances, the level of output as a whole and its movement were determined. This gave birth to a new branch of economics, macro-economics, distinguished by the fact that unlike the prevailing economic theory it made empirical hypotheses concerning the behaviour of groups or categories of individuals, the validity of which could be refuted, by observation if not by experiment, and which made it possible to make quantitative forecasts of how the 'economy' would behave in response to either policy changes introduced by the Government, or to external changes due *e.g.* to new inventions or spontaneous changes in expectations.

Thus the main reason why Keynes's book found such a widespread echo so soon after its publication was that it brought economics 'back to earth' – back to its original purpose of being an instrument for formulating rational policies concerning the economy.

Though the initial reactions by the economics profession was almost uniformly adverse – as shown by the reviews of the book by leading economists in English or American journals – the new ideas made rapid strides among academic economists of the younger generations, and also among civil servants, advisers to Ministers and even financial journalists. No doubt the outbreak of the war greatly lessened the normal resistance to new ideas. Thus in Britain in 1941 Keynes (by that time an adviser to the Chancellor of the Exchequer) managed to embody the new principles in the Budget, which meant aiming at the 'right amount' of fiscal deficit – a notion which only made sense in terms of a Keynesian model of the economy. From then on, and until the end of the 1970s, the annual 'Budget judgement' meant that the primary function of taxation was regarded as the avoidance of inflationary pressures whilst securing the right climate for expansion in the economy. And well before the end of the war, the Coalition Government gave a solemn undertaking that henceforth 'the maintenance of a high and stable level of employment' would be one of the Government's principal obligations and responsibilities.[1] Much the same intellectual change occurred in the United States where the new principles of economic management were embodied in the Employment Act of 1946. They were also embodied in the new French Constitution of 1946, in Article 55 of the Charter of the United Nations, and Article 104 of the Rome Treaty. None of this would have occurred without the appearance of Keynes's *General Theory* – since 'maintaining full employment' would not have occurred to economists or politicians as a feasible policy objective.

In the following quarter of a century – up to 1973 – the Western world did in fact experience an unprecedented period of economic expansion, combined in most countries with full employment or even 'over-full employment' in the sense that the demand for labour could only be satisfied through the various states allowing a considerable immigration from the surplus labour areas of less developed countries – whether from overseas dependencies or ex-dependencies (as in the case of Britain or France) or from the less developed countries of Europe (as in the case of Germany, Holland, Switzerland, Austria, etc.). How far this was the result of the adoption or the deliberate pursuit of Keynesian policies, or how far it would have happened in any case as a consequence of a prolonged economic boom is a complex question which admits of no simple answer. There were some countries (such as France) where the acceptance of Keynesian ideas led to state investment planning in the form of a succession of five year plans, carried out in cooperation between the state and private enterprises – with the result that France became the fastest growing country in Europe. The results for Britain were not nearly as good (mainly I think because there was too little investment at home and too much abroad; and a strong inborn resistance, absent in France, to the State 'meddling' in the affairs of business). Nevertheless the 25 years 1948–73 recorded a higher rate of progress than any earlier period of comparable length in British history, and, except for the last few years of that period, unemployment

---

[1] This obligation was formally abandoned only with the arrival of Mrs. Thatcher's Government in 1979 – some 36 years later; although in practice it was abandoned after 1973 for various reasons (mentioned later), one of which was that Keynesian demand management proved incompatible with our membership of the Common Market.

remained consistently low (well below Beveridge's 3 per cent target) despite considerable immigration.[2]

In the 1970s this happy era came to an end with a rapid inflation of both commodity prices and industrial wages; as a result of which the Governments of industrial countries became pre-occupied with the dual problem of inflation and balance of payments deficits, both of which they believed could be corrected by monetary and fiscal policies. Hence the international conditions which Keynes had always regarded as essential for national full employment policies ceased to hold, and the cumulative process of credit contraction which he had much dreaded was finally unleashed in the post-war world.[3]

Hence recession hit a number of countries and it became generally believed (rightly or wrongly) that 'Keynesian' instruments of economic policy were unavailable for coping with this situation. At the same time the anti-Keynesian school of economists, the 'new' monetarists, rapidly gained followers among influential people more or less simultaneously in a number of countries and this was combined by widespread and rapidly growing antagonism to Keynesian ideas. The reason for this antagonism, not openly acknowledged, was the change in the power structure of society which the pursuit of Keynesian policies has brought about. This was foreseen well before the adoption of Keynesian methods of demand management. Thus in an article in *The Times* in January 1943 on post-war Full Employment it was stated:

Unemployment is not a mere accidental blemish in a private-enterprise economy. On the contrary, it is part of the essential mechanism of the system, and has a definitive function to fulfil. The first function of unemployment (which has always existed in open or disguised forms) is that it maintains the authority of masters over men. The master has normally been in a position to say: 'If you don't want the job, there are plenty of others who do'. When the man can say 'If you don't want to employ me there are plenty of others who will' the situation is radically altered.[4]

---

[2] R. C. O. Mathews (*Economic Journal*, September 1968) tried to demonstrate that all this owed little to Keynesian fiscal management, since it was the increase in *private* investment (in relation to the national income) which filled the pre-war gap in effective demand. However, as I argued (*Economic Journal*, March 1971, p. 9) the main effect of the Government's fiscal policy was to ensure a continued *growth* in demand, which *induced* the increase in investment. (Investment is very dependent on the actual (and expected) rate of growth of demand.)

[3] See in particular his remarkable speech in the House of Lords on 23 May 1944, reproduced in J.M.K., xxvi, p. 16.

[4] The doctrine is usually associated with Karl Marx who argued that capitalism can only function with a 'reserve army' of unemployed labour. But Marx himself owes these ideas (though he never seems to have acknowledged it) to Adam Smith, who wrote in the *Wealth of Nations* that normally there is always a scarcity of jobs relative to job-seekers: 'There

The change in the workers' bargaining position which should follow from the abolition of unemployment would show itself in another and more subtle way. Unemployment in a private enterprise economy has not only the function of preserving discipline in industry, but also indirectly the function of preserving the value of money. If free wage bargaining as we have known it hitherto, is continued in conditions of full employment, there would be a constant upward pressure upon money wage-rates. This phenomenon also exists at the present time, and is kept within bound by the appeal of patriotism. In peace-time the vicious spiral of wages and prices might become chronic.[5]

The second main point is that whereas the main proposition of Keynes's *General Theory* concerning the critical role of demand in determining aggregate output and the possibility or likelihood of an 'under-employment equilibrium' with involuntary unemployment, withstood the attacks launched against it, many of the theoretical constructs which he invented or employed by way of proof or explanation did not. In other words his famous passage on Marshall (written on the occasion of his obituary of Marshall in the *Economic Journal* of 1924) sounds almost prophetic since it appears to be far more applicable to his own future work than to that of his great teacher:

It was an essential truth to which he held firmly that those individuals who are endowed with a special genius for the subject and have a powerful economic intuition will often be more right in their conclusions and implicit presumptions than in their explanations and explicit statements. That is to say, their intuitions will be in advance of their analysis and their terminology.

To this should perhaps be added the famous concluding paragraph to the Preface of the *General Theory* written in December, 1935:

The composition of this book has been for the author a long struggle to escape, and so must the reading of it be for most readers if the author's assault upon him is to be successful – a struggle of escape from habitual modes of thought and expression . . . The difficulty lies, not in the new ideas, but in escaping from the old ones which ramify, for those brought up as most of us have been, into every corner of our minds.[6]

could seldom be any scarcity of hands nor could the masters be obliged to bid against one another in order to get them. The hands, on the contrary, would in this case, naturally multiply beyond their employment. There would be a constant scarcity of employment and the labourers would be obliged to bid against one another in order to get it. If in such a country the wages of labour had ever been more than sufficient to maintain the labourer and to enable him to bring up a family, the competition of the labourers and the interest of the masters would soon reduce them to the lowest rate which is consistent with common humanity' (Book I, ch. VIII, p. 24).

[5] 'Planning Full Employment – Alternative Solutions of a Dilemma', *The Times*, 23 January 1943. (A 'turnover' article; the article was unsigned but its authorship is generally attributed to Joan Robinson.)

[6] *General Theory*, p. viii.

The result was an extraordinary paradox in that while Keynes took every opportunity to emphasise the novelty of his approach, and his rejection of the 'fundamental postulates' of the 'classical economists' (by which he meant everybody who figures in 'mainstream' economics from Adam Smith to Marshall) this merely disguised the extent to which his theory suffered from an almost slavish adherence to prevailing (Marshallian) doctrine – to which his own ideas were 'fitted' more in the manner of erecting an extra floor or balcony here or there, while preserving the pre-existing building. This, I hope to show, applies to Keynes's most radical novelties, such as the principle of effective demand, the liquidity preference theory of interest, his 'revision' of the quantity theory of money as well as his retaining the fiction of a 'closed economy' which prevented him from analysing the more basic (or intriguing) question of why unemployment looms so much larger in some countries than in others.

In the following section I shall deal with each of these aspects in turn.

THE PRINCIPLE OF EFFECTIVE DEMAND

The core of Keynes's theory is the principle of effective demand which is best analysed as a development or refinement of Say's law, rather than a complete rejection of the ideas behind that law. Say, like Ricardo or John Stuart Mill (or later Walras), takes as his starting point the proposition that ultimately all economic activity consists in the exchange of goods and services between different 'agents', hence 'demand' and 'supply' are merely different aspects of the same thing; when two economic agents exchange two commodities, x and y between them, the supply of x by A is at the same time A's demand for y; the supply of y by B is B's demand for x. If, for sake of convenience, prices are expressed in a common medium the *numéraire*, the situation is not fundamentally altered; the money value of things sold is equal to the money value of things bought for *each* individual and *therefore* for all individuals taken together. Hence the total value of the things sold in terms of money is identical to the total value of things bought; or, as Mill put it, 'could we suddenly double the productive powers of the country, we could double the supply of commodities in every market; but we should by the same stroke, double the purchasing power'.[7] Hence 'Supply creates its own demand.'

However the application of this idea takes different forms at different stages of economic development. In a simple barter economy, when goods are exchanged against goods but each commodity is valued in terms of a

---

[7] Mill, *Principles of Political Economy*, Book III, ch. XIV, para. 2.

common unit, the value of the initial bundle of commodities of each participant is no greater or less than the value of the final bundle – at any rate if we abstract from the 'tâtonnement' problem, the possibility that some of the commodities are exchanged at 'false' prices. When however we go a step further and allow for the existence of money as a medium of exchange this equivalence no longer holds – or not necessarily, because some of the money obtained by sellers may not be used for the purchase of goods of equivalent value on the *same day*; the peasant who brought a bundle of produce to the market may end up with a smaller bundle of goods (in terms of value) and with some unspent money (i.e. with some 'savings', even if only from one market day to the next); conversely, some participants may buy things with money left over from the trading of earlier days, and which supplement their purchases from current sales. The existence of durable money which can be stored thus destroys the necessary equivalence between demand and supply in the aggregate – on a particular 'market day' the one can be larger or smaller than the other.[8]

All this applied to what Keynes called, in an early draft, a 'co-operative economy' – where different producers satisfy at least some of their needs through exchanges of their own produce with those of others. He distinguished this sharply from the 'entrepreneur economy'[9] which corresponds to what Marx called 'capitalism', where production is carried on in large-scale units by hired labour, with the entrepreneur deciding how much to produce (i.e. how many people to employ) in the light of their expectation of sales-proceeds from different levels of output. In other words the entrepreneurs incur costs which become 'factor incomes' in the hands of the recipients[10] and which are the primary source of purchasing power for the goods produced. To that extent it is true to say that 'supply creates its own demand'. But the two are not (or need not be) equivalent to one another; demand generated by supply may not be enough to satisfy the expectation of entrepreneurs for two primary reasons (as we shall see, there can be several others): *first*, because the recipients of incomes may not devote all of it to the purchase of goods (or not immediately); *second*, even if they spent it fully and on the same day, the entrepreneur would only

---

[8] Neo-classical economists would argue that the existence of durable money necessarily leads to a 'money market' where those with surplus money lend it out to those who are deficient of it for a consideration which takes the form of interest. It is Keynes's contention however that the mere existence of a market of 'loanable funds' will not suffice to restore the overall equality of demand and supply at all levels of output.

[9] See J.M.K., XXIX, pp. 66–8.

[10] Each individual entrepreneur incurs costs in buying goods or services from other entrepreneurs, as well as hiring labour. However these are also resolvable into 'factor incomes', once double counting is eliminated.

succeed in recovering his costs, leaving nothing over for his own remuneration. To induce entrepreneurs to stay in business the sales proceeds must exceed the costs incurred in production – in other words firms must make a profit – and profits cannot be treated as part of 'factor incomes', fixed in advance; they reflect the *outcome* of the whole operation, and they can be negative as well as positive. One can say (as Keynes does) that entrepreneurs require a larger total profit for a larger output; but if so, such profits form part of a *minimum* 'supply price' which can be smaller (as well as larger) than the realised sales-proceeds. If realised sales proceeds are inadequate, the entrepreneur will be induced to contract operations. Supply will be reduced, but this in turn, by reducing factor-incomes, will reduce Demand, thus leading to a further reduction of supply, etc.[11]

The originality in Keynes's conception of effective demand lies in the division of demand into two components, an endogenous component and an exogenous component. It is the endogenous component which reflects (*i.e.*, is automatically generated by) production, for much the same reasons as those given by Ricardo, Mill or Say – the difference is only that in a money economy (*i.e.* in an economy where things are not directly exchanged, but only through the intermediation of money) aggregate demand can be a *function* of aggregate supply (both measured in money terms) without being *equal* to it – the one can be some fraction of the other. To make the two equal requires the addition of the exogenous component (which could be one of a number of things, of which capital expenditure – 'investment' – is only one) the value of which is extraneously determined. Given the relationship between aggregate output and the endogenous demand generated by it (where the latter can be assumed to be a monotonic function of the former), there is only one level of output at which output (or employment) is in 'equilibrium' – that particular level at which the amount of exogenous demand is just equal to the difference between the value of output and the value of the endogenous demand generated by it. If the relationship between output and endogenous demand (which Keynes called 'the propensity to consume') is taken as given, it is the value of exogenous demand which determines what total production and employment will be. A rise in exogenous demand, for whatever reasons, will cause an increase in production which will be some multiple of the former, since the increase in production thus caused will cause a consequential increase in endogenous demand, by a 'multiplier' process. How large this secondary increase will be will depend on a lot of

---

[11] Major Douglas, who saw this point but was not able to see further, derived from this the conclusion that a capitalist economy necessarily tends to shrink with more and more unemployment unless factor incomes were supplemented by a 'social dividend'.

things such as the distribution of the additional output between wages and profits, and the change in productivity (or in costs per unit of output) associated with the increase in production, etc.

The critical role played by exogenous demand in the process of income generation has another aspect, less frequently emphasized – i.e., that given the basic behavioural relationships (such as the consumption function) an increase in resources, whether of labour or capital (or in their efficiency due to technical progress, etc.) will not serve to increase actual production unless the exogenous component of demand is increased at the same time. In many cases the same factor may operate on both but this is not necessarily so, nor is there any presumption that the rate of growth of the one will be closely geared to the rate of growth of the other. A capitalist economy (for reasons explained below) is not 'self-adjusting' in the sense that an increase in potential output will automatically induce a corresponding growth of actual output. This will only be the case if exogenous demand expands at the same time to the required degree; and as this cannot be taken for granted, the maintenance of full employment in a growing economy requires a deliberate policy of demand management.

This was the chief message which Keynes intended to convey. It was also the message which economists found most difficult to accept – at least all those who regarded the Walrasian model of the economy as the valid paradigm of the functioning of a market economy (and they comprised a far wider group than those who actually studied Walras). Walras' general equilibrium model presupposes the universal rule of perfect competition and constant returns to scale, the twin assumptions necessary to ensure that all markets 'clear' (i.e. that all resources are fully utilized and the production of each commodity is at its attainable maximum, given the production of all other commodities.[12])

But in the absence of these twin assumptions the mere existence of competition between sellers ('firms') will not in itself ensure the full utilization of resources unless all firms *expand in concert*. Any one firm, acting in isolation, may find that the market for its own products is limited, and will therefore refrain from expanding its production even when its marginal costs are well below the ruling price. Under these conditions involuntary unemployment could only be avoided if something – the growth of some extraneous component of demand – drives the economy forward.

Keynes was no student of Walras. However, there was enough in Marshall (particularly in Book v, the short period theory of value) to raise

---

[12] For a simple demonstration of this, see my paper, 'What is Wrong with Economic Theory', *Quarterly Journal of Economics*, August 1975.

the same kind of qualms – *why* don't all markets behave in such a way to *compel* the full utilization of resources? Marshall's own theory suggested that saving represents an indirect demand for commodities in the same way as consumption which sets up direct demand. Savings provide the supply of 'loanable funds' which, given an efficient capital market which equates supply and demand, governs the amount of capital expenditure incurred. This amounts to a denial of the whole idea of an exogenous source of demand – the latter notion presupposes that the supply and demand for savings are brought into equality by changes in income and employment, and not by the 'price' of savings in the capital market, which is the rate of interest. In order to explain why the market for loans is not 'market-clearing' in the same sense as other markets, Keynes introduced the liquidity-preference theory of interest – which, as is evident from his own later writings, was added more or less as an afterthought.[13]

But for Keynes's critics it was the key assumption needed for showing why the Rate of Interest does *not* behave in the manner required to generate capital expenditure that equals full employment savings. In other words, but for the downward rigidity of interest rates, involuntary unemployment would not exist, and classical economics would be vindicated.

This was the origin of the view that Keynesian economics depended on a 'liquidity trap' which could be effectively countermanded by an appropriate policy on interest rates.[14] It was the basis of the post-war 'neo-classical synthesis' according to which the notion of general equilibrium (of producers and consumers) guided automatically by the price-mechanism remains valid provided only that monetary policy (which meant interest rate policy) is so directed as to make the market for savings 'market-clearing' just like all the other markets. The 'micro-foundations of macro-economics' appeared to have shown that so long as one sticks to neo-classical micro-economics, Keynesian macro-economics amounts to very little.

[13] 'Alternative Theories of the Rate of Interest,' *Economic Journal*, June 1937, pp. 241–52, reprinted in J.M.K., XIV, pp. 201–15: 'As I have said above, the initial novelty lies in my maintaining that it is not the rate of interest, but the level of incomes which ensures equality between savings and investment. The arguments which lead up to this conclusion are independent of my subsequent theory of the rate of interest, and in fact I reached it before I reached the latter theory . . . But the result of it was to leave the rate of interest in the air . . . It was only when the search [for a productivity explanation] led repeatedly to what seemed to be circular reasoning that I hit on what I now think to be the true explanation . . . the rate of interest has to be established at the level which . . . equalises the attractions of holding idle cash and of holding a loan. It would be true to say that this does not carry us very far. But it gives us firm and intelligible ground from which to proceed . . . To speak of the "liquidity-preference Theory" of the Rate of Interest is indeed to dignify it too much. It is like speaking of the "professorship theory" of Ohlin or the "civil-servant theory" of Hawtrey.'

[14] The term 'liquidity trap' was first used by D. H. Robertson.

However the *main* attributes of Keynes's 'under-employment equilibrium' cannot be ascribed to the 'liquidity-trap' – to liquidity preference holding up interest rates. For the very notion of production in the aggregate being limited by demand pre-supposes a state of affairs in which the production of individual firms in industries of all kinds is limited by lack of orders and not by productive capacity. 'Keynesian' unemployment, as numerous writers have pointed out,[15] as distinct from 'classical' or 'Marxian' unemployment presupposes unutilized or under-utilized capacity as well as involuntary unemployment of labour. The existence of excess capacity on the other hand implies that the individual producer faces a *limited* demand for his product – not an infinitely elastic demand curve.

The discovery that competition in a capitalist economy does not conform to the assumption of pure or perfect competition was, just as Keynes's *General Theory*, the product of the intellectual ferment of the 1930s.[16] But for reasons that have never been satisfactorily explained, these latter discoveries were never properly integrated – though not because they were found either unimportant or irrelevant. In a paper published in early 1935[17] I showed that imperfect competition requires the assumption of falling long run cost curves (increasing returns to scale) up to some minimum level of output which is significant in relation to the size of the market as a whole. Given this fact, the competition of potential new producers will come to a halt when any benefit gained from selling a smaller output at a higher price is offset, or more than offset, by the higher cost per unit of the smaller output – when the demand curve for the products of the firm becomes 'tangential' to the cost curve. If on the other hand the long run cost curves are horizontal (i.e. there are constant returns to scale over the whole range – however small or however large the production) the process of the inflow of new producers (or new 'substitute' products – these come to the same thing since the products of different producers are never

[15] See e.g. Malinvaud, *The Theory of Unemployment Reconsidered*, Oxford, 1977.

[16] As is often the case, the original work in this field was done by economists such as A. A. Young at Harvard and G. F. Shove in Cambridge (England) who never published a systematic exposition of their ideas developed in their lecture courses; instead they left this task to their pupils, E. H. Chamberlin, the author of *The Theory of Monopolistic Competition* and Joan Robinson, the author of the *Economics of Imperfect Competition*, two books independently written which were published more or less simultaneously. However, just because the implications of the imperfect competition and oligopoly proved too difficult to incorporate into traditional theory, these doctrines (unlike Keynes's theory of employment) were gradually ignored and forgotten; the massive post-war work on the theory of general economic equilibrium – by Samuelson, Debreu, Arrow, Hahn and innumerable others – simply assumed away their existence (without attempting to justify this procedure either on empirical grounds or by showing that it is a harmless simplifying assumption which makes no difference to the conclusions).

[17] 'Market Imperfection and Excess Capacity', *Economica*, February 1935, reprinted in *Essays in Value and Distribution*, pp. 62–80.

wholly identical with each other) will not come to a halt until the output of the typical producer becomes small enough for the elasticity of demand to become infinite – when prices become equal to *both* average and marginal costs. Hence constant returns to scale (a consequence of an infinite divisibility of all factors) is sufficient to create perfect competition. I concluded 'We see therefore that the mathematical economists in taking perfect competition as their starting point, weren't such fools after all. For they assumed perfect divisibility of everything; and where everything is perfectly divisible, and consequently economies of scale are completely absent[18] perfect competition must necessarily establish itself solely as the result of the free play of economic forces. No degree of product differentiation and no possibility of further and further product variation will be sufficient to prevent this result, so long as all kinds of institutional monopolies and all kinds of indivisibilities are completely absent.'[19]

I *should* have added that under these conditions the 'free play of economic forces' will necessarily *also* establish (and maintain) a state of full employment. Unfortunately the above was published a year before the appearance of the *General Theory*, and the notion of a macro-economic 'under-employment equilibrium' was as yet unknown.[20] However, more recently, Mr M. L. Weitzman has demonstrated[21] that constant returns to scale, strictly interpreted, are a sufficient condition for the absence of 'involuntary unemployment'. The latter arises because a worker who is not offered a job cannot turn himself into his own employer (in the manner originally suggested by Wicksell) since he cannot compete effectively with firms organised for large-scale production.[22] But under these conditions no

---

[18] I have since changed my mind on the question whether perfect divisibility is a sufficient (as distinct from a necessary) condition of constant returns to scale (see 'The Irrelevance of Equilibrium Economics', Appendix on Indivisibilities and Increasing Returns, *Economic Journal*, December 1972, reprinted in *Further Essays in Economic Theory*, pp. 196–201).

[19] *Ibid.* p. 71.

[20] The most widespread explanation for unemployment at that time was that put forward by Pigou in the *Theory of Unemployment* (1933) which is best summed up by saying that unemployment was caused by the downward rigidity of money wages resulting from trade unions and collective bargaining, but which did not indicate (or not necessarily) that real wages correspond to the real supply price (or marginal disutility) of labour.

[21] 'Increasing Returns and the Foundations of Unemployment Theory', *Economic Journal*, December 1982, pp. 781–809.

[22] 'On the other hand with perfect divisibility, when unemployed factor units are all going about their business spontaneously employing themselves or being employed, the economy will automatically break out of unemployment. While the simple story of supply creating its own demand can be told in a closed barter economy, I do not see the existence of money, savings, investment or international trade *per se* invalidating the basic proposition that a logical inference of strict constant returns to scale and perfect competition is full employment. With sufficient divisibility of production, each unemployed factor unit has an

single firm finds it profitable to hire more workers and to produce more output, even though the marginal cost is well below the price set by the firm (but which is strongly dependent upon the prices set by other firms). If all firms acted in collusion, in *all* industries, it would be a different matter, since the increased output of all firms would increase the demand for every one of them sufficiently to justify the increased output. But in the absence of such co-ordinated action the system can be in equilibrium at *any* level of employment and output; Keynes has shown that it will gravitate to a level set by the exogenous components of demand. 'There is a sense therefore in which the natural habitat of effective demand macroeconomics is a monopolistically competitive micro-economy. Analogously, perfect competition and classical macroeconomics are natural counterparts.'[23]

The implication of this analysis however is that most of the debate around the legitimacy of Keynes's notion of 'underemployment equilibrium' was misplaced. It is the notion of a 'full employment equilibrium' which is an artificial creation, the consequence of the artificial assumption of constant returns to scale in all industries and over the whole range of outputs which implies infinite divisibility of everything. Once the artificial assumption of pure (or perfect) competition is abandoned, a Walrasian equilibrium with market-clearing prices in every market becomes a mirage, not in any way descriptive as a 'first approximation' of the conditions obtaining in the real world.

Hence in my view, most of the voluminous literature concerning the reconciliation of Keynesian analysis with Walrasian general equilibrium – in terms of 'disequilibrium' economics, inverted velocities of price and quantity adjustments, absence of the 'heavenly auctioneer', etc. – is beside the point. The two kinds of theory cannot be reconciled, simply because one concerns a purely artificial world of perfect competition, etc., whilst the other attempts to generalise about the real world.

Keynes himself was by no means fully conscious of this contrast. He

incentive to produce itself out of unemployment and market the product directly. In fact the unemployed are induced to create on their own scale an exact replica of the full employment economy from which they have been excluded' (Weitzman, *op. cit.* p. 793). It is not necessary of course that increasing returns with price-*making* firms should be the rule in every single industry. It is quite possible that some sectors of the economy (like parts of agriculture or mining) should conform to the rules of perfect competition, where sellers are price-*takers*, and where equilibrium output involves price = marginal cost. However the demand for their products will largely be determined by the incomes earned in the rest of the economy and provided that in the aggregate there is insufficient pressure for a balanced and simultaneous expansion in all markets – i.e. in other words, provided that the forces making for self-generated expansion are too weak, the economy will conform to the same characteristics as if increasing returns extended to every branch of the economy.

[23] *Ibid.*, p. 801.

accepted neo-classical theory (in its Marshallian version) as regards micro-economics – he assumed that prices of individual commodities are equal to, or determined by, marginal costs; that (real) wages reflect the marginal productivity of labour and that marginal productivity declines with increasing employment, so that, as he believed in the *General Theory*, there is an inverse relationship between real wages and employment. There is no mention of imperfect competition or its consequences in the *General Theory*. This prompted Jean de Largentaye, the French translator of the *General Theory*, to say that the acceptance of Marshallian micro-economics by Keynes made it possible for his opponents 'to invoke the authority of the *General Theory* in favour of views directly contrary to its essential teaching'.[24] Clearly the assumption of the prevalence of in-voluntary unemployment (which implies that the real wage is in excess of the marginal disutility of labour) is less plausible, or less intuitively obvious, when one assumes that increased employment is associated with lower real wages than when one assumes, on the contrary, that a larger volume of production and employment would be associated with *higher* real wages.

In an important article published in 1939,[25] written in response to the criticisms of Tarshis, Dunlop and Kalecki, Keynes retracted his earlier views concerning real wages and employment, saying that his assertions in the *General Theory* were based on Marshall's empirical findings (and not just on the theoretical requirements of neo-classical value theory) which however related to a succession of boom and depression periods prior to 1886. Investigating the cyclical variation in real wages since that date he found that the relationship was reversed; real wages were higher in periods of high employment than in depression periods, and he attributed this to the practical workings of the laws of 'imperfect competition in the modern quasi-competitive system' characterized by the fact that the individual producer 'is normally operating subject to decreasing average costs'.[26]

However while this 1939 article was a laudable attempt to rectify erroneous statements (both empirical and theoretical) in the *General Theory*, it would be an exaggeration to say that Keynes even then showed full awareness of the critical importance of increasing returns and imperfect competition to his general theory of employment. Had he done so, a great

---

[24] Jean de Largentaye, 'A Note on the General Theory', *Journal of Post-Keynesian Economics*, Vol. 1, No. 3, p. 9. (This is an English translation of the *Introduction* to the second French edition of the *General Theory*, published by Payot, Paris 1968.)

[25] 'Relative Movement of Real Wages and Output', *Economic Journal*, March 1939, pp. 34–51, reprinted in J.M.K., VII, pp. 394–412.

[26] *Ibid.*, p. 46 and 406–7.

deal of the post-war controversy concerning the *nature* of Keynesian theory might have been avoided. And as de Largentaye pointed out in the paper referred to above, by the time his 1939 article appeared the harm was done, and there were a number of influential writers who maintained, in line with Milton Friedman later, that the increase in employment associated with a Keynesian policy of demand management was both inflationary and temporary: the policy depended for its effectiveness on a misperception of future prices and hence in over-estimation of the expected real wage relatively to the money wage and the *actual* real wage. Such doctrines could not have gained a foothold had the existence of increasing returns in industry been appreciated and had it been recognised, in consequence, that any 'misperception' arising out of the expansion of demand and of employment is more likely to consist of an under-estimation rather than an over-estimation of the expected real wage relative to the actual wage.[27]

Mr Weitzman also shows that 'in an increasing return system, the equilibrium trade-off between real wages and employment will tend to make ordinary wage adjustment mechanisms ineffective or unstable'. Indeed 'a successful attempt to depress real wages would actually *increase* the equilibrium level of unemployment. The implication would seem to be that aggregate wage and price flexibility cannot make this kind of economy self-correcting. Under such circumstances wage stickiness may actually be a blessing.'[28]

This is very much in line with the spirit of the *General Theory* and, indeed, it is expressly stated in Chapter 19 on 'Changes in Money Wages' (p. 267) that 'money wage flexibility is not capable of maintaining full employment'. However the argument leading up to this conclusion is by no means as decisive and clear-cut as the conclusion itself, and no doubt Keynes would have been very grateful for Mr Weitzman's support had it been available to him – the more so since the latter's argument (unlike Keynes's) relates to *real* wages and not merely to money wages.

THE MONETARIST COUNTER-ASSAULT

The controversy over the question whether a capitalist economy is necessarily 'resource constrained' or whether it can be in under-

---

[27] It is in this respect that Kalecki's original model of unemployment equilibrium (read at the Leyden meeting of the Econometric Society in 1933 and published in *Econometrica*, 1935) which takes monopolistic competition as its starting point, is clearly superior to Keynes's. I heard Kalecki's exposition at Leyden but it was not until Keynes published his *General Theory* that I understood the notion of effective demand.

[28] *Ibid.* pp. 800–801.

employment equilibrium constrained by effective demand, is related to, though not identical with, another controversy concerning the role of money in the economy. This second controversy (or rather the second aspect of the controversy) has become far more vociferous and virulent in the past fifteen to twenty years and it has raised the question of alternative economic policies in a far more acute form.

It would be impossible to give a comprehensive review of the various issues raised by this controversy within the confines of a conference paper. I am handicapped also by the fact that I have published a number of papers in this field in the last few years[29] so that most of my views are fairly well-known – at least in those aspects of the controversy which fall within a realm of discourse that I feel confident of understanding. These relate to what Tobin called Monetarism Mark I – which concerned the question whether changes in prices are the consequence of *prior* changes in the amount of money in circulation, or whether, on the contrary, it is changes in incomes and prices caused by other factors which cause an accommodating change in the 'money supply' in consequence. Monetarism Mark II, on the other hand, raised far more subtle issues that are only relevant in a kind of super-neo-classical world where markets are continuously clearing, and where they also have the additional property that they enable 'economic agents' to foresee the future correctly and thereby neutralize the effects of Governmental economic policies – as, for example, the effects of switching from taxation to borrowing.

Leaving aside the Rational Expectations Hypothesis, as something which does not belong to the same universe of discourse, we are still left with the issue whether money is 'important' or 'unimportant' as a factor determining output, employment and prices.

To understand how this controversy developed, two things need to be borne in mind. First, the fact that during most of his working life Keynes (along with other Cambridge economists such as D. H. Robertson) was a true follower of the Quantity Theory of Money in the form developed by Marshall, on which he lectured for many years, and which he wished to develop further, both in the *Tract on Monetary Reform* in 1923 and in the *Treatise on Money* in 1929. Second, that the years in which the *General Theory* was written were years of easy money, with very low interest rates, and where the rate of credit expansion was far more effectively limited by a lack of credit-worthy borrowers than by the Bank's inability or unwilling-

---

[29] See (with James Trevithick), 'A Keynesian Perspective of Money', *Lloyds Bank Review*, January 1981; *Origins of the New Monetarism* (the Page Lecture, Cardiff, 1981; *The Scourge of Monetarism*, (Oxford University Press, 1982) (this includes the full text of my Evidence to the Treasury and Civil Service Committee of July 1980); *Limitations of the General Theory* (a British Academy lecture published by Oxford University Press, 1973).

ness to expand the base of bank credit. Hence the question of how the equation determining the equilibrium level of demand, looked at as the sum of business expenditures on investment and personal expenditures on consumption, was reconciled with aggregate demand as determined by monetary factors, MV, had never really occurred to him; the liquidity preference theory of interest, as we have seen on p. 10 above, served the function not of reconciling the quantity theory with the effective demand theory but of explaining what determines the money rate of interest. Its function as 'underpinning' Keynes's concept of under-employment equilibrium (which lent it such importance in the eyes of Dennis Robertson and other writers) was not one that would have naturally occurred to Keynes himself.

Nevertheless it is possible to show in terms of a few equations how monetary and 'real' factors relate to each other in both pre-Keynesian and post-Keynesian economics.

The first equation is the traditional Fisher equation $MV = PT$ substituting output Q for Fisher's T (which includes transactions in stock and shares, etc., as well as in newly produced goods and services). Hence

$$P = \frac{MV}{Q}$$

where P = the price level
            M = quantity of money   (1)
            $V \equiv$ velocity of circulation
            $Q \equiv$ output or income in real terms

The second is the 'Pigou amendment' to the quantity theory (so named because of its original appearance in Pigou's *Theory of Unemployment*)

$$P = (1 + \eta)\, \frac{dL}{dQ} w$$

where L = labour
            w = the money wage rate per unit of L (2)
            η = the reciprocal of the elasticity
                 of demand facing the individual
                 producer

Taking these two equations alone, we have two dependent variables, P and Q, while all other terms (including w, the money wage rate) are assumed to be given extraneously. Formally, the two equations jointly determine both P and Q; in fact it will depend on the elasticity of the short-period cost function – the variability of dL/dQ or simply L/Q with respect to changes in Q – whether P is *mainly* determined by equation (1) and Q *mainly* determined by equation (2) or *vice versa*.

The difference between the above system of two equations and the original quantity theory, equation (1), is that the above takes the level of money wages as an extraneous factor (i.e. *not* determined by the requirements of a market-clearing price in the labour market).[30]

This system of two equations summarised the prevailing view on unemployment which amounted to saying that as the demand curve for labour in the aggregate is falling, the amount of unemployment depended on a level of money wages, w, which exceeded the level compatible with full employment.

Keynes introduced a new concept, effective demand, which can be represented by an equation in *real* terms. To represent his theory of real demand in terms of a simple equation we assume that consumption, C, is a simple linear fraction of income ($C = cQ$) and the condition of equilibrium $I = S$ (investment equals savings) can be written as $I = (1 - c)Q$ (since the model also assumes $S = sQ$ and $s = 1 - c$). Hence

$$D \equiv Q = \frac{1}{1-c} I \tag{3}$$

This equation introduces two new exogenous variables, $(1 - c)$ and I, but no new dependent variables. The question now is can equation (3) be reconciled with the 'Pigou' model, represented by equations (1) and (2)?

Keynes's solution was to introduce a further equation, the 'liquidity preference relation' which he put as $M = L_1(Y) + L_2(r)$ but which can be expressed more generally in the form

$$M = L(Y,r) \qquad \text{where } Y \equiv PQ \tag{4}$$

which makes the demand for money a function both of income and the rate of interest. This implies that the quantity theory equation (equation (1)) should be re-interpreted in the form of

$$V(r) = \frac{Y}{M} \tag{4a}$$

where $V(r)$ is an alternative form of the liquidity preference function ($L = 1/V$ is the demand for money as a proportion of income).

The replacement of a constant V in equation (1) with $V(r)$ adds in fact two new dependent variables, since V will vary with r, and r must be such as

---

[30] Hence the two equations provide for an under-employment equilibrium due to excessive wages relatively to the demand for labour – the unemployment however is not 'involuntary' in Keynes's sense.

to satisfy equations (4) and (4a), *i.e.* it must equate the demand for money with the supply. However, apart from *P* and *Q* all other variables are exogenous – including *M*.

The consequence of this interpretation of Keynes (which was the generally accepted one, following Hicks's 1937 article, by Keynesians and non-Keynesians alike) was the whole burden of making equation (1) consistent with equation (3) – the quantity theory of money with the Keynesian theory of employment – fell on *V(r)*; on the change in the velocity of circulation which adapts itself to changes in aggregate demand due to (3).[31]

It fell to a young economist Milton Friedman to discover that this model makes Keynes's theory one that can be refuted (or confirmed in the sense of not refuted) by empirical investigations based on time series. For the model predicts on the above presentation that there should be a high correlation between variations in *V* and variations in *Y*, which in turn *implies* the absence of any correlation between *M* and *Y*. So Friedman went to work on this with all possible speed, and lo and behold! he found the very opposite – that *M* and *Y* were invariably highly correlated (subject only to a variable time lag) whereas *V* was far more stable and its variations were, if anything, positively correlated with *M* and not negatively. He then pronounced against Keynes and in favour of the quantity theory, and kept on supplying more and more 'proofs' of this kind from 1956 to the present day.

The obvious point that correlation says nothing about the direction of causality was raised of course very early in the controversy; Friedman put forward at different times a whole series of points in 'evidence', of which the time lag was the most famous (and also the most hotly contested). Moreover he had written a book with Anna Schwartz[32] of some 800 pages in support of the view that changes in the money supply in the U.S. were exogenous, but as several reviewers pointed out, there is nothing in the book that would really support this, and quite a lot that would support the contrary.[33] He attributed (in his Presidential address to the American

---

[31] Hence the statement by H. G. Johnson, James Tobin, G. Akerlof and numerous others that the difference between the 'Keynesian' and the monetarist position turns on an empirical question, the interest-elasticity of the demand for money.

[32] Milton Friedman and Anna Schwartz, *A Monetary History of the United States, 1867–1960*, Princeton University Press, 1963.

[33] The book was subjected to a scathing attack by an American economic historian, Robert R. Russel, in *Fallacies of Monetarism* (Western Michigan University, 1981) who also pointed out that 'the basic statistical tables in the appendixes of the *History* do not confirm the authors' findings' (*ibid.* p. 17). He also points out (p. 11) that at the end of the book (on p. 695) – the fifth from the final page of the text – they wrote a wholly unexpected ambivalent statement about causality: 'While the influence running from money to economic activity has been predominant, there have clearly also been influences running

Economic Association in 1967) the Great Contraction of the U.S. 1929–1933 to the *deflationary* policies of the Federal Reserve System 'which *forced or permitted* a sharp reduction in the monetary base'. The facts are that the Federal Reserve *increased* the monetary base in a vain attempt to stimulate the economy, as indeed Friedman's own statistics show.[34]

The extraordinary feature of all the monetary writing in this century both in Britain and in the U.S. has been that the exogenous character of the money supply was almost never questioned, despite the fact that most money assets originate in bank credit – through borrowing either by the public sector or the non-bank private sector. It was assumed by most writers that ultimately the total amount of money held by the public (i.e. outside the banking system) is determined by the monetary authorities, independently of the demand for money (or the demand for credit). The monetary authorities have wide powers through fixing the Bank Rate (or the discount rate) supplemented by open market operations, to provide the banking system with the particular amount of 'liquidity' which conforms to the authorities' policy. Yet there was plenty of evidence to show that the supply of bank credit was elastic (it responded to fluctuations in demand) and the monetary authorities' power to counteract such fluctuations was severely circumscribed by their function of 'lender of last resort' – a function that became all the more important the more the business of banking was concentrated in fewer hands. In addition, under the British banking system, an automatic increase in bank credit is provided in the form of guaranteed over-draft facilities, while the commercial banks have plenty of means at their disposal to replenish their reserves through the creation of inter-bank loans which give rise to negotiable paper in the form

the other way, particularly during the shorter-run movements associated with the business cycle. . . . Changes in the money stock are therefore a *consequence* as well as an independent source of change in money *income* and *prices*. *Mutual interaction*, but with money rather clearly the senior partner in longer-run movements and in major cyclical movements, and more nearly an equal partner with money income and prices in shorter-run and milder movements – *this is the generalization suggested by our evidence.*' (Italics in the original.)

It is worth quoting Prof. Russel's comment which follows the above quotation:

'Now I find the above statement pretty hard to parse. What explanation of business cycles does it imply? What explanation of price changes? If changes in the money stock cause the longer-run movements and the big booms and busts, why do they not also cause the shorter-run and milder movements and the little business expansions and milder recessions? And, if changes in prices, wages, profits, interest, and rents can cause mild changes in the money stock, why can they not also cause big changes in the money stock? And what, by the way, is a longer-run *movement* or a shorter-run *movement?* Movement of what? And why after 694 pages of evidence and positive thinking must we be content with a 'generalization *suggested* by the evidence' when we had been led to expect a Q.E.D.? It looks very much like a hedge or a cop-out.'

[34] *Op. cit.*, Table B-3, pp. 800–8.

of 'certificates of deposit' that can be discounted in the discount market.

Moreover the whole mechanism by which changes in the quantity of money will cause a rise in prices postulates a world of commodity money (where gold or silver are the main forms of money and convertible bank notes a subsidiary form): in that world, an increase in the amount of gold in circulation may cause the 'supply' of gold, at the existing gold price level, to exceed the demand for it; and since all the gold which is anywhere must be somewhere, the only way the 'excess supply' can be eliminated is through a rise in prices (i.e. a fall in the value of gold in terms of other commodities). As a result of, say, the discovery of a new gold mine, the circulation of gold will be accelerated until gold has lost enough of its value so that the new amount is no longer regarded as excessive in relation to the amount of real purchasing power which individuals wish to hold in the form of money.

But there is no analogy to any such process in the case of credit money. Since credit (and hence bank money) varies in response to the demand for bank loans, the 'money supply' cannot be assumed to vary *relatively* to the money demand; the supply of money can never be in excess of demand for it; if there was such an excess (say, on account of an unexpected fall in business turnover or in incomes and prices) the excess supply would automatically be extinguished through the *repayment* of bank loans, or what comes to the same thing, through the purchase of income yielding financial assets from the banks.[35] It was for this reason that Friedman and his followers were never able to give an intelligible account of how an increase in the 'money supply' will lead to an equi-proportionate rise in money incomes eighteen months to two years later. This 'transmission mechanism' remains a 'black box'.

In Britain, monetarism of the Friedmanite type became extremely fashionable in the late 1970s; however since a new 'monetarist' government of Mrs Thatcher came into power, these beliefs have fairly quickly evaporated among intellectuals. For the money supply, on the Government's chosen definition, £M3, rose nearly twice as fast as formerly, and it became clear to everyone that the monetary authorities had no direct means at their disposal of controlling its movement, but only indirect means through influencing the growth in the *demand* for money through deflationary fiscal policies. At the same time, a rigid pay policy in the public sector combined with strong pressure on business profits (caused by the over-valuation of the pound) have greatly reduced both the rate of increase in money wages and of prices of imported commodities. Hence the rate of

---

[35] The commercial banks always hold a large proportion of their assets in 'investment' (Government bonds) which is the marginal employment of their assets, and which enables them to expand credit, or to repay deposits by corresponding variations in their investment portfolio.

inflation fell from 22 per cent in their first year in office to 5.3 per cent in the last twelve months. But this very fact puts paid to the orthodox monetarists, according to whom the money explosion of the first two years should by now have caused a *high* rate of inflation of around 20 per cent or more.

Most of the stir created by Friedman's activities might have been avoided if Keynes had explicitly recognised that the quantity of money M is also an *endogenous* variable; at any given rate of interest it is determined by demand. This could have been incorporated in the model by a slight change in the liquidity preference function, writing

$$M(r) = L(Y,r) \tag{4}'$$

or

$$Y = \frac{M(r)}{v(r)} \tag{4a}'$$

Since this adds another variable $M(r)$ it requires another equation, which in its simplest form could be put

$$r = \bar{r} \tag{5}$$

when $\bar{r}$ is the rate of interest as determined by monetary policy.[36] $\bar{r}$ can change of course with changes in policy, but for any given $\bar{r}$ the supply of money is infinitely elastic – or rather it cannot be distinguished from the demand for money; whereas the quantity theory asserts, *per contra*, that it is changes in the supply of money *relative* to the demand which are the sole cause of changes in the general price level.

Once this is seen, the importance attached to the interest elasticity of demand for money (reflecting 'liquidity preference') disappears. If this elasticity is small or non-existent (as recent experience suggests with regard to M3) this does not argue in favour of the efficacy of monetary controls but of the very opposite – of the impotence of the authorities to vary the quantity of money otherwise than in response to a variation in demand. Of course interest policy may be effective in influencing the level of investment (though hardly as powerful, in my view, as Keynes thought) and in this way would influence the level of incomes generated in the economy; and this in turn would influence the demand for money. In that case, however, monetary policy does nothing more than fiscal policy; it is a particular instrument of demand management in the Keynesian sense.

---

[36] Diagrammatically, the difference in the representation of the supply and demand for money, is that in the original version (with M exogenous) the supply of money is represented by a vertical line, in the new version by a horizontal one, or a set of horizontal lines, representing different stances of monetary policy.

In a Keynesian model the price level of an industrial society depends on the money costs of production of commodities which, in a closed economy, depends on the level of efficiency wages – on money wages relative to output per head. At any given moment these factors are given exogenously, as a heritage of the past. But there is nothing in the model to determine the rate of change of money wages relative to the rate of change in productivity. It has been the universal experience of industrial countries in the present half century that the former invariably rises faster than the latter, though the gap is habitually greater in some countries than in others. This is a problem which Keynesian methods of demand management leave unresolved – except perhaps in the suggestion that wage-induced inflation would be more serious and show a stronger tendency to accelerate in boom periods with fast-rising profits and high employment than in slack periods with low profits and high unemployment.

The solution of this problem may require far-reaching changes in the institutional arrangements concerning the division of the national product between the different groups and classes which contribute to its formation.

THE TERRITORIAL ASPECT

Though Keynes was only too conscious of the role of foreign trade in Britain's unemployment problem – one need only refer to his opposition to the gold standard, to his numerous pamphlets and papers (of which *The Economic Consequences of Mr Churchill*[37] is justly the most famous) – in the *General Theory* he wished to concentrate on the domestic causes of unemployment, and for this purpose he adopted the traditional fiction of a closed economy.[38]

The analysis of the properties of a closed economy could in principle be applied to a region (such as, say, Scotland) or to a country in the sense of a sovereign entity with its own laws and customs, a common currency, and a single central authority deciding on how economic policy should be conducted – whether this concerns interest policy, public investment, etc. Or it could be related to the economy of a whole world – which is the only definition of a closed system that is literally true.

However, Keynes recognised and emphasized that his analysis relates to

[37] J.M.K., IX, pp. 207–30.

[38] There are rare references (as for example on p. 270 of the *General Theory*) that his conclusions relating to 'a closed system' may also be applicable to an 'open system', 'provided equilibrium with the rest of the world can be maintained by means of fluctuating exchanges', but this was no more than an indication that the important issues concerning the causes and cure of unemployment must arise within the system and not be brought in from outside.

an advanced industrial society, such as Britain, which is dependent on imports of food and raw materials and exports manufactured goods to pay for them (or used to); and that its main propositions could be equally applied to other 'entrepreneurial economies' such as the U.S. or Germany or France. He believed however (in company with all classical economists or their successors) that the labour supply of each 'economy' can be taken as given – in other words, there is no *international* mobility of labour (and capital?), whereas *within* the 'economy' space presents no problems, and limitations on the internal mobility of resources which might cause labour bottlenecks in some industries and under-employment in others could, in the first approximation, also be left out of account.

There is certainly no indication to suggest that foreign trade can be a cause of a failure of effective demand, even when, thanks to fluctuating exchange rates or other causes, exports and imports are in balance. In his chapter on Mercantilism (chapter 23) he retracted his earlier extreme views on the free trade question, according to which 'If there is one thing Protection can *not* do, it is to cure Unemployment. There are some arguments for Protection, based upon its securing possible but improbable advantages, to which there is no simple answer. But the claim to cure Unemployment involves the Protectionist fallacy in its grossest and crudest form'.[39]

In the *General Theory*, he quotes the above passage as an example of how wrong he was when – in company with all other economists – he asserted that foreign trade is irrelevant to the problem of unemployment. But the 'element of scientific truth' which he then (in 1936) conceded to mercantilism was the proposition (which followed directly from the effective-demand theory) that *net* foreign investment, as reflected in the surplus of the current account of the balance of payments, constitutes 'investment' in much the same way as 'home investment'; and hence, for a country suffering from insufficient investment opportunities, foreign investment (in this sense) can serve as a useful adjunct to home investment in raising production to the full employment level. He pointed out however that this concession to the mercantilist view is full of pitfalls and dangers, since foreign investment, by raising interest rates, can make home investment less attractive; also an export surplus by one country is an import surplus of another: the gain in employment is thus a 'beggar-my-neighbour' policy of curing unemployment (though the actual expression 'beggar-my-neighbour' is of later origin).

But there is no hint of an indication that the *volume* of exports and their

---

[39] *The Nation and Athenaeum*, 24 November 1923 (quoted in the *General Theory*, p. 334. Italics in the original).

rate of growth (irrespective of whether they represent a current account surplus or not) are powerful factors determining the level of employment – more powerful perhaps than investment. (There was no mention in the *General Theory* of R. F. Harrod's 'Foreign trade multiplier', despite the fact that the latter made its first appearance three years earlier in a Cambridge Economic Handbook of which Keynes was the General Editor.)[40] In so far as exports can be regarded as an *exogenous* component of demand (which they certainly can, so long as they are not in the nature of a direct payment for goods and services imported from abroad) they have very much the same kind of multiplier effects as domestic investment; with the important difference that in calculating the multiplier, the marginal propensity to import has to be taken into account and not (or not only) the marginal propensity to save. Assuming that the two propensities stand in the same relation to each other as the value of the two exogenous components of demand (i.e. that I/s is the same as E/m) and ignoring any autonomous element (not geared to income) either in savings or in imports, the action of the multiplier will result both in an equality of (home) investment with (home) savings and also in a zero current balance – in an equality of exports and imports. If the two ratios are not equal (say $E/m > I/s$) the process will yield a positive current account balance and a corresponding shortfall of domestic investment over domestic savings; with $E/m < I/s$ the opposite will occur. The latter situation is likely to impose a more binding constraint on employment than the former since it is easier to deal with a chronic tendency towards a balance of payments surplus than to find finance for a chronic deficit.

There is moreover a further important point which Keynes (as distinct from his followers, from Harrod onwards)[41] failed to take into account. Business investment is only partly an exogenous factor; partly it arises from the need, in a *growing* economy, to keep productive capacity growing in line with sales.[42] Such 'induced investment' which is often expressed in the form of the acceleration principle is no different from other induced elements of demand such as consumption; in the view of some writers, such as Hicks, the two ought to be lumped together, in the notion of

[40] *International Economics*, by R. F. Harrod, 1933, ch. 6, pp. 104–20.

[41] See Harrod, *The Trade Cycle*, Macmillan, 1938.

[42] Under increasing returns each firm attempts to maintain capacity at a level that is more than adequate for current sales, or sales expected for the immediate future, partly because the unit cost of a plant that is somewhat larger than that required for optimal use may have lower costs than the 'optimal' plant; partly also because (for reasons first explained by Marx) each firm is striving to enlarge its market share and thereby gain a cumulative advantage over its rivals; the ready availability of surplus plants alone puts it in position to exploit any chance increase in its selling power.

a 'super-multiplier' to gauge the true effect of an increase in exogenous demand.[43]

The final reason which makes exports, and not the export surplus, the important factor for employment and prosperity is that in a growing world economy (where growth may be ultimately governed by increases in the availabilities of primary products, such as foodstuffs, industrial materials or sources of energy) exports emanating from a particular country or region may be the governing factor in determining, not just the *level* of employment, but the growth of employment and productivity in the secondary and tertiary sectors (i.e. industry and services) over longer periods.

In most countries (if not all) there are latent labour reserves in agriculture and in traditional service industries so that it is not possible to say that any recorded level of employment (or unemployment) conforms to the full-employment assumption, in the sense that the general level of output is the maximum attainable in the short period. This may be true in the *very* short period since labour mobility takes time, though it is much accelerated in times of buoyant industrial demand; moreover, since the growth of industrial productivity is highly correlated with the growth of output, the *effective* supply of labour is itself enlarged beyond the growth in actual numbers. Internal mobility, moreover, is supplemented by international mobility – as post-war experience has shown, political barriers to international migration are almost automatically lifted whenever a growth-area becomes congested – and, taking the world as a whole, the magnitude of disguised unemployment is such that it is safe to assume that, from the point of view of any particular industrial growth-region, there are potentially unlimited supplies of labour; this means that it is not the *supply* of labour which is given to an 'economy', however defined, but only the *supply price* of labour (or rather the *minimum* supply price – for the extent of migration depends not so much on earnings-differences as on the availability of jobs in the immigrant areas).[44]

As increasing returns are a prominent feature of manufacturing industries, and because they operate more as a consequence of *large* production than of *large-scale* production, they take the form of an ever-increasing differentiation of processes and of specialisation of human activities – which in turn depends for its success on easy communication of ideas and experience, and the constant emergence of new market opportu-

[43] Hicks, J. R. *A Contribution to the Theory of the Trade Cycle*, Oxford, 1950, p. 50.

[44] This is amply shown by the enormous cyclical variation in the rate of labour migration from Europe to the U.S.A. in the period 1865–1914 without any corresponding change in earnings differentials.

nities, features emphasised in the famous paper by A. A. Young.[45] For these reasons industrialisation is invariably connected with urbanisation; industrial development tends to get polarized in certain growth points or in 'success areas' which become centres of vast immigration either from surrounding or from more distant areas. This process of polarization – what Myrdal calls 'circular and cumulative causation' – is largely responsible for a growing division of the world between rich and poor areas as well as for the persistent differences in growth rates between different industrial countries. Countries which succeed in increasing their share of the world market – because they are relatively more successful in introducing innovations, etc. – impose an increasing handicap on those whose market share is diminished in consequence.

Thus the introduction of the 'territorial aspect' or 'space aspect' does not diminish, but on the contrary serves greatly to enhance, the emphasis to be placed on demand as a factor determining not just the short-run level of employment, but the long-run development of particular regions of the globe. However, in contrast to the framework of assumptions of neo-classical theory, the actual line of progress is not predictable – except perhaps for short periods in which the range of possibilities is severely circumscribed by whatever exists at a given moment, as a heritage from the past. But with each step that modifies the environment, new opportunities for change open up which make the future less and less predictable – owing to a powerful feed-back mechanism the events of each period of historical time can only be explained in terms of the actual sequence through which the system has progressed.

The main stimulus to growth and prosperity is not just more investment – though faced with the alternative of idleness, and its psychological frustration, the kind of investment programme advocated by Keynes in 1929 (in his pamphlet *Can Lloyd George Do It?*) would undoubtedly have meant a very considerable improvement in the performance of the British economy. But it would not have facilitated (or at least not nearly so much) an export-led growth which alone could ensure the long-run prosperity of these islands.

The latter would have required instruments which go beyond those needed for the maintenance of the pressure of demand by ordinary fiscal and monetary policies. It would have involved the deliberate encourage-ment of industries with a high export potential and a high technological potential, requiring a policy of positive guidance and direction of private as well as public investment (like Japan's 'administrative guidance' and France's post-war five-year plans). Unfortunately, the dominance of

[45] 'Increasing Returns and Economic Progress', *Economic Journal*, December 1928.

laissez-faire philosophy in Britain for 100 years or more ensured that this kind of State guidance was universally regarded as distasteful and inefficient.

But whatever criticism can be made of the limitations imposed by the intellectual method of 'equilibrium economics' (which Keynes inherited and was unable to discard) there can be no question of the greatness of his achievement. Perhaps it is fitting to quote one of his best known critics, Don Patinkin, for a final word:

> One need only study the literature which preceded the *General Theory* to appreciate both the novelty and importance of the message of the equilibrating role of changes in output generated by discrepancies between aggregate demand and supply at the time when Keynes presented it. And the force of that message is not much diminished by the existence of errors or confusion about the exact nature of the demand and supply curves and of the related dynamic process.[46]

COMMENT

James Tobin

I deeply appreciate the honor of participating in this celebration, especially because I cut my teeth on the *General Theory*. A Harvard sophomore all of eighteen years, I was just beginning study of economics when my young tutor said 'Here's a new book, maybe quite important, just published in England. Let's you and I read it for tutorial this year.' Not knowing enough to be properly scared, I plunged in. It was an exciting time in that Cambridge too; the contagion spread to undergraduates. Here was an intellectual revolution challenging encrusted and irrelevant orthodoxy, opening intriguing avenues for young minds, and promising to save the world.

Thanks to that initiation, I spent a large part of my career on Keynesian economics – trying to tidy it up and provide more solid foundations for key equations, giving it empirical content, applying it in policy, teaching it, and defending it against infidels. Much of my work was critical of Keynes in detail, but I think it was faithful in spirit. Though I dislike being pigeonholed, I wear the label Keynesian with pride, especially nowadays.

Discussing Nicky Kaldor's paper is a particular honor. From my student days on, I learned from every article of his I read; there were many, and

---

[46] Don Patinkin, 'Keynes's Theory of Effective Demand', *Economic Inquiry*, Vol. 17 (1979), p. 175.

many more I should have read. I learned even when I disagreed. In those cases I later found deeper messages that had escaped me at first, an experience also common in reading Keynes. Kaldor, like Keynes, has combined imaginative and perceptive theorizing, intense concern for real world events, and resourceful contributions to public policy. His paper today, like his extensive testimony to the Select Parliamentary Committee, shows how he just keeps rollin' along.

Keynesian economics has been suffering hard times, both in the public arena and in the economics profession. Stagflation, misread to discredit Keynesian theories and policies, is an obvious reason. It has intensified professional skepticism of long standing. Kaldor's paper refers to the chronic professional turbulence about the *General Theory*, and I take this as my topic also.

Why all this turbulence, he asks. Basically, I think, it stems from the evident discrepancy between Keynes's propositions and the theoretical paradigm central to our discipline. That is the theory of general competitive equilibrium, in which rational individuals optimize and markets for all commodities are simultaneously cleared by prices. In the Walrasian model no lapses from full employment, let alone permanent equilibria with excess supplies, can occur.

This construction, for sociological and psychological reasons I will not elaborate, has a powerful fascination for the best analytical minds attracted to our discipline, especially those of post-Depression vintage. Theorists whose trained instincts lead them to presume that the Invisible Hand really works cannot credit the massive market failures alleged by the *General Theory*. They presume instead that Keynesian propositions rest on attribution of irrational behavior to economic agents – for example, money illusion or misperception of government policy – and accordingly dismiss them.

The so-called neoclassical synthesis of earlier postwar decades never effected a complete reconciliation. In recent years of disillusionment with government interventions of all kinds, faith in the optimality of 'market solutions' solidified. Skepticism of the 'microfoundations' of macro-economics grew, and heavier burdens of proof were loaded on allegations of market failures. Modern classical theorists bring to the fray more powerful ammunition than Keynes's classical targets and opponents five decades ago.

Keynes did indeed allege massive systematic market failure, orders of magnitude more serious than the items in the standard welfare economics catalog of exceptions to the optimality of market outcomes. According to Keynes, interconnected failures occur both in labor markets and in capital markets. I condense and paraphrase. Workers are unemployed even though they are willing to work for real wages no greater than their marginal productivities, and even though they and their employers would willingly buy the products of their labor if the capital markets correctly matched interest rates to intertemporal preferences.

General equilibrium theory itself has been refined and elaborated in the years since the *General Theory* appeared. Walras's conjectures have been rigorously proved, but with considerable sacrifice of their applicability. As a succession of notable theorists – Wald, Arrow, and Debreu are important names – made Walras's vision rigorous, they had to introduce restrictive assumptions that made the Invisible Hand less reliable than Smith or Walras or Marshall or Pigou or Hayek thought. It is easier now than it was for Keynes in 1936 to describe in the language of the paradigm itself the sources of his alleged market failures. Yet even if, as Kaldor says, Keynes was no student of Walras, he understood surprisingly well his own heresies.

Keynesian market failures may be ascribed to several complementary sources: (1) the incompleteness of markets, in particular the absence of most 'Arrow–Debreu' markets for future and contingent deliveries; (2) the intrinsic indeterminacy of the expectations on which agents must act in the absence of those markets; (3) the essential non-neutrality of money, which indeed would have no function in a full Walras–Arrow–Debreu world; (4) interdependence among individuals in utilities or preferences, a phenomenon arbitrarily excluded from individualistic general equilibrium models; and (5) imperfections of competition, such that many agents are not price-takers but price-makers.

Keynes was quite explicit about all of these except the fifth. Kaldor makes that last one, imperfect competition, the sole genesis of macroeconomic difficulties. Pure competition implies full employment equilibrium, he says, while imperfect competition implies Keynesian macroeconomics. He therefore blames Keynes for failing to see, or at least to say clearly, that his General Theory requires microfoundations encompassing increasing returns to scale and consequently monopoly, oligopoly, or monopolistic competition.

Why did Keynes not exploit the microeconomic revolution fomented in this very town by his own colleagues and disciples in the same years he was revolutionizing macroeconomics? That certainly is a puzzle, as Kaldor says. To try to win the game on the other side's home field and with their book of rules was a mistake. But faithful neoclassicals on both sides of the Atlantic had no compunctions dismissing imperfect competition from microeconomic theory, as a trivial exception proving the rule of pure competition. They probably would not have found Keynes's macroeconomics any more appealing if he had based it on imperfect competition.

I agree with Kaldor that imperfections of competition are necessary at some stages of Keynes's argument; I am not sure they are sufficient. Anyway, the other four departures from modern Walrasian conditions are also essential, and I suspect sufficient to generate some kind of macro difficulties even if all extant markets were properly flexprice-cleared.

Kaldor admiringly cites Martin Weitzman's observation that constant returns to scale implies that any unemployed worker can employ himself by replicating in microcosm the economy from which he has been excluded. This shows, according to Kaldor and Weitzman, that increasing returns technology is a necessary condition of unemployment. But doesn't the unemployed worker need the other factors of production? And if he has the wealth or credit to obtain their services, what prevents the unemployed from likewise establishing individually or collectively enterprises with U-shaped cost curves in industries with either homogeneous or differentiated products?

Weitzman's construction is one of a number of ingenious non-Walrasian parables in the current literature. They have the virtue of showing how Keynes-like problems can arise among rational optimizing agents. They generally show how an economy may get stuck in an inferior member of a family of equilibria. But these stories are usually told wholly in terms of real variables, and in my opinion miss the essential monetary and intertemporal features of macroeconomics.

I return to the four items in the above list which, I argue, are reasonably explicit in the *General Theory*. On the first, the absence of markets for most future and contingent commodities, it is sufficient to quote Keynes:

An act of individual saving means – so to speak – a decision not to have dinner today. But it does *not* necessitate a decision to have dinner or to buy a pair of boots a week hence or a year hence or to consume any specified thing at any specified date. Thus it depresses the business of preparing today's dinner without stimulating the business of making ready for some future act of consumption. It is not a substitution of future consumption-demand for present consumption-demand, – it is a net diminution of such demand . . . If saving consisted not merely in abstaining from present consumption but in placing simultaneously a specific order for future consumption, the effect might indeed be different. For in that case the expectation of some future yield from investment would be improved, and the resources released from preparing for present consumption would be turned over to preparing for the future consumption . . .

The trouble arises, therefore, because the act of saving implies, not a substitution for present consumption of some specific additional consumption which requires for its preparation just as much immediate economic activity as would have been required by present consumption equal in value to the sum saved, but a desire for 'wealth' as such, that is for a potentiality of consuming an unspecified article at an unspecified time.

The non-neutrality of money has two dimensions in Keynes: (1) Prices are generally quoted whether in organized markets or by price makers and negotiators, in the society's nominal unit of account. So are numerous financial assets and debts – there are well-developed futures markets for currency. This is a natural feature of a monetary economy, for it enables the society to reap the 'public good' fruits of using a common unit of account. But it does contribute to inertia in nominal wealth holdings and debts, and if prices are themselves decision variables for individual agents, to inertia in nominal price paths. (2) Money and other nominally denominated assets are imperfect substitutes for other stores of value, including real goods. The stocks of money and other nominal assets, inside and outside, and the expectations of their real rates of return, affect demands for commodities for consumption and investment. The so-called classical dichotomy is a misleading guide to monetary analysis and policy. It certainly cannot apply to conventional central bank operations or to the asset exchanges by which commercial banks and other financial institutions alter the volume of deposits. These are not equivalent to simple and universal changes in the unit of account; they do not alter proportionately all existing individual positions with respect to present and future money.

Keynes stressed the incalculable uncertainties of returns to long-term investments, and the consequent element of exogeneity in the states of business confidence – 'animal spirits' – that drive capital investment. The point has long been rightly emphasized in this Cambridge, notably by Joan Robinson and Kaldor. I think it was not sufficiently acknowledged across the Atlantic. Two uncertainties are involved. One concerns future demands for and earnings from specific capital goods now put in place, as indicated in the quotation above. The other concerns asset prices. What savers are willing to pay for assets today depends on their guesses what future buyers will pay them, which in turn depends on their guesses, etc. Bubble phenomena are endemic and epidemic. Keynes's discussion has a modern ring. Consider the current vogue of overlapping generation models, where each generation, in order to consume in retirement, must sell its assets to the next. Recent statistical studies, moreover, find that stock and bond prices are much more volatile than justified by the variability of pay-outs.

Although Keynes, like modern classical macroeconomists, saw the importance of expectations, he would dissent from their faith that 'rational' expectations can take the place of the missing markets. This is a principal reason why in Keynesian economics, in contrast to monetarism old and new, exogenous demand shocks are an important source of business fluctuations, why instability does not arise solely from erratic government policy, and why there is opportunity and need for compensatory demand management. As Kaldor emphasizes, moreover, growth in potential supply does not automatically generate the demand to purchase it.

I included interdependence of utilities as the fourth item in my list because of the role it plays in Keynesian wage theory, which I discuss below. Some hint of it may also be detected in Keynes's propensity to consume, which he regarded as a social-psychological phenomenon rather than a simple aggregation of individual behaviors. General equilibrium models conventionally stick to individualism, because externalities in preference, or technologies, are analytically inconvenient. But rationality does not exclude dependence of one consumer's preferences on the actual consumptions of others.

Why are labor markets not always cleared by wages? Keynes begins the *General Theory* with this central question. His answer is usually interpreted to depend on an *ad hoc* nominal rigidity or stickiness in nominal wages, and thus to attribute to workers irrational 'money illusion'. This interpretation, for which sympathetic expositors of Keynes bear no little responsibility, is the main reason neoclassical theorists reject Keynesian macroeconomics.

I now think, however, that Keynes provides a theory free of this taint. At least he almost does, and the gap can be filled with the help of Kaldor's recommendation of attention to non-competitive elements in labor and product markets. This is not to say that a permanent equilibrium with involuntary unemployment can be proved. That is not an important operational issue. It is enough that inertia in nominal wage and price paths last long enough for unemployment to be a serious social problem and a costly economic waste, and for demand management policies to work.

The several elements in such a theory are these:
(1) Wages are set or bargained in the nominal unit of account. As Keynes was aware, things would be different if they were set in terms of commodities labor produces or fully indexed to consumer goods prices.
(2) Wage-setting is decentralized.
(3) Workers are principally concerned with relative wages – here enters interdependence of utilities. An economy-wide increase in prices reduces all real wages proportionately, and that makes it more acceptable to every group of workers than a local reduction in their money wages, which they perceive as damaging their relative position. Evidence accumulated in labor economics strongly supports Keynes's observation of the crucial importance of relative wages.

These three assumptions together explain, without resort to any 'money illusion' at all, why it is easier, as Keynes saw as early as his criticism of Mr Churchill's return to the old gold parity, to lower real wages by raising prices than by lowering money wages. The argument is perfectly clear in the *General Theory*. I don't know why it is so widely ignored.

But the argument is not complete. The three assumptions do not explain why unemployed workers would not prefer jobs at lower relative money, and real wages to idleness, or why employers would not hire them or threaten to hire them in place of relative-wage-conscious employees. This would happen if labor markets were competitive-wage-auction markets. In fact, another well-established finding of labor economists is that queues at factory gates have little direct effect on wages paid inside. Wage patterns do not give way until employers are in such financial straits that insiders' jobs are credibly in jeopardy. But for the power of the insiders we need explanation Keynes did not provide, except for hints that he really had in mind wage-setting mechanisms other than auction markets.

Kaldor informs us of Keynes's interesting distinction between an 'entrepreneur economy' and a 'cooperative economy.' The former is characterized by large-scale production units hiring large numbers of wage laborers. That implies wage scales which are decision or negotiation variables – that already gives them inertia. Furthermore, workers are not hired or rehired daily but with mutual expectations of continuity. Trained on the job, they acquire individually and, I stress, collectively firm-specific human capital. Heavy turnover disrupts teamwork and damages productive efficiency. Inside workers can exploit this fact even without union organization or the threat of unionization – better with than without. Whether by contract or by unilateral decision of the employer, periodic revision of wage scales always involves, implicitly or explicitly, negotiation with existing employees. In this way increasing returns to scale and non-competitive features of 'markets' are the missing but essential ingredients of Keynes's theory of nominal wage inertia.

The case can be further strengthened by noting the prevalence of non-competitive average-cost-based pricing of products. These prices too are made not taken, and here too a case can be made for rationality of behavior apparently deviant from Walrasian assumptions. For example, oligopolistic rivals cannot know for sure whether a drop in sales or orders is local or sectoral or economy-wide (a type of confusion Robert Lucas, the leading new classical theorist, exploits in a different context). The rivals therefore are reluctant to cut margins and prices for fear of triggering price warfare. Their behavior in turn strengthens labor's resistance to wage cuts.

Excess capital capacity, highly correlated with unemployment of labor, is a problem for equilibrium theorists. They can scarcely argue that machines and plants are unemployed because they prefer job search or the dole. It could be argued that technological complementarity idles capacity whenever employment falls for whatever reason. But factor substitutability, usually assumed in neoclassical models, is frequently feasible. Entrepreneurs expecting fluctuations in labor supplies and real wages would plan installations to allow such substitutions. Keynes worried about this problem in his appendix on marginal user cost. His idea was that entrepreneurs would keep capacity idle in bad times because using it would impair its productivity in a more remunerative future. This was not a convincing resolution of a puzzle he trapped himself into by insisting on competitive product markets where firms continuously equate price and marginal cost.

Keynes's theory of wages and unemployment involved a second argument, the proposition that downward flexibility of money wages would not in any case eliminate unemployment due to deficiency of aggregate demand. Product prices would just chase wages down, and no incentive to expand output and employment would arise. The standard criticism has been that this is true, as Keynes himself appears to admit later in the book, only in the liquidity trap – and not even then if the Pigou–Patinkin real balance effect works. The latter is dubious: differences in marginal propensities to consume from wealth between debtors and creditors could swamp the stimulus of increased real value of base money and public debt. More important in practice, the very process of deflation or disinflation may, as Keynes observed, move demands for commodities and labor perversely – a destabilizing effect that can occur even if nominal interest rates have plenty of room to fall. It is no accident that even in the good old days when agriculture unsuccored by governments was the main industry and occupation, when prices and wages were much more flexible, deflationary times were hard times.

Once it is recognized that for whatever reason money wages and prices cannot and do not continuously clear markets, then some substitute or supplementary mechanism of equating demand and supply must come into play. A great contribution of the *General Theory*, foreshadowed of course by Richard Kahn, was recognition that quantity adjustments will play this role and development of the calculus of quantity adjustment for the system as a whole. Recent rediscovery by mathematical economists under the label 'disequilibrium theory' adds precious little of macroeconomic significance to what Keynes and Keynesians long knew. Keynes's principle of effective demand says it all quite clearly: your demand is constrained by what you actually can sell, not determined by what you would like to sell and buy at prevailing prices. Walrasian critics to the contrary, it was not a vulgar mistake for Keynes to relate consumption to realized income rather than to wage rates and prices.

I agree with most of what Kaldor says concerning the 'monetarist counter-assault'. It was indeed a tactical mistake for Keynes and Keynesians to acquiesce, uncritically and inadvertently, in the formulation that the stock of money M is an exogenous policy-determined variable. It was especially a mistake when M was identified empirically with aggregates consisting largely of 'inside' money, and when central banks themselves were not playing by monetarist rules but were 'leaning against the wind'. It was also clearly a mistake for open economies committed to fixed exchange parities. Endogeneity of Ms explained many of the pseudo-reduced-form correlations that helped to popularize Milton Friedman's monetarism. But perhaps more than Kaldor realizes, the mistakes were corrected and his points made in the debates on monetarism in the United States in the 1960s.

I interject here a Keynesian point of practical relevance in the 1930s, and quite possibly today. It relates to asymmetries of expectations and perceived risks as between savers and investors, lenders and borrowers. Keynes would not have approved the current fashion of models where all agents are identical in tastes, expectations, and circumstances (except for age in some models). They leave unexplained the great bulk of daily transactions on financial markets. He was worried that lenders' expectations of restoration of 'normal' interest rates would keep long rates high in the depression, whereas borrowers had no equivalent expectations of normal earnings to justify borrowing and investing at such rates. At the time short rates were so close to zero that monetary authorities could not bring further downward pressure on long rates via short rates. But I have the impression that Keynes regarded lenders' expectations and fears as an obstacle to recovery independent of the floor to short rates. A similar asymmetry of expectations appears to be an obstacle to recovery now, in the United States anyway, intensified by lenders' fears that expansionary monetary measures spell future inflation and by the central banks' fears of those fears.

The interest-elasticity of the demand for money was, I think, not as irrelevant to the monetarist debates as Kaldor says. It is the shape of the Hicksian LM curve that matters, for the effects of fiscal policies and the responses of the economy to real demand shocks and to financial shocks. The shape depends jointly on the interest-elasticities of money demands and supplies; supply elasticities depend both on the behavior of depository institutions and on the policies of central banks. I do agree, however, that this aspect of the monetarist-Keynesian debate is less crucial than the questions of unemployment, inflation, and demand management to which most of Kaldor's paper and my discussion are addressed.

On the compatibility of full employment and price stability Kaldor leaves us up in the air when he says, 'The solution . . . may require far-reaching changes in the institutional arrangements concerning the division of the national product between the different groups and classes.' Earlier he quotes a stronger statement to the same effect published in the *Times* of London in 1943 and generally attributed to Joan Robinson. This is still the major dilemma of policy. As an economics student can expatiate in an exam paper, incomes policies entail distortions and deadweight losses. But those have to be weighed against the social costs of the massive market failures to which Keynes and Keynesian economics call attention.

As positive theory, Keynesian macroeconomics had one immense advantage over its old and new classical rivals: It can explain, and they cannot, the main repeatedly observed characteristics of business fluctuations. As guide to policy, Keynesian macroeconomics can claim considerable credit for the successful performance of capitalism since the second world war. Keynesian ideas will survive the counterrevolutions. The synthesis that emerges from their challenges will, I expect, be more theoretically acceptable to the profession than the earlier 'neoclassical synthesis'. The crisis in economic theory is as much one of microeconomics as of macroeconomics, and it will have to be resolved by systematic rebuilding on non-Walrasian foundations.

COMMENT

A.P. Thirlwall

Kaldor does two things in this paper. First he restates with characteristic lucidity some of the fundamental Keynesian truths relating to the functioning of modern aggregate economies. Secondly, he outlines some of the weak aspects and limitations of the *locus classicus* of Keynesian economics, *The General Theory of Employment, Interest and Money*, particularly the short-period Marshallian constructs on which much of the theory is based and the assumption of a closed economy. Since I agree with the spirit of most of what he says (if not all the detail), I come to praise Kaldor not to bury him! I praise him in this his 75th year, not only for his present contribution but also for his own development and extension of Keynesian modes of thinking to issues of growth and distribution, which has made him a leader and one of the foremost architects of the post-Keynesian school of economists. Kaldor and Keynes share many characteristics and intellectual gifts, particularly a strong intuition and insistence that a scientific theory cannot require the facts to conform to its own assumptions. The description that Lord Robbins gave of Keynes at Bretton

Woods paints an image that history may have of Kaldor: 'the quick logic, the bird-like swoop of intuition, the vivid fancy, the wide vision, above all, the incomparable sense of the fitness of words, all combine to make something several degrees beyond the limit of ordinary human achievement'.[1]

Kaldor addresses himself to three major issues: first to the principle of effective demand and the theory of employment and unemployment; secondly to the relation between money and inflation, and thirdly to the territorial aspect of Keynesian theory. In deference to this structure, my own simple thoughts will be organized around these themes, and I shall be quite fundamentalist in my approach in homage to the man we are honouring. I shall argue that if Keynes was to be reborn, he would react to monetarism and the new classical macroeconomics in exactly the same way as he reacted in the *General Theory* to classical theory. Remember that Keynes prefaced his theory as 'General' to contrast it with what he regarded as the special case of classical theory; that special case being the limiting point of the possible positions of equilibrium. But as he observed, 'the characteristics of the special case assumed by classical theory happen not to be those of the economic society in which we actually live, with the result that its teaching is misleading and disastrous if we attempt to apply it to the facts of experience'.[2] Likewise, today, the tenets and assumptions which constitute the Keynesian counter revolution do not accord with reality or the facts of experience. In consequence, I believe, we have been led up a blind alley, and I predict that when the virulence of the monetarist disease has abated, the corpus of Keynesian economics and thinking on vital issues will emerge largely unscathed. I shall leave aside the intriguing and fascinating question posed by Kaldor of how economists and politicians caught the monetarist bug in the first place. It will probably require an economic historian with a training in psychology to provide us with a full explanation. Kaldor suggests a reaction to the shift in the balance of economic power towards organized labour. Another favourite theory is to say that in the 1970s Keynesian economics failed, and nature abhors a vacuum. But failed in what sense? Economic performance was certainly poor by post-war standards, but the combination of inflation on the one hand and unemployment on the other is readily explicable in Keynesian terms, if the aggregate supply function is not conveniently forgotten. I sometimes wonder how carefully those of anti-Keynesian

[1] From Robbins's Journal 24 June 1944, cited in R. F. Harrod, *The Life of John Maynard Keynes*, Macmillan, 1951, pp. 576–7.

[2] J. M. Keynes, *The General Theory of Employment, Interest and Money*, Macmillan, 1936, p. 3.

persuasion have read the *General Theory*. If the book had been digested properly there should never have been the divorce between Keynesian economics and the economics of Keynes, nor would we have had to suffer the ridiculous jibe that in Keynes 'money does not matter'. On the contrary, money matters too much!

From current discussions of the causes of high unemployment, the denial of the existence of involuntary unemployment, and from the concept of the natural rate of unemployment and how it is measured, one might also be forgiven for wondering whether the new orthodoxy has absorbed the fundamental criticisms made by Keynes of the classical assumptions of how aggregate labour markets function. In my view, it certainly has not answered them satisfactorily.

One of Kaldor's central points is that whereas the main proposition concerning the critical role of demand in determining output and employment has withstood attacks launched against it, many of the theoretical constructs, which Keynes invented or employed by way of proof or explanation, have not. This may be true, but seems to me incidental. The fact that Keynes assumed such things as diminishing returns to labour, and made no explicit assumption about the state of competition, except that it is given, makes no essential difference to the thrust of the main argument. The key innovation was to alter the assumptions concerning labour supply, and this insight is as valid as it ever was. The major issue dividing Keynesians from non-Keynesians is not whether involuntary unemployment is impossible if the unemployed can become self-employed in a perfectly competitive economy with no barriers to entry, but whether, in the real world, flexible real wages are necessary and sufficient for full employment. On this score, to read Professor Friedman, or our own home-spun Professor Minford,[3] one could still be reading Pigou: 'with perfectly free competition among workpeople and labour perfectly mobile . . . there will always be at work a strong tendency for wage rates to be so related to demand that everybody is employed . . . The implication is that such unemployment as exists at any time is due wholly to the fact that changes in demand conditions are continually taking place and that frictional resistances prevent the appropriate wage adjustments from being made instantaneously.'[4] Aggregate labour demand is a negative function of the real wage; labour supply is a positive function of the real wage, and the real wage serves to equilibrate the supply of and demand for labour so that all those who wish to work at the current real wage can do so. In effect all

[3] See P. Minford, *Unemployment: Cause and Cure*, Martin Robertson, Oxford, 1983, and my review of the book in the *Times Higher Education Supplement*, 22 April 1983.

[4] A. C. Pigou, *The Theory of Unemployment*, Macmillan, 1933, p. 252.

unemployment is either frictional or voluntary due to a refusal of workers to accept a cut in the real wage, and this point locates the natural rate of unemployment, below which there will be ever-accelerating inflation. What is wrong with this theory is exactly what Keynes said was wrong with it nearly 50 years ago. First, it is a fallacy of composition to construct an aggregate demand curve for labour like the demand curve for labour for an individual firm. Keynes states this quite clearly: 'the demand schedule for particular industries can only be constructed on some fixed assumptions as to the nature of the demand and supply schedules of other industries and as to the amount of effective demand. It is invalid, therefore, to transfer the argument to industry as a whole unless we also transfer our assumption that the aggregate effective demand is fixed. Yet this assumption reduces the argument to an *ignoratio elenchi*. For whilst no one would wish to deny the proposition that a reduction in money wages accompanied by the same aggregate effective demand as before will be associated with an increase in employment, the precise question at issue is whether the reduction in money wages will or will not be accompanied by the same aggregate effective demand as before.'[5] There is also the question to confront of whether real wages and employment must be inversely related. As Kaldor mentions, Keynes unfortunately accepted the neo-classical orthodoxy in the *General Theory*, although later he changed his mind.[6] If there are increasing returns to labour, two awkward questions immediately arise. How would those of classical/monetarist persuasion then draw the aggregate labour demand curve, and what happens to the concept of the natural rate of unemployment, premised as it is on the assumption that unemployment and real wages are positively correlated?

Secondly, and equally serious, the supply of labour is not a function of the real wage and, even if it was, it is doubtful whether workers could ever position themselves on the supply curve without the power to determine their own real wage. Keynes remarks: 'ordinary experience tells us, beyond doubt, that a situation where labour stipulates (within limits) for a money wage rather than a real wage, so far from being a mere possibility, is the normal case. Whilst workers will usually resist a reduction of money wages, it is not their practice to withdraw their labour whenever there is a rise in the

[5] *Op. cit.*, p. 259. This point has been made ad nauseam by post-Keynesians but with apparently little impact on those unable to think outside the confines of static micro analysis. For a proper construction of the aggregate labour demand curve see, for example, P. Davidson and E. Smolensky, *Aggregate Supply and Demand Analysis*, Harper Row, 1964, and for a more recent and simple restatement, P. Davidson, 'The Dubious Labour Market Analysis in Meltzer's Restatement of Keynes' Theory', *Journal of Economic Literature*, March 1983.

[6] See J. M. Keynes, 'Relative Movements in Real Wages and Output', *Economic Journal*, March 1939.

price of wage goods'.[7] On the second point, Keynes observes 'the assumption that the general level of real wages depends on the money wage bargains between the employers and the workers is not obviously true. Indeed, it is strange that so little attempt should have been made to prove or refute it.'[8] 'There may be *no* method available to labour as a whole whereby it can bring the wage-goods equivalent of the general level of money wages into conformity with the marginal disutility of the current volume of employment. There may exist no expedient by which labour as a whole can reduce its *real* wage to a given figure by making revised *money* wage bargains with the entrepreneurs. This will be our contention.'[9] In other words, the real wage is a dependent variable in the system, not an independent variable. The treating as exogenous of what is endogenous is the source of most fallacies in economics. In the classical view of employment determination we have a prime example. It was Keynes's great insight to reverse the direction of causation between real wages and employment, and I see no reason for rejecting it: 'The propensity to consume and the rate of new investment determine between them the volume of employment, and the volume of employment is uniquely related to a given level of real wages – not the other way round.'[10]

The fact that workers may be off their (classical) labour supply curve for most of the time has profound implications, of course, for the diagnosis of unemployment and for public policy. But as Hahn sarcastically remarks in his brilliant and scathing dissection of monetarism 'apparently the notion of involuntary unemployment is beyond monetarist comprehension and in some way meaningless'.[11] Rising unemployment due to a progressive lack of effective demand also makes nonsense of estimates of the so-called natural rate of unemployment derived from expectations-augmented Phillip's curves where all the parameters of the equations themselves depend on the pressure of demand.[12]

---

[7] *General Theory*, p. 9.

[8] *Ibid.*, p. 12.

[9] *Ibid.*, p. 13.

[10] *Ibid.*, p. 30. For an excellent fundamentalist defence of Keynesian employment theory along these lines, see J. Brothwell, 'Monetarism, Wages and Employment Policy in the U.K.', *Journal of Post-Keynesian Economics*, Spring 1982; also my own paper, 'Keynesian Employment Theory is not Defunct', *Three Banks Review*, September 1981 and *Problèmes Économiques*, 24 February 1982.

[11] In more vindictive mood he goes on 'I confess that I sometimes hope that monetarists may come to learn by personal experience what the notion is all about', F. Hahn, *Money and Inflation*, Blackwells, Oxford, 1982, p. 105.

[12] See A. P. Thirlwall, 'What are Estimates of the Natural Rate of Unemployment Measuring?', *Oxford Bulletin of Economics and Statistics*, May 1983.

We now have Weitzman's[13] rigorous demonstration of what Keynes's intuition told him all along that, even if it could be engineered, an all round reduction of real wages cannot cure unemployment: 'firms would find it cheaper to hire labour, but this effect is outweighed by a simultaneous decline in the demand for their products . . . a successful attempt to depress real wages would actually increase the level of unemployment'.[14] The reason for this result is the pro-cyclical nature of movements in productivity and real wages arising from increasing returns and the imperfectly competitive market structures that falling long run costs give rise to. To his credit, Kaldor seems to have recognized as early as 1935[15] that, as Weitzman puts it, 'the natural habitat of effective demand macroeconomics is a monopolistically competitive micro economy. Analogously, perfect competition and classical macroeconomics are natural counterparts',[16] but he lacked the concept of effective demand. Kaldor's conclusion now that 'most of the voluminous literature concerning the reconciliation of Keynesian analysis with Walrasian general equilibrium is beside the point' would, I imagine, have wide support. 'The two kinds of theory cannot be reconciled simply because one concerns a purely artificial world of perfect competition . . . . whilst the other attempts to generalise about the real world.'

MONEY AND INFLATION

In his discussion of money and inflation, Kaldor chides Keynes's revision of the quantity theory of money as suffering from 'slavish adherence to prevailing (Marshallian) doctrine', and argues that most of the stir created by Friedman's activities would have been avoided if Keynes had explicitly recognized that the quantity of money is an endogenous variable. I understand what he means but I think he is slightly unfair to Keynes and underestimates the commitment and ingenuity of those who wish to use evidence for political motives. What Keynes does in Chapter 21 on 'The Theory of Prices' is to provide a clear and comprehensive scheme for organising our thoughts about the relation between money, costs and prices, which has not been surpassed, and which recognizes that money does adapt to variations in the cost unit.

Keynes's important contribution in his restatement of the quantity

---

[13] M. L. Weitzman, 'Increasing Returns and the Foundations of Unemployment Theory', *Economic Journal*, December 1982.

[14] *Ibid.*, p. 800.

[15] N. Kaldor, 'Market Imperfections and Excess Capacity', *Economica*, February 1935.

[16] Weitzman, *op cit.* p. 801.

theory of money was to draw attention to the dichotomy between the theory of value on the one hand and the theory of money and prices on the other. He expressed surprise with classical doctrine that while value theory teaches that prices are governed by conditions of supply and demand, costs and supply are forgotten entirely when it comes to the determination of the aggregate price level. There is no economic or logical reason for this dichotomy. If the price level in a single industry depends partly on the rate of remuneration of the factors of production which enter into marginal cost and partly on the scale of output, there is no reason to modify this conclusion when we pass to industry as a whole. The most significant change that needs to be taken into account at the aggregate level is the effect of changes in demand both on costs and the volume of output. For Keynes, the relation was a complex one, and so it is, the problem being what variables to take as independent. It is true that in his discussion he proceeds *as if* prior monetary expansion is the source of increased demand, but only to tackle the mechanical quantity theory on its own ground. Strict adherence to this view would be inconsistent with both his theory of investment and consumption behaviour. There is also clear recognition that the cost unit can change independently of monetary expansion and that when money is 'relatively scarce' (as he puts it) some means is found to increase the effective quantity of money. Indeed, this is given as the reason why in the long run a stable proportion between the national income and the quantity of money may be observed.[17]

Keynes had already observed in the *Treatise*[18] that 'if there are strong social or political forces causing spontaneous changes in the money rates of efficiency wages, the control of the price level may pass beyond the power of the banking system'.[19] In this important chapter 21 of the *General Theory* we have modern cost push and structural theories of inflation precisely anticipated. We also have an explanation of stagflation; that shifts in the supply price of output not accompanied by equivalent increases in effective demand lead to both inflation and unemployment. The contrary view that Keynesian theory cannot explain the simultaneous existence of both underemployed resources and rising prices must be attributed largely to ignorance of the *General Theory* and to the pervasive use of the 45° line diagram in the teaching of Keynesian economics.

Kaldor has performed an impressive demolition job here and else-where[20] in undermining the key monetarist assumption of exogeneity of the

[17] *General Theory*, p. 307.

[18] J. M. Keynes, *Treatise on Money*, Macmillan, 1930. J. M. K., VI, p. 314.

[19] *Ibid.*, Vol. 2, p. 351.

[20] See particularly N. Kaldor, *The Scourge of Monetarism*, Oxford University Press, 1982.

money supply and the monetarist explanation of the apparent stability of the demand for money function. The idea that institutional factors operating independently of prior changes in the supply of money cannot affect the absolute price level always defied common sense, confirming the astute observation once made by Voltaire that 'common sense is not very common'! In the world of practical affairs, the Keynesian theory of prices has already been rehabilitated. Monetarism Mark I (to use Tobin's classification)[21] is dead, at least in the United Kingdom. We are now told by Conservative Ministers that a precondition of stable prices is moderate wage claims: a far cry from the heady monetarist days of 1979 when it was confidently asserted that only money matters, and the outcome of collective bargaining was irrelevant.

THE OPEN ECONOMY

There is no time to discuss my views on Keynesian theory in an open economy except to say that I think we are in need of a simple model which brings to the fore the importance of the balance between exports and imports in both a static and dynamic context in the same way that Keynes and Harrod brought to the fore the importance of the balance between investment and saving for the determination of the equilibrium level and growth of income in the closed economy. As Kaldor says, this may be important not only because exports are a more important component of autonomous demand than investment but because an imbalance between full employment imports and exports may be much more difficult to rectify than an imbalance between full employment saving and investment. I happen to think that the dynamic Harrod trade multiplier,[22] with extensions for capital flows and terms of trade changes, is a very useful starting point and it is this that I and several colleagues have been trying to develop and apply in recent years.[23]

---

[21] J. Tobin, 'The Monetarist Counter-Revolution Today – An Appraisal', *Economic Journal*, March 1981.

[22] The static Harrod trade multiplier can be found in R. F. Harrod, *International Economics*, Cambridge, 1933.

[23] See, for example, A. P. Thirlwall, 'The Balance of Payments Constraint as an Explanation of International Growth Rate Differences', *Banca Nazionale del Lavoro Quarterly Review*, March 1979, and A. P. Thirlwall and M. Nureldin Hussain, 'The Balance of Payments Constraint, Capital Flows and Growth Rate Differences Between Developing Countries', *Oxford Economic Papers*, November 1982. Individual country studies of Italy, Brazil, Australia and New Zealand are also available.

DISCUSSION

There were two tests as to whether views claimed as 'Keynesian' were consistent with the *logic* of Keynes's theory concerning the relationship between aggregate demand and aggregate supply, on the one hand, and Say's Law, on the other. In a Say's Law world aggregate demand and aggregate supply always coincided giving an infinite number of equilibrium levels, but there were no obstacles (said Keynes) to full employment. (Clower argued that coordination failures could trap the economy in an under-employment equilibrium.) Keynes, however, insisted that actual income in a monetary production economy could not constrain aggregate demand which consisted of two components D_1 (consumption expenditures) and D_2 (investment expenditures). As long as there is saving (which can reside in non-reproducible assets) and investment (with given long-run expectations) is constrained by the money rate of interest, there is a unique level of equilibrium income, which may be associated with involuntary unemployment. Keynes also insisted that the object of the production process (and the banking process) was to end up with more money at the end than was started with, so that 'money matters' in both the short run and the long run.

It was next suggested that Lord Kaldor seemed to have implied that the theory of effective demand was a requirement of Say's Law – Keynes would have turned in his grave.

Turning to the role of competition and Keynes's alleged neglect of imperfect competition, it was suggested that, in a very general manner, Keynes *had* taken account of the latter; for the *Treatise* dealt entirely in averages while marginals, a principal characteristic of imperfect competition theory, figured prominently in the *General Theory*. Moreover, to argue that Keynes's results needed imperfect competition and increasing returns creates problems. Keynes was aware of Sraffa's criticism of Marshall in 1926 (when he argued that the only consistent assumption for economic theory was constant returns), of Joan Robinson's 1933 book and of Richard Kahn's 1929 fellowship dissertation which suggested that imperfect markets could cause unemployment in the economy as a whole. Perhaps Keynes wanted to explain unemployment without bringing in imperfect competition which was sufficient but not necessary for it. Keynes himself said it was not and empirically business cycles go back to the 18th century with fluctuations in employment and something near perfect competition ruling. Weitzman's argument that you cannot have unemployment without increasing returns rests on the special case, that any one person could become a firm.

As to the closed economy assumption, the *General Theory* was written when Britain had a floating exchange rate whereas in the *Treatise* international capital movements played a big role under a different regime, i.e., historical perspective is needed. It was a pity that Lord Kaldor had viewed the *General Theory* within the framework of equilibrium analysis; under-employment equilibrium is equilibrium only in the very rough sense that even if money wages fell, employment need not increase.

It was noted that discussions of employment bargains somehow assume that employers and employees are in the same boat. There is a tacit understanding that workers may be sacked – forces external to the firm or industry are the cause – but not that wages may be cut for this brings to the fore the conflict of interest between employers and employees.

Returning to the cause of unemployment, it was argued that nominal wage rigidity was absolutely crucial for Keynes's theory (and that it together with the concept of liquidity preference were Keynes's principal innovations). However, as wages have been rising rapidly in recent years, the argument is empirical nonsense. It could be replaced with the idea of *real* wage rigidity – the very gradual adjustment of the real wage to what it 'should' be, i.e., to its 'market clearing' level – for Keynes himself had assumed a constant price level over the long haul. A counter argument was advanced that real wage rigidity would not do the trick because of the Pigou effect.

Finally the discussion turned to the quote from Keynes in Professor Tobin's comment in which coordination problems were associated with saving decisions and a desire for wealth as such. A number of possible outcomes in the short run and the long run to the impact of an increase in the desire for wealth on a growth equilibrium were identified and analysed. They ranged from the monetarist case where the shock does not occur through a long-run real balance effect if prices and money wages are flexible, the neoclassical case where real capital accumulation occurs, to the usual Keynesian multiplier case whereby output falls in order to offset the new desire for wealth. The role of expectations in each was raised and the intriguing suggestion was made that if people really expected Keynesian policies to be applied, they would be required *only* as signals, and perfect demand management would occur.

Lord Kaldor replied to the comments as follows:

Keynes never assumed wage rigidity – Chapter 19 of the *General Theory* is devoted to changes in money wages. He would have agreed with the view that resistance is encountered to wage reductions more than to wage increases. He did not emphasize downward inflexibility of wages too much, possibly because it was a relatively new phenomenon at the time, though he did oppose the return to gold at pre-war parity, as it would have required a large allround reduction in money wages.

The real author of the so-called 'neo-classical synthesis' was not Paul Samuelson, it was Keynes himself. Keynes produced a synthesis between Marshall and himself; Marshall was a neo-classical economist but very different in many ways from Walras. Walras explored the logical implications of a competitive market to the point of absurdity in a way Marshall never did. Though Marshall frequently asserted that prices will tend to equal the marginal costs of production, when he considered the individual firm he emphasized the fact that firms do not reduce their prices during a recession for 'fear of spoiling the market' – something which could not happen under Walrasian perfect competition.

Guillebaud once gave a special lecture on Marshall in the course of which he put a diagram on the blackboard showing a horizontal demand curve and a U-shaped cost curve and said 'This is *not* Marshall, Marshall *always* assumed a downward sloping demand curve, never a horizontal curve.' At the same time Marshall believed in competition – he did not believe that individual firms can charge whatever prices they like, they were confined by the market. Yet he never explored the full implications of these assumptions, or succeeded in bringing them into full logical consistency. Kaldor thought that in many ways Keynes suffered from the same thing.

There are two types of markets in this world, those in which the initial signal of an exogenous change in demand is a price change and those where the initial signal is a quantity change (which may or may not be followed by a price change). In the second category – which is far more widespread in an industrial economy – competition and markets obey different laws from the Walrasian model. Competition in this sense underlies Marshall and therefore Keynes, who did not draw the distinction between perfect and imperfect competition in the way we would do it now.

He felt very sorry for more than one reason that Joan Robinson could not be present. Joan often told him that she tried to interest Keynes in imperfect competition for many years, and its relevance to the problem of the insufficiency of effective demand – but she never succeeded. However, later Kalecki succeeded, as is shown in the article which Keynes published in the March/1939 issue of the *Economic Journal*, where Keynes spoke about 'our prevailing *quasi*-competitive system'. This is the nearest that he came to dealing with a situation in which average costs were falling and marginal costs were well below average costs and so were at variance with the general rule which he enunciated all through the *General Theory*, that prices are equal to marginal costs, that the wages are equal to the marginal product of labour, and that, as a universal rule, there is an inverse relationship between employment and real wages.

Short period analysis was invented by Marshall and it remains the peculiarity and distinguishing mark of the Cambridge School to this very day. It implies a flow equilibrium which ignores certain adjustments, for example, the mobility of labour from outside the industry, or the adjustment of the capital stock. Keynes was thinking in terms of the Marshallian short period.

While there is a clear concept of 'full employment equilibrium' in the short period, it has no equivalent in the long period and this is where the neo-classical equilibrium approach falls apart. In the long period there is no such thing as an exogenous supply of Labour or Capital whether in terms of quantities or in terms of growth rates, either for an individual region or a particular country or nation, or even the world as a whole. It is in long period analysis (which was never developed by Keynes himself) that Keynesian economics really parts company with neo-classical economics.

He agreed with Martin Weitzman, that if one takes the assumption of constant returns to scale literally, extending from an infinitely small output to an indefinitely large one, anyone who fails to get a job is free to do his own production and sell the products of his labour, instead of hiring out the services of his work capacity. Free entry will be sufficient to generate both falling costs and 'full employment', since so long as prices are higher than costs per unit, the markets of existing sellers will be shrinking owing to the inflow of new producers. This process can only come to an end when real earnings are no longer higher than the marginal disutility of labour. Under the assumptions of general equilibrium theory, strictly interpreted, there would be no scope for exchanges and markets, since each man could satisfy all his own needs by his own production on no worse terms than the market can offer.

2

On Keynes and Monetarism*

ALLAN H. MELTZER

It is an honor to be invited to speak at a conference honoring Keynes. His work has probably stimulated more pages of analysis, discussion and controversy than the work of any other economist.[1] Many of the controversies proved sterile, but others have had lasting effects and some continue to shape economics.

The particular controversy about which I have been asked to speak – the monetarist controversy – remains one of the more productive controversies. The controversy stimulated developments in micro and macro economics, in econometrics, in the theory of expectations and the relation of expectations to econometrics and to micro and macro economics. At times, some disputants ignore these gains and appear to see only retrogression where there is progress. Kaldor (1982) is one example, but an example familiar to this audience. Other economists, who undertake to read the literature – though highly critical of recent developments and distressed by their policy implications – recognize that the monetarist controversy has caused them to rethink and change their views – Modigliani (1977) – and, more importantly, has caused lasting changes in economic theory – Tobin (1981, pp. 41–2). I take as given and obvious that both monetarism and our understanding of Keynes's theory continue to change, the former because it is part of economic science, the latter to considerable degree as a result of the excellent volumes containing Keynes's papers and letters produced for the Royal Economic Society.[2]

---

* I owe an enormous debt to Karl Brunner who contributed in many ways to shape this essay, and my thinking and activity as an economist. My first exposure to the subtleties of the *General Theory* and its stock–flow analysis came as a student in his classroom. Our joint work on what is known as monetarism developed later. Frank Hahn pointed out an error in an earlier draft.

[1] The most probable rival is Karl Marx.

[2] I refer, of course, to *The Collected Writings of John Maynard Keynes*. I will follow the practice of referring to the volumes as J.M.K. followed by a Roman numeral indicating the particular volume.

Keynes died in 1946. The term 'monetarism' originated, I believe, in Karl Brunner's (1968) article, so we cannot expect to find Keynes's responses or know how his criticisms would have changed the development of monetarism or how his own theory might have been altered by the development of monetarist theories. Many of the hypotheses that constitute monetarism have their origins in classical and neo-classical economics, but the same can be said of Keynes's hypotheses in the *General Theory* both before and after. Partly for these reasons, I regard as fruitless any attempt to offer a final assessment of the degree to which Keynes was or would have been a monetarist.[3]

A further difficulty in relating Keynes to monetarism is the absence of widely accepted statements of either Keynes's main differences from classical economics or of monetarist theory. There are many statements and restatements of both hypotheses, but none is definitive. My recent attempt to offer a different interpretation of Keynes, Meltzer (1981), summarized and criticized some of the alternative interpretations of Keynes's *General Theory* but made no effort to summarize all of the literature or to reconcile differences.[4] I continue to believe that '[N]o single set of statements is *the* correct restatement of the *General Theory*.' Meltzer (1981, p. 37). The same must be said for monetarism also. There are at least four types of monetarist theory, and there are differences within each type. Some of these differences are likely to remain, but some will close and others widen as work continues.

Mayer's collection of essays on monetarism and his own contribution, Mayer (1978), show some of the difficulties that are inherent in any effort to obtain agreement about the unique features of a developing theory. Mayer recognizes that any listing of 'principal' monetarist or Keynesian propositions will vary with the author and the date on which the list is drawn. Nevertheless there is some overlap. Recent efforts to state and analyze differences between monetarist and Keynesian analysis have produced agreements on some propositions that are distinctively monetarist. See Brunner (1970), Stein (1976), Laidler (1981) and Mayer (1978). One principal reason for the persistence of differences is that many arise from unresolved issues about relative magnitudes, speeds of adjustment, relative frequency of different types of shock and the relation of these issues to

---

[3] Hicks (1974, pp. 31–2) renders such a judgment based on the weak effect of nominal money on real activity, but Keynes (XIV, p. 79) explained in a letter to Hicks that the ineffectiveness of (anticipated) money is an implication of classical theory which had been neglected.

[4] Patinkin's (1982) recent effort to state the contribution that is uniquely Keynesian recognizes also (*ibid.*, p. 5) that 'there is no unanimity on this question'. Both Patinkin's book and other recent writing, e.g. Ohlin (1978), suggest that issues of priority are unsettled also.

short-run non-neutrality of money. A second reason is that economists differ about the risks that policymakers should run in an effort to reduce unemployment or to reduce inflation and the net benefit of any reductions achieved.[5] My views on issues of this kind are available elsewhere.[6]

Some of the participants in the disputes about policy claim more of a relation to Keynes than Keynes is likely to have reciprocated. We do no honor to Keynes by identifying him with many of the prescriptions offered by his followers. Keynes was a theorist with an active interest in policy and practice and a sense of empirical magnitudes. Like his teacher, Alfred Marshall, he avoided elaborate theorizing, had no interest in econometric models and cautioned against their use. He often preferred a simple assumption of constancy to rigorous analysis or careful computation of variables that have relatively low amplitude of fluctuation.[7] Many of the empirical issues about which monetarists and Keynesians dispute, such as the slope of the Phillips curve or the relative responses of output to monetary and fiscal policy, are not central issues in the *General Theory*, and some are unrelated. Keynes wrote about a world in which the price level can change, but there is no inflation.[8] There is no basis for a claim that he would have favored the type of 'Keynesian' policies that try to trade inflation for employment. There is, on the contrary, much reason to believe that he strongly opposed inflation and accepted the (long-run) neutrality of money in the *General Theory* and after.[9]

This paper compares an interpretation of Keynes's *General Theory* to some specific monetarist theories. It does not further treat 'Keynesian' theories or discuss how these theories are related to either Keynes's theory or to monetarist theories. To reduce ambiguity, I introduce an explicit monetarist hypothesis from the early 1970s and indicate some changes introduced later to incorporate rational expectations. I compare these types of monetarist theory to a restatement of Keynes's theory. The

---

[5] Differences of this kind are not limited to economics. Physical scientists have differed sharply about the safety of nuclear power plants, the disposal of wastes, the relative advantages of different treatments for cancer and other policy issues.

[6] Economists who write down the same model may impose different restrictions when they draw policy implications. See, also, Brunner (1983).

[7] One example is illustrative. Keynes (1939, p. 48) treats the wage share as stable and describes the stability as surprising and well-established. In a footnote, he defined stability implicitly. For the U.S. and Britain, his maxima are respectively 13% and 6% greater than the minima.

[8] In August 1936, he wrote to Hicks, '[A] great part of my theory ceases to be required when the supply of output as a whole is inelastic' (J.M.K., XIV, p. 71). In the *General Theory* (1936, p. 303), he defines this position of supply inelasticity as 'true inflation'.

[9] For examples of the latter see (1936, p. 142) (J.M.K., XIV, p. 79).

comparison suggests some distinguishing features and, of course, some similarities.

There are many interpretations of Keynes and many versions of monetarism, as noted earlier. In my interpretation, the *General Theory* is Keynes's attempt to explain why the economy fluctuates around a stable equilibrium level that is below the level of output that society is capable of producing. In Meltzer (1981, 1983), I present and defend this interpretation by referring to specific passages in his *General Theory* and the papers and the letters that followed and by quoting extensively from Keynes's writings. Here, I rely on the previous work and repeat only those parts required for the discussion.

MONETARIST THEORIES

Nobay and Johnson (1977) identify four distinct types of theory as 'monetarist'. The first, developed in the fifties and sixties, consists of empirical tests of single equations and relatively small models. These models and tests tried to distinguish, both analytically and empirically, between various monetarist and Keynesian propositions. Most of the studies neglected the foreign sector and the influence of international currency movements or exchange rates. The second distinct type, concentrating mainly on the role of money in an open economy, is associated with the work of Harry Johnson (1971), Robert Mundell (1968) and their students. In this tradition, the money stock is controlled only if exchange rates are flexible. Under fixed exchange rates the stock of money adjusts in response to commodity price (and interest rate) movements. 'Money' refers to base money (or currency). Debt and real capital are perfect substitutes, so there are only two distinct assets – base money and either bonds or real capital. In the third type of monetarist theory, developed by Karl Brunner and Allan H. Meltzer (1968, 1972), there are three distinct assets – base money, bonds and real capital. The (conventional) stock of money is determined in the asset markets with the demand for money and the demand for the supply of bank credit. There is opportunity for intermediation and for differences in interest rates on short- and long-term assets. The fourth, distinct, type of monetarist theory is the rational expectations monetary theory developed by Robert Lucas (1972, 1975), Robert Barro (1976), Thomas Sargent and Neil Wallace (1975), Finn Kydland and Edward Prescott (1977) among others.

To reduce the scope of this essay, I impose two restrictions. One removes issues raised by an open economy. Although the *General Theory* mentions foreign trade in a few places and devotes a chapter to mercantilism, the theory is properly regarded as applicable to a closed economy. The other restriction follows, without endorsing, the procedure used by such critics of monetarism as Modigliani (1977) and Tobin (1981). These critics refer mainly to the works of Milton Friedman and a small number of rational expectations theorists as examples of monetarist theory.

Milton Friedman

Friedman (1974) is an effort 'to set out explicitly the general theoretical framework that underlies them' [the series of monographs on money written with Anna J. Schwartz]. Friedman offers two main versions of his theory that he calls the quantity theory and the theory of nominal income. A third version, with prices fixed, is attributed to Keynes.[10] Friedman notes (1974, p. 46) that his theory of nominal income is close to my own interpretation of the theory underlying Friedman and Schwartz (1963), developed in Meltzer (1965), but he misstates the main difference.[11]

The demand for nominal money (M^d) depends on nominal income (Y) and the nominal rate of interest (r), as shown in (1).

$$M^d = L(r)Y \tag{1}$$

Friedman assumes that the demand for nominal money is proportional to nominal income (*ibid.*, p. 34) and independent of the distribution of income between prices and real income. At times, the supply of money (M^s) depends on r, but more often international capital movements and intermediation are ignored, and M^s is exogenous to the model. Let $M^s = M_t$ so that, in equilibrium,

$$M_t = L(r)Y_t. \tag{2}$$

Friedman then rewrites the money equations as a quantity equation, a procedure I adopt below.

Decisions to consume or save and to invest depend on the real rate of interest (ρ) and real income (Y/P). Let C and I be real consumption and investment respectively. Friedman assumes

$$C = f_1(Y/P, \rho), \tag{3}$$

$$I = f_2(\rho) \tag{4}$$

---

[10] A more accurate statement is that Keynes held the expected equilibrium price level fixed throughout. In the early chapters, prices are constant, but later this restriction is removed.

[11] Friedman (1974, n. 28) disagrees with my (1965) statement because he regards as 'ad hoc' the way real income and changes in real income enter the analysis. Friedman's statement about expected income does not differ from my interpretation, and his equations for real income changes seem no less ad hoc. The principal difference, in my view, is that Friedman's version includes interest rates but, in his development of the theory, he removes any difference that might arise from this source. This point is developed below.

and

$$C + I = Y/P.$$

The *IS* curve is, then,

$$Y/P = f_3(\rho). \tag{5}$$

To relate the nominal and real rates of interest, Friedman assumes that

$$r = \rho^* - g^* + \frac{1}{Y}\frac{dY}{dt} \tag{6}$$

where g^* is the expected rate of growth of real income and ρ^* is the expected real rate of interest. Recognition of the effects of inflation on market rates is a significant step away from Keynes and toward a more general theory.

Friedman offers several alternative assumptions about ρ without expressing a preference for any. The simplest is to treat the difference as a constant, (k_0), so he writes (*ibid.*, p. 29)

$$\rho^* - g^* = k_0, \tag{7}$$

but a few pages later (*ibid.*, p. 39) he also makes ρ^* a constant. This assumption fixes the value of real income. The *IS* curve is now degenerate, as can be seen in equation (5). The theory of nominal income becomes a version of Friedman's quantity theory. Real income is constant in both. Substituting (7) into (6) and the result into (2), we obtain (8) as a linear equivalent. Real income is given by (5), so, for given M, the theory of nominal income reduces to an equation relating current nominal income to its rate of change.

$$\frac{Y_t}{M_t} = V_1\left(\frac{1}{Y}\frac{dY}{dt}\right) + V_0 \tag{8}$$

Friedman recognizes that the constancy of the real rate in the *IS* equation is unsatisfactory.[12] He maintains that (1974, p. 40) 'it seems entirely satisfactory to take the anticipated real interest rate . . . as fixed for the demand for money'. His reason is that fluctuations in the real rate, and deviations of actual from expected real rates, have at most a minor role in financial markets.

Random deviations of actual from expected real income affect nominal rates of interest and the price level, but they do not affect expected real income. Friedman's discussion of the adjustment process is not developed

---

[12] Friedman (1974, p. 40) mentions some other omissions, principally the neglect of wealth, anticipations of inflation and the difference between measured and permanent income.

as an implication of his theory but appears compatible with the interpretation of the Phillips curve suggested in his Presidential address (1968). He relies on errors and misperceptions to explain the deviations of output and employment from expected values.

Friedman, like Keynes, offers a theory of the level of income. Real income fluctuates around its expected value, and prices change so, in this sense, Friedman's theory is a theory of nominal income. His framework differs from Keynes on two major points. The level of equilibrium real income does not depend explicitly on the variability of income, and inflation is incorporated.

What determines the expected value of real income? Here, and elsewhere, Friedman's expected income is a weighted average of past real income. This has proved a useful empirical simplification in many applications, but it falls short as a response to Keynes's theoretical challenge. Friedman does not explain why expected real income is higher in some times and places than in others. There is no relation between expected real income and the risks or uncertainties that society bears. And unlike Keynes, Friedman does not suggest a relation between expected income and institutional arrangements that cause risks to be reduced or augmented.

But, Friedman's treatment of fluctuations is similar to Keynes's in a broad sense. Both offer static theories of income determination. Although both discuss fluctuations, fluctuations, or business cycle dynamics, are not part of either theoretical framework.[13] For a 'monetarist' theoretical perspective on business cycle dynamics, we turn to rational expectations monetarism.

Rational expectations

Emphasis on rational expectations in macro economics began with Lucas (1972), and he has remained a major contributor. Lucas (1981) contains many of Lucas's contributions up to the time of publication. He describes his research as 'concerned almost exclusively with the attempt to discover a useful theoretical explanation of business cycles' (*ibid.*, p. 2).

Economists from Thornton (1802, pp. 119, 189–90) through Marshall (1920, pp. 709–10) to Keynes (1936) relied on wage rigidity, at least in part, to explain the severity or persistence of unemployment during business cycles.[14] Neither these authors, nor others, offered an explanation of the

---

[13] Meltzer (1965) discusses the latter point more fully and notes that 'transitory income' is difficult to distinguish from the cyclical deviation. I return to this discussion below when I compare Keynes and monetarism.

[14] Keynes's principal explanation for the duration of recessions is the durability of capital and the slow recovery of the marginal efficiency (1936, p. 317).

labor supply curve consistent with maximizing behavior. Marshall, like many who followed, refers to the power of labor unions. In the passage just cited, and elsewhere, Marshall finds some merit in the increased real wages received by those who continue to work during recessions.[15] In Marshall's view, there are both welfare gains and losses during recessions. Keynes (1939) criticized Marshall's work on the grounds that Marshall had not provided a theory of labor supply useful for explaining the supply of output.

A major problem posed in the rational expectations literature on employment (or unemployment) and business cycles is to explain why people choose to vary hours of work instead of varying wages. The same general problem arises for other factors of production; for example, capital is used more intensively at the peak of the cycle than at the trough; time series on investment spending show relatively large cyclical changes. There is a presumption in much of the rational expectations literature, however, that once economists can explain how tastes and constraints combine to induce people to choose the patterns that produce aggregate unemployment, other aspects of the cycle will be easier to explain. This presumption differs from Keynes's view that the duration of business cycles depends mainly on the relation of expectations to the marginal efficiency of capital and the carrying costs of inventories.

As in any scientific endeavor, there are rules or conventions guiding the procedures. Rational expectations business cycle theory can be described as an attempt to develop a theory of business cycle dynamics consistent with maximizing behavior. Although some markets may be missing, all existing markets clear (up to a stochastic component). Information is used efficiently; expectations are rational in the sense of Muth (1961). Business cycles arise because people misperceive what is happening, as in the Friedman (1968) and Phelps (1968) versions of the natural rate hypothesis. Some type of accelerator sustains the cycle and produces persistence, as in Lucas (1975).

The basic idea, relating fluctuations to misperceptions, errors or misjudgements, is not novel. Uncertainty and errors of judgement have long been recognized in discussions of 'over-investment' or 'under-consumption' and more recently in some models of adaptive learning. Many models can be made to appear 'rational' by appealing to costs of acquiring information or similar costs. Explanations of this kind introduce what Lucas calls free parameters; they are useful for some purposes but

---

[15] Keynes (1939) refers to Marshall's view and notes that Marshall based his conclusion about real wages on studies he and others had done in the 19th century. For references see Meltzer (1981, p. 51). Subsequent research does not support Marshall's conclusion about real wage changes. The pattern is mixed.

leave major questions unanswered. Why do we tolerate particular forms? Can institutional arrangements be found to lower costs of information and reduce uncertainty? Would different arrangements reduce the amplitude of fluctuations? Attempts to answer questions of this kind have produced a burgeoning literature on the role of money in the asset portfolios of optimizing households, the use of money as a medium of exchange and on alternatives to the Walrasian auctioneer as an institutional device for clearing markets. This literature has not reached the stage at which a professional consensus has formed, and it has not produced an explanation of contracts and institutions that is sufficiently general and parsimonious to be useful for a large class of problems.[16] But it has given major impetus to the search for micro foundations that explain *why* we tolerate the costs of information and institutional or contractual arrangements that impose these costs. This impetus is broadly similar to the impetus that Keynes's work gave to the analysis of existence and stability of general equilibrium micro foundations.

A considerable gap remains between the goal of producing micro foundations compatible with observations at the macro level and current monetary theory. As Grossman (1983) notes in a recent essay, the market clearing, rational expectations model of a business cycle that is driven by monetary surprises survives despite the failure to achieve a theory that is compatible with observations at the macro level.

The Walrasian auctioneer who clears the market also provides costless information about market clearing prices. At these prices, we aggregate individual demands to get market demands, and, with some additional restrictions, aggregate market demands to get aggregate demand. The range of problems to be solved after using the auctioneer to dispose of the problem of price setting in individual markets is greatly reduced.[17] It takes a lot of ingenuity to derive the persistence of aggregate excess supply or demand, or to derive persistent deviations of actual from expected values, using a micro foundation in which everyone has the same information and is permitted to recontract until a general equilibrium is reached. The auctioneer has proven to be a useful institutional arrangement for many issues addressed by economic theory, but it does not seem to be useful for investigating the non-neutrality of money. Once the auctioneer is removed

---

[16] I find it difficult to fathom why most of this literature remains separate from the theory of public choice and ignores the perceptive insights in, for example, Hayek's (1959) discussion of the formation and development of institutions. Equally difficult to justify is continued reliance on the assumption that governments do not alter the allocation of resources or that debt and capital are perfect substitutes.

[17] Alchian (1977) contains some early efforts to develop alternatives and some applications to prolonged recessions. Patinkin (1965) states the relevant assumptions.

and prices are 'rationally' set for one period, using all available information, there is no problem in showing that unforeseen changes in money growth cause fluctuations in inventories, aggregate demand, employment and real wages. If, in addition, people cannot instantly distinguish persistent and transitory changes in money growth, changes in money growth (or real variables) are sufficient to generate fluctuations broadly similar to those we observe. See Brunner, Cukierman and Meltzer (1983).

Current rational expectations macro models differ from Friedman's (1974) framework not only by giving more explicit attention to the way information and disturbances (or shocks) affect market participants but also by introducing a supply equation, or Phillips curve, as a part of the model. The micro-foundations for the latter are not fully developed. A popular linear version of the rational expectations model, used in McCallum (1980), is reproduced in equations (9) to (11).

$$y_t = a_0 - a_1[i_t - E_{t-1}(p_{t+1} - p_t)] + v_{1t} \qquad (9)$$

$$m_t - p_t = c_0 + c_1 y_t - c_2 i_t + v_{2t} \qquad (10)$$

$$y_t = \alpha_0 + \alpha_1(p_t - E_{t-1}p_t) + \alpha_2 y_{t-1} + u_t \qquad (11)$$

The three equations are, respectively, the *IS*, *LM* and supply curves representing equilibrium solutions for the expenditure, money, and output sectors of the economy. Productive capacity is assumed constant throughout. Real income (y), price level (p), and money stock (m) are in logarithms; i is the nominal rate on a one-period asset. $E_{t-1}p_{t+j}$ is the expectation of the price level expected to prevail in period $t + j$ based on all information available at the end of period $t - 1$. The v_t and u_t are random variables with zero mean, constant variance and other properties useful for removing covariances, serial correlation and other complications.

For given values of money and rational price expectations, the model determines y, p, i and the real rate of interest. Output and the real rate are not fixed, as in Friedman's theory; output can vary around the predetermined level of productive capacity. McCallum's use of y_{t-1} introduces persistence, but there is no reason given for a persistent difference between y_{t-1} and capacity output. By assumption there is no relation between the size or frequency of random disturbances and the level of capacity output.

The convenient assumption that excludes any effect of past or current disturbances on productive capacity is not innocuous. Lucas's (1981, pp. 104–30) critique of econometric models implies that structural parameters of the investment, consumption, production and asset equations are not constant but depend on policy rules and, more generally, on institutional structure. Structures or policies that reduce or dampen fluctuations can be expected to induce different behavior from structures or policies that augment fluctuations. Lasting effects of fiscal and monetary policies on capacity output can occur if policies increase (or reduce) the variance of prices and output or if government debt, issued to finance consumption, is held in asset portfolios in place of claims to real capital issued to finance investment.[18] A potential link between Keynes and rational expectations models lies in the relation of policy rules and procedures to investment, the size of the capital stock, the choice of labor or leisure, the size of the labor force and expected output.

A basic problem in models of this kind arises from the assumption that all bonds are one period assets. It is hard to see how this assumption can be reconciled with observations on the term structure of interest rates. Risk or liquidity premiums are difficult to reject empirically. If risk premiums differ, there must be at least two asset markets in which people trade claims to assets with different risk premiums. One of these markets is missing. Its absence from a model of long-run equilibrium may be a useful simplification; its absence from a model of the business cycle that relies on misperceptions and expectations is more difficult to accept.

One of the main implications of rational expectations monetarism is known as the policy ineffectiveness proposition. See Sargent and Wallace (1975). This proposition states that real variables are independent of systematic – known or predicted – changes in money. McCallum and Whitaker (1979) extend this result to include the systematic part of a feedback rule for fiscal policy, using a linear model in which policy-makers and the public have the same information. Built-in stabilizers can reduce the variance of real variables but, as before, the variance of output does not affect the interest rate, the level of capacity output or the size of the capital stock.[19]

Another major development of rational expectations policy analysis is the time inconsistency proposition of Kydland and Prescott (1977). These authors build on Lucas' result (1981, pp. 104–30) showing that the choice of policy rules affects the structure of the policymakers' model of the economy. Since changes in policy rules induce changes in structure, a policy that is optimal for a particular structure does not remain optimal. Kydland and Prescott show that the choice of policy (or politician) affects

---

[18] McCallum (1980, pp. 726–9) considers effects on capacity arising from a real balance effect and cites some previous discussion of this problem. See also Barro (1976). The effect of debt arises if debt is not a perfect substitute for money or real capital and if the government spending financed by debt alters the allocation of resources between consumption and investment. Brunner and Meltzer (1972) suggest some of the reasons for an effect of debt on capacity output (crowding out) by treating debt, money and capital as distinct assets.

[19] McCallum (1980) shows that the policy ineffectiveness proposition remains in a limited class of structures that have prices set in advance if the price incorporates expected policy.

expectations, the structure of the model and, therefore, the optimal policy. They demonstrate, also, that in some (specified) structures frequent policy changes can destabilize an economy.

These studies do not establish specific conditions under which any particular rule is optimal, but they show that, under rather general conditions, known (announced) policy rules are superior to discretionary policy changes. The main reason is that surprises are costly to individuals and to society. Surprises, or shocks, cannot be avoided but they can be reduced to the minimum inherent in nature and market processes. Unless policymakers have an uncommon advantage in forecasting future shocks, they are unable to predict shocks or offset them, and their attempts to reduce variability will fail. These policy implications of rational expectations models are more closely related to one of the main issues Keynes addressed in the *General Theory* than they may appear. Keynes directed attention to the relation of institutional structure to expectations, to the variability of output and to the distribution of risk between the public and private sectors. The main policy recommendation of the *General Theory* is a proposal for a policy rule that, Keynes believed, would reduce fluctuations in investment.

KEYNES AND THE MONETARISTS

Keynes would not object to the monetarist proposition that the systematic portion of monetary policy has no effect on the equilibrium value of real variables. He wrote that he had difficulty understanding Irving Fisher's theory of interest because (1936, p. 142)

[I]t is not clear whether the change in the value of money is or is not assumed to be foreseen . . . [I]f it is foreseen, the prices of existing goods will be forthwith so adjusted that the advantages of holding money and of holding goods are again equalized, and it will be too late for holders of money to gain or to suffer a change in the rate of interest which will offset the prospective change during the period of the loan in the value of the money lent.

A few lines later, Keynes added (*idem*):

The prices of *existing* assets will always adjust themselves to changes in expectation concerning the prospective value of money. (Italics in the original.)[20]

Keynes corresponded with J. R. Hicks, after Hicks sent his classic (1937) article. Keynes commented that Hicks had not stated the classical position

---

[20] The argument is part of Keynes's effort to establish that the effect of *expected* price changes on output arises mainly by changing the marginal efficiency of the given stock of capital *relative* to the rate of interest.

accurately. Early classical writers had been free of the inconsistency that crept into later classical doctrine (J.M.K., xiv, 79).

> The inconsistency creeps in, I suggest, as soon as it comes to be generally agreed that the increase in the quantity of money is capable of increasing employment. A strictly brought up classical economist would not, I would say, admit that. We used formerly to admit it without realizing how inconsistent it was with our other premises.

In these passages and elsewhere, Keynes is free of the belief that employment, output and other real variables depend on the expected nominal stock of money. He rejects the type of non-neutrality that is prominent in the Keynesian tradition and in criticisms of rational expectations. Viewed in the context of these statements, Keynes's frequently quoted proposition about the ineffectiveness of monetary policy is an early statement of the rational expectationists' policy ineffectiveness proposition.[21]

The major differences between Keynes and the monetarists are not about money illusion or the effect of nominal money on equilibrium real output. Keynes is not guilty of these vulgar errors that are identified as Keynesian. The differences between Keynes's theory and monetarists' theories are more basic. In the remainder of this section, I compress the differences under four headings that bring some main differences and similarities into focus but are not meant to be either exhaustive or exclusive.

Impulses

Keynes and the monetarists reach very different conclusions about the dominant impulses affecting the economy. For Keynes, changes in the marginal efficiency of capital are the main cause of fluctuations in investment and output. During periods of expansion, investors become excessively optimistic about the future returns to investment. A sudden shift in sentiment causes a collapse of investment and an increased demand for money. The latter drives up the rate of interest and intensifies the decline in investment, 'but the essence of the situation is to be found, nevertheless, in the collapse in the marginal efficiency of capital' (1936, p. 316).

Keynes does not deny that monetary surprises can affect investment by changing the rate of interest or affecting expectations, but his emphasis is on non-monetary factors. Principal among the latter is 'confidence'. Confidence affects current (private) decisions by changing investors' subjective beliefs about the quality of forecasts (1936, p. 48) and, thus,

---

[21] The proposition, in Chapter 19 (1936, p. 267), denies that 'open market monetary policy is capable unaided of achieving this result [continuous full employment]'.

confidence is a major determinant of the marginal efficiency of capital.

Monetarists typically treat the private sector as stable. Government policies, particularly monetary policies, are the major cause of instability. Shifts in sentiment (or confidence) are seen, principally, as a response to shifts in 'underlying conditions', but the principal shifts discussed in much of this literature remain in the classical tradition; emphasis is on changes in money and in the rate of money growth.

In the rational expectations literature changes in 'confidence' and in conditional expectations do not occur haphazardly as a consequence of 'animal spirits'. Changes in belief are a rational response to perceived changes in the environment or, in contemporary jargon, the information set. For rational expectations monetarists, changes in the environment are dominantly, but not exclusively, monetary.

Expectations and risk

Keynes's treatment of expectations and risk differs from the rational expectationists and Friedman. Neither Friedman nor the rational expectationists directs attention to perceived changes in risk, whereas risk and uncertainty are of major importance for Keynes's interest rate theory and for liquidity preference. Keynes distinguishes between short- and long-period expectations. The distinction is used to explain why short-term rates of interest differ from long-term rates. In contrast, Friedman assumes that the real rate of interest is fixed, and the rational expectationists either do not distinguish between short- and long-term rates or, at times, omit the interest rate. See Lucas (1975).

Keynes defines a person's short-term (sales) expectations in a way that rational expectationists can find attractive. Sales expectations are the expectations of proceeds which, if held with certainty, would lead to the same behavior as does the bundle of vague and more various possibilities which actually make up his state of expectation when he reaches his decision (1936, p. 24, n. 3).

In Keynes's 1937 lecture notes, we find a clear statement of his intention to keep these expectations equal to actual outcomes.

All one can compare is the expected and actual income resulting . . . from a particular decision. Actual investment may differ through unintended stock changes, price changes, alterations of decision . . .
I began as I said by regarding this [the mistake in short-period expectations] difference as important. But eventually I felt it to be of secondary importance, emphasis on it obscuring the real argument. For the theory of effective demand is *substantially the same if we assume that short-period expectations are always fulfilled.* . . .
I now feel that if I were writing the book again I should begin by setting forth my

theory on the assumption that short-period expectations were always fulfilled; and then have a subsequent chapter showing what difference it makes when short-period expectations are disappointed. (J.M.K., XIV, pp. 180–1. Italics added.)

The lecture notes then discuss differences between Keynes's theory and the theories of Robertson, Hawtrey and the Swedish economists. These writers 'find the whole explanation in the *differences* between effective demand and income . . . in my treatment *this is not so*' (J.M.K., XIV, p. 181). Keynes remarks: 'I'm more classical than the Swedes, for I am still discussing the conditions of short-period *equilibrium*' (*ibid.*, p. 183. Italics added).[22]

The discussion of long-term expectations starts off in a similar way. 'We are assuming, in effect, that the existing market valuation, however arrived at, is uniquely *correct* in relation to our existing knowledge of the facts which will influence the yield of the investment' (1936, p. 152) (Emphasis in the original). Keynes continues, '[A]n investor can legitimately encourage himself with the idea that the only risk he runs is that of a genuine change in the news *over the near future*, as to the likelihood of which he can attempt to form his own judgement, and which is unlikely to be very large' (*ibid.*, pp. 152–3).

The problem is that the stability of long-term expectations depends on the assumption that our beliefs about the future will not be very different tomorrow. This assumption, or convention, breaks down, Keynes believed, because market valuations are dominated by the opinions of speculators who are either ill-informed or unconcerned about the more distant future. When there are changes in opinion, Keynes's 'bulls and bears' produce sudden changes in the marginal efficiency of capital.

Keynes regarded the economic system and equilibrium output as stable, despite the volatility of long-term expectations. Shackle (1967, p. 129) interprets Keynes's discussion of long-term expectations as evidence of Keynes's belief that expectations are not only volatile but irrational. This interpretation is a radical departure from Keynes's early work on probability, work to which he refers the reader of the *General Theory* (1936, p. 148) to supplement the explanation he offered there.

A random walk with relatively large permanent variance and relatively small transitory variance captures the central idea. Suppose, for example, that the yield or price of each durable good, p^i, follows a random walk, as in equation (12).

$$p_t^i = p_{t-1}^i + u_t^i, \qquad (12)$$

---

[22] In a letter to Ohlin, Keynes explained that he assumed perfect competition and diminishing marginal productivity (J.M.K., XIV, p. 190). See also (1936, p. 114) where Keynes assumes diminishing marginal productivity. Ohlin (1978, p. 147) regarded these simplifications as radical.

where u_i^j and Δp_i^j are normally distributed with zero mean and variances σ_u^2 and $\sigma_{\Delta p}^2$ respectively. Prices (or yields) are subject to discrete changes which, for relatively large $\sigma_{\Delta p}^2$, produce rapid adjustment in the market for the particular good. If changes in the prices of durables are correlated, as Keynes's examples of uncertainty (XIV, pp. 113–14) suggest, large changes in expected prices can induce the swings in the marginal efficiency of capital and in investment that Keynes placed at the center of his theory.[23] The larger the price changes, the greater is the induced change in investment and the variability of output.

The *General Theory* differs from Keynes's earlier work by giving greater attention to the relation of variable expectations to risk premiums, and of risk premiums to interest rates and the level of equilibrium output. Keynes tells us that the 'necessary condition [for a liquidity preference for money as a means of holding wealth] is the existence of *uncertainty* as to the future of the rate of interest, i.e., as to the complex of rates of interest for varying maturities which will rule at future dates' (1936, p. 168). The premium for uncertainty or risk raises the equilibrium market and the effective (risk augmented) real rate of interest and lowers equilibrium investment, the capital stock and the level of output. The more volatile are expectations, the larger the size and frequency of fluctuations in the marginal efficiency of capital and, therefore, in the level of income. The larger and more frequent are fluctuations in actual income, the greater the risk borne by society and embedded in risk premiums.

These considerations are not reflected in the monetarist theories of Friedman and the rational expectationists. On these issues, Keynes's and monetarists' theories are distinct.

Supply and demand

Although Friedman (1968) is a principal reference for the rational expectations supply curve, the supply curve of output is not an integral part of Friedman's framework. In one version, real output is fixed at its equilibrium value. In the other, the division of nominal output between prices and real output is one of the less satisfactory features, as I noted earlier.

The rational expectations model, in equations (9) to (11), has *IS* and *LM*

---

[23] This type of uncertainty is compatible with the method called rational expectations. See Brunner, Cukierman and Meltzer (1980, 1982). An alternative interpretation of uncertainty, based on Bayesian theory, allows people to learn gradually about changes in the conditional distributions of structural parameters. See Cyert and DeGroot (1974).

equations and a supply equation for aggregate output.[24] A principal difference between this model and Keynes's is that the rational expectationists assume that capacity output is given. Keynes's principal concern on the supply side is the position or level of capacity output. He wrote to Lerner (J.M.K., XXIX, p. 215):

> It was an important moment in the development of my own thought when I realized that the classical theory had given no attention at all to the problem *at what point* the supply of output as a whole and the demand for it would be in equilibrium. When one is trying to discover the volume of output and employment, it must be this point of equilibrium for which one is searching.

The same idea is repeated many times. In his discussion of the classical theory of interest, Keynes points out that an equation is missing.[25] In letters to Robertson, who commented extensively on early versions of the text, he explained that the equilibrium level of employment is unique (for given risk). (J.M.K., XIII, pp. 513–14):

> I argue that there is only one value of N for which $D = D'$ and that this may have a lower value than the N given by the classical theory. In this case actual employment is given by the lower value . . .[26]
> The notion that supply is never heard of again suggests that you think that I like yourself throw over all my fundamental principles when I come to study fluctuations.

Keynes's 1937 restatement makes a similar point (J.M.K., XIV, pp. 122–3).

> In a system in which the level of money income is capable of fluctuating, the orthodox theory is one equation short of what is required to give a solution . . . [I]t has always tacitly assumed that income *is* given, namely, at the level corresponding to the employment of all the available resources.[27]

The particular form and arguments of the supply curve are not critical for exposition of Keynes's theory or its differences from classical and monetarist theories. We are in the realm of Keynes's theory as long as the supply curve of output is not inelastic. In this range, the expected level of equilibrium output can be increased by reducing risk or uncertainty.

---

[24] Keynes would not have written the same equations. I repeat below two of Keynes's three equations used in my interpretation, Meltzer (1983).

[25] '[T]he functions used by the classical theory . . . do not furnish material for a theory of the rate of interest; but they could be used to tell us what the level of income will be, given (from some other source) the rate of interest' (1936, p. 181). See also *ibid.*, pp. 178 and 183.

[26] D is aggregate demand; D' is aggregate supply; and N is the volume of employment.

[27] See also Keynes (1936, p. 276, p. 181 and pp. 183–4) for other references to the indeterminacy in the classical model caused by failure to determine the position of supply.

The principal points can be made using two equations.[28] Once again, there are two interest rates, a long-term rate r^e, that changes much less during cycles than the short-term rate, r.

$$IS: \frac{Y}{W} = A \left(r, \frac{Y}{W}, E \right) \tag{13}$$

$$LM: \frac{Y}{W} = B \left(r, r^e, \frac{M}{W} \right) \tag{14}$$

Y/W and M/W are income and money stock in wage (W) units; r is the rate of interest; E is the expected level of equilibrium income based on available technology *and* the prevailing institutions that determine the risk that society must bear; r^e is the (long-term) real rate of interest that includes that risk. In Keynes's words, r^e is the 'rate of interest which will preserve the *status quo*' (1936, p. 234). Generally, r^e is not the optimum or '*neutral* rate . . . which is consistent with *full* employment' (*idem*).

The two interest rates, r and r^e, can be taken as measures of long- and short-term rates. The long-term rate (r^e) includes the risk factor that is relevant under prevailing institutions. The long-term rate changes much less during business cycles than the short-term rate, r.

A permanent reduction in risk reduces r^e and reduces the demand for money. The reduction in money lowers r and increases real income (in wage units). Once everyone expects the increase in income to persist, employment is expected to remain at a higher level, on average. The demand for labor increases. The economy experiences small fluctuations around a higher (average and expected) level of income. For Keynes, the limit to increases of this kind is full or maximum employment – the position at which the elasticity of the supply of output reaches zero.

Business cycle dynamics

The *General Theory* analyzes an economy in which output fluctuates around its equilibrium value. It is not a dynamic theory of fluctuations or of the business cycle. It is true that the *General Theory* includes a chapter called 'Notes on the Trade Cycle', but the chapter is written to show that Keynes's theory is applicable to the business cycle and consistent with its principal characteristics.

Rational expectations monetarist theory *is* a dynamic theory of fluctuations. Misperceptions, errors and unforeseen changes introduce devi-

[28] Meltzer (1981, 1983) relates these equations to some of Keynes's specific statements and includes a supply curve of output that, following Keynes (XIV, pp. 71, 104; 1936, p. 26, 243) becomes inelastic at full employment (potential output).

ations of actual from anticipated values. The principal observations, as seen by Lucas (1981, p. 15), include the volatility of business investment and the volatility of employment over the cycle. These observations are the principal observations that, Keynes believed, lacked a satisfactory explanation.

Both Keynes and the rational expectationists develop and use equilibrium theories. Keynes's equilibrium is a stable equilibrium *level* that lies below the level that the economy has the potential to achieve. His problem is to explain the relation of institutional structure to expectations and of expectations to the *size* of fluctuations in investment, employment and output. The main proposition in his book is that the size of fluctuations affects the position of stable equilibrium that the economy reaches. Most of his book is concerned with developing a framework for analyzing the determinants of this position and showing how the equilibrium can be changed. He then proposed changes to dampen fluctuations and raise the level of equilibrium output to (or toward) potential output.

Neither Friedman's model nor the rational expectations model addresses Keynes's central concern. Both reach equilibrium with full use of resources. The rational expectations model remains in equilibrium up to a stochastic component that, at times, is large enough to produce cyclical patterns. Rational expectations theorists have not attempted to relate the size or frequency of shocks to the equilibrium level of capacity (or potential) output or to relate the efficiency of policy rules to capacity output.

CONCLUSION

Keynes's theory differs in several ways from the monetarist theories represented by Friedman (1974) and by recent rational expectations theories. One difference is methodological. Methods in economics have changed in the direction of increased formalism since Keynes's time. Keynes never wrote down an algebraic statement of his theory, although he accepted Hicks's (1937) algebraic restatement with some important, specific qualifications. Rational expectations theories and, to a more limited extent, Friedman's theory are stated algebraically, so the logical structure is often clearer for these theories than for Keynes's. Further, Keynes's theory is static; his discussion of business cycle dynamics is a postscript written to sketch the application of his theory to an important problem that was one of his lifetime concerns. Rational expectations monetarism is a dynamic theory of fluctuations. Friedman (1974) takes an intermediate position. His theory is static, but he devotes many pages to the dynamics of adjustment and the fluctuations induced by unforeseen changes in monetary and real variables.

Differences are not limited to the method of presentation or to the choice of statics or dynamics. The *General Theory* touches on many topics that are not closely related to Keynes's theory. The chapter on mercantilism seems out of place in a book developing the theory of a closed economy. Keynes's lengthy discussions of user cost and the measurement of national income have no counterpart in monetarist theory. These differences are clearly peripheral.

The most important difference is in the issues that the theories address. Keynes's main criticism of classical theory is that the equilibrium position is assumed to be given. Fluctuations occur around the equilibrium level, but neither the size of fluctuations nor their frequency affects investment, the size of the capital stock and equilibrium output. Classical theories assume that the level of equilibrium income is at society's maximum or potential income. The rate of interest reaches equilibrium at a value consistent with the efficient use of the economy's resources. Keynes called this rate of interest the 'neutral' rate (1936, p. 183), and he denied that it is the relevant rate.

The monetarist theories of Friedman and the rational expectationists, considered here, are open to Keynes's criticism of classical theory. They treat the level of full employment income as a given, or what is the same, as determined by factors that are given. There is, at most, one rate of interest, *the* equilibrium rate.

The *General Theory* offers an explanation of the factors that determine the level of output at which the economy reaches equilibrium and the forces causing changes in that level. Keynes states this objective in the preface and repeats the point many times.[29] Keynes's problem is to explain *why* fluctuations in income have their observed size and frequency and *how* the size and frequency of fluctuations affect the *level* of equilibrium income. His answer is that the variability of long-term expectations depends, *inter alia*, on the institutional structure; change relevant institutions and policy rules and the size and frequency of fluctuations will change. Risk and risk premiums in interest rates will change, and these changes, in turn, will change the *level* of equilibrium income that the economy achieves.

For given institutions, changes in expectations may arise because of misperceptions, as in the monetarist theories discussed here. Keynes offers some additional reasons. These include differences in expectations (bulls and bears), and uncertainty about the timing or occurrence of major events.

In his summary of the *General Theory*, Keynes wrote: (1936, p. 249–50):

---

[29] 'This book . . . has evolved into what is primarily a study of the forces which determine changes in the scale of output and employment' (1936, p. vii).

[I]t is an outstanding characteristic of the economic system in which we live that, whilst it is subject to severe fluctuations in respect of output and employment, it is not violently unstable. Indeed it seems capable of remaining in a chronic condition of sub-normal activity for a considerable period without any marked tendency towards recovery or towards complete collapse. Moreover, the evidence indicates that full, or even approximately full, employment is of rare and short-lived occurrence ... [A]n intermediate situation which is neither desperate nor satisfactory is our normal lot.

I interpret this summary as a restatement of the main point of the *General Theory*: the equilibrium level of income lies below the level that could be achieved with different institutions that engender different expectations.[30] Keynes argued in the very next paragraph (and throughout the book) that the higher level of income cannot be achieved unless it is expected to persist. And it cannot be expected to persist unless risk is reduced.

Monetarist theories build on the micro foundations of Walrasian general equilibrium. Keynes assumes perfect competition, but he was not a Walrasian and, I believe, he would regard the impressive work of Arrow (1964) and Debreu (1959) as an inadequate foundation for macroeconomics. The reason is that, currently, Walrasian general equilibrium micro theories do not include relevant institutions that augment or reduce risk. A valid theory of the risk premium, the liquidity premium and the role of money remain among the missing elements of a micro foundation for Keynes's macroeconomics.

Keynes describes his reasons for departing from classical theory as 'definitive', his policy recommendation as 'not definitive' (J.M.K., xiv, p. 122). His main policy recommendation in the *General Theory*, state direction of investment, is offered as a possible solution to the problem he saw. Later, he appears to have changed his mind about state direction. He favored rules and the type of pre-announced fiscal policy called 'build-in stabilizers'. He opposed counter-cyclical tax changes to stimulate consumption.[31]

Keynes's recommendations, like most policy advice given by economists, neglect a major difference between governmental and private decisions in democratic, market economies. Governments, particularly elected governments, cannot forever ignore voters' preferences as expressed in the polling place. The voting rules under which governments are elected to office may be inconsistent with the policy rules designed to minimize risks in the process of achieving the Pareto-efficient outcomes that lie on the (dynamic) production frontier.

[30] Keynes refers to the environment and the psychological propensities instead of institutions and expectations. He considers both 'ultimate independent variables'.

[31] See the memos to James Meade discussed in Meltzer (1981, p. 42). Keynes (1936, p. 203) favored a stable *rule* for monetary policy.

In the *General Theory*, Keynes blamed the private sector for the relatively high and persistent unemployment experienced in Britain during the twenties and in most market economies during the thirties. He looked to government for a solution and presumed that government would act to reduce variability. Monetarists give greater emphasis to instability caused by the absence of policy rules, the types of government policy and the variability induced by frequent, large changes in public policy. Issues about the relative effect of impulses introduced by the private and public sectors and the degree to which they contribute to variability have received far more attention in the monetarist than in the non-monetarist literature.[32] The central policy difference between Keynes and the monetarists is unlikely to be resolved as long as this neglect continues.

REFERENCES

Alchian, A. A. (1977). *Economic Forces at Work*. Indianapolis, Liberty Press.
Arrow, Kenneth J. (1964). 'The Role of Securities in the Optimal Allocation of Risk Bearing', *Rev. of Econ. Stud.*, 31 (April), 91–6.
Barro, Robert J. (1976). 'Rational Expectations and the Role of Monetary Policy', *J. of Monetary Econ.* 2 (Feb.), 1–32.
Brunner, Karl (1968). 'The Role of Money and Monetary Policy', *Review*, Federal Reserve Bank of St. Louis, 50, 9–24.
   (1970). 'The "Monetarist Revolution" in Monetary Theory', *Weltwirtschaftsliches Archiv* 105, 1–30.
   (1983). 'Has Monetarism Failed?' *The Cato Journal* (May).
Brunner, Karl, Alexa Cukierman and Allan H. Meltzer (1980). 'Stagflation, Persistent Unemployment and the Permanence of Economic Shocks', *J. Monetary Econ.* 6 (Oct.), 467–92.
   (1983). 'Money and Economic Activity, Inventory and Business Cycles', *J. Monetary Econ.* 9 (May).
Brunner, Karl and Meltzer, Allan H. (1972). 'Money, Debt and Economic Activity', *J. Political Economy* 80 (September), 951–77.
   (1968). 'Liquidity Traps for Money, Bank Credit and Interest Rates', *J. Political Economy*.
Cyert, Richard M. and Morris H. De Groot (1974). 'Rational Expectations in Bayesian Analysis', *J. Political Economy* 82 (May), 521–36.
Debreu, Gerard (1959). *Theory of Value*, New Haven: Yale.
Friedman, Milton (1956). *Studies in the Quantity Theory of Money*, Chicago.
   (1968). 'The Role of Monetary Policy', *Am. Econ. Rev.* (March), 1–17.
   (1974). *Milton Friedman's Monetary Theory: A Debate with His Critics*, R. J. Gordon, ed., Chicago.
Friedman, Milton and Anna J. Schwartz (1963). *A Monetary History of the United*

---

[32] Lindbeck (1976, p. 17) recognizes that 'the functioning of the political system is not always in good harmony with the requirements of stabilization policy'. He proposes changes in both political and economic arrangements to improve stability.

States, 1867–1960, Princeton University Press for the National Bureau of Economic Research.

Grossman, Herschel (1983). 'The Natural Rate Hypothesis, the Rational Expectations Hypothesis and the Remarkable Survival of Non-Market Clearing Assumptions', in *Carnegie-Rochester Conference Series on Public Policy*, 19, Fall, (forthcoming).

Hayek, F. A. (1959). *The Constitution of Liberty*, Chicago.

Hicks, John R. (1937). 'Mr. Keynes and the "Classics": A Suggested Interpretation', *Econometrica* 5 (April) 147–59.

(1974). *The Crisis in Keynesian Economics*, New York: Basic Books.

Johnson, Harry G. (1971). *Inflation and the Monetarist Controversy*. Amsterdam: North-Holland.

Kaldor, Nicholas (1982). *The Scourge of Monetarism*, Oxford.

Keynes, J. M. (1923). *A Tract on Monetary Reform*, Reprinted as Vol. IV, *The Collected Writing of John Maynard Keynes*, ed. Donald Moggridge. London: Macmillan, 1971.

Keynes, J. M. (1936). *The General Theory of Employment, Interest and Money*. London: Macmillan.

(1939). 'Relative Movements of Real Wages and Output', *Econ. J.* 49 (March), 34–51.

(1973a). *The Collected Writings of John Maynard Keynes*, Vol. XIII. *The General Theory and After, Part I, Preparation*, ed. Donald Moggridge. London: Macmillan; N.Y., St Martin's.

(1973b). *The collected Writings of John Maynard Keynes*, Vol. XIV. *The General Theory and After, Part II, Defense and Development*, ed. Donald Moggridge. London: Macmillan; N.Y., St Martin's.

(1979). *Collected Writings*, Vol. XXIX. *The General Theory and After: A Supplement*, ed. Donald Moggridge.

Kydland, Finn and Edward C. Prescott (1977). 'Rules Rather than Discretion: The Inconsistency of Optimal Plans', *J. Polit. Econ.* 35 (June) 473–92.

Laidler, David (1981). 'Monetarism: An Interpretation and an Assessment', *Econ. Journal* 91 (March) 1–28.

Lindbeck, Assar (1976). 'Stabilization Policy in Open Economies with Endogenous Politicians', *American Economic Review*: 66 (May), pp. 1–19.

Lucas, Robert E., Jr. (1972). 'Expectations and the Neutrality of Money', *J. Econ. Theory* 4, 103–24.

(1975). 'An Equilibrium Model of the Business Cycle', *J. Political Economy* 83 (November) 1113–44.

(1981). *Studies in Business Cycle Theory*. Cambridge: M.I.T. Press.

Mayer, Thomas (1978). *The Structure of Monetarism*. New York: Norton.

McCallum, Bennett (1980). 'Rational Expectations and Macroeconomic Stabilization Policy', *J. Money, Credit and Banking* 12, Part 2 (November) 716–46.

Meltzer, Allan H. (1965). 'Monetary Theory and Monetary History', *Schweizerische Zutschreft* 4 (Spring), 409, 22.

(1981). 'Keynes's General Theory: A Different Perspective', *J. Econ. Lit.* 19 (March) 34–64.

(1983). 'Interpreting Keynes', *J. Econ. Lit.* 21 (March) 66–78.

Modigliani, Franco (1977). 'The Monetarist Controversy, or Should We Forsake Stabilization Policies?' *Am. Econ. Rev.* 67 (March) 1–19.

Mundell, Robert A. (1968). *International Economics.* New York: Macmillan.

Muth, John F. (1961). 'Rational Expectations and the Theory of Price Movements', *Econometrica* 29 (July) 315–35.

Nobay, A. R. and Johnson, H. G. (1977). 'Monetarism: A Historic-Theoretic Perspective', *Journal of Economic Literature* 15 (June) 470–85.

Ohlin, Bertil (1978). 'Keynesian Economics and the Stockholm School: A Comment on Don Patinkin's Paper', *Scandinavian J. of Econ.* 80, 144–7.

Patinkin, Don (1965). *Money, Interest and Prices*, 2nd. ed. New York: Harper and Row.

  (1982). *Anticipations of the General Theory?* Chicago.

Phelps, Edmund S. (1968). 'Money Wage Dynamics and Labor Market Equilibrium', *J. Polit. Econ.* 76 (July) 687–711.

Sargent, Thomas J. and Neil Wallace (1975). 'Rational Expectations, the Optimal Monetary Instrument, and the Optimal Money Supply Rule', *J. Polit. Econ.* 83 (April) 241–54.

Shackle, G. L. S. (1967). *The Years of High Theory.* Cambridge: Cambridge University Press.

Stein, Jerome L. (1976). 'Inside the Monetarist Black Box', in *Monetarism*, J. L. Stein, ed. Amsterdam, North Holland, 183–232.

Thornton, Henry (1802). *An Enquiry into the Nature and Effects of the Paper Credit of Great Britain.* N. Y. Kelley, 1965.

Tobin, James (1981). 'The Monetarist Counter-Revolution Today – An Appraisal', *Econ. J.* 91 (March) 29–42.

Tumlir, Jan (1983). 'J. M. Keynes and the Emergence of Post-WW2 IEO'. Xeroxed GATT, Geneva (March).

COMMENT

F. H. Hahn

Professor Meltzer has given a lucid and fair account of some of the more important recent discussions in macro-economics. He has reached a conclusion which I regard as surely correct when he writes of Keynes: 'he was not a Walrasian and I believe that he would regard the impressive work of Arrow and Debreu as an inadequate foundation for macro-economics' (p. 69). Meltzer also notes, again correctly, that Classical theories assume that the level of equilibrium income is at society's maximum or potential income. The rate of interest reaches equilibrium at a value consistent with efficient use of the economy's resources (p. 68). He does not note that classical theories have no business assuming this. Indeed my complaint is that Meltzer writes as if adherence to one view or another is at present largely a matter of taste or at least a matter on which in the present state of knowledge nothing can be said. This is not the case.

I am not a 'Keynes scholar' and I can offer no comments on what Keynes would have thought of Mrs Thatcher or of Professor Lucas. Nor do I consider that an interesting question. My prime interest in Keynes arises from two circumstances: his insights into the pathologies of a capitalist economy seem to me to be correct and his attempt to forge these insights into a coherent theory seem to me to have failed. For instance as Professor Meltzer notes he never abandoned the postulate of perfect competition or diminishing returns and so made a theory of 'effective demand' almost impossible. In any case the challenge of constructing a theory which without abandoning the sine qua non of greedy and rational agents allows one for instance to describe states where people cannot find work which they want to do at the current wage, makes an economist's life worthwhile. It may also make it useful.

Now the first thing to be said about the Monetarists' theories which Professor Meltzer describes is that they *assume* away almost every problem which Keynes was concerned with. Thus for instance all markets including that for labour are at all times and in all states in competitive equilibrium. There is always a unique equilibrium deducible from the fundamentals of tastes and technology. Bootstrap equilibria are thus impossible. And so on. The second thing to be said is that these *are* assumptions; they are not logically deducible from the axioms of classical theory.

For instance there are many, mostly a continuum of rational expectations equilibria over a finite horizon and generally there may be many for an infinite horizon. Now take the banal proposition that if every agent's money stock doubles, if all debts denominated in money double then every real equilibrium that existed before this event will still be a real equilibrium. How does one deduce from this that any existing money price and wage will double?

If one looks at the more careful rational expectations literature one finds that to get the well known results one must assume, (a) that there is a unique stationary or quasi stationary state which is a saddle point and (b) that expectations must be rational over the *infinite* future. For many plausible models (a) is not true and for practical purposes (b) seems rather dotty. And the new macroeconomists claim to pronounce on current events!

I want to show now by a simple example why these points are not purely 'academic' in the bad sense. Consider an economy where there are constant returns to labour and the labour market has not yet cleared in the Lucas sense, there is excess supply of labour at the going real wage. I am quite happy to suppose, (a) that this is due to past mistakes and (b) that in due course if left to itself the labour market may clear. As is well known under these assumptions, with the real wage equal to the marginal product, firms do not care how much or little they supply. If money wages fall so do prices and increased employment comes entirely from the real cash balance effect. Suppose we agree that this takes more time than we wish to allow and we give every agent a gift of money. Certainly if prices and wages rise in the same proportion as has the money stock then neglecting distribution effects between borrowers and lenders the economy will be where it was before. On the other hand an alternative outcome consistent with rational agents is that output and employment are higher, money prices or wages are unchanged and the extra money is held just because money incomes are higher. Which, or which combination will happen will depend on expectations which, however, are always rational. So the multiplicity of outcomes is here of central importance. The monetarists have done us the disservice of inducing agents to hold the least helpful rational expectations.

One can go on in this vein for a long time. Without departing from classical economics one can get some very non-classical macro-economics.

Professor Meltzer writes that typically the classical macro-economists assume 'complete markets for contingent claims'. I think this must be a mistake since on such an assumption the economy would not, in the absence of transaction costs, have a sequential structure which gives rise to the need for the postulate of rational expectations. Typically rational expectation equilibria are not Pareto-efficient precisely because there are insufficient insurance markets. The habit of writing down log-linear equations in the conditional mathematical expectation of a variable is not only a restricting one but it also leads to muddle which is avoided in a proper 'state of the world' formulation.

I am also a little unhappy with the way in which the problem of 'real fluctuations' has been formulated. It is a mistake widely made to believe that for instance an Arrow–Debreu equilibrium is incompatible with fluctuation as time and states unfold. It is not. The question then is not, why real fluctuations but why fluctuations which seem greater than warranted by this theory and seem also inefficient. I think that the *explanation* which turns on mistakes made by agents will turn out to be tautologous. However, Lucas's more recent work which treats the serial correlation of mistakes occasioned by these being embodied in durable goods seems in the right direction. It however raises the question of how in such a world agents can learn since they must know the mistakes made or to be made by other agents.

I conclude by returning to Keynes. I interpret him as saying that there are available co-operative strategies which lead to outcomes which are superior to the non-co-operative outcomes to be expected from the invisible hand. This makes all economists think of externalities and increasing returns. In fact I think that the recent works of Diamond and Weitzman are the only ones so far produced which give this Keynesian contention a theoretical chance. In a non-perfect competition economy externalities are intrinsic and indeed allow one to formulate a meaningful theory of effective demand. Since I do not subscribe to Friedman's 'as if' methodology I am impressed by the wide divergence of what one observes from what classical theory assumes. I want to see the gap closed.

It took us almost two hundred years to translate Adam Smith's vision into something sufficiently precise to allow us to argue about it. It will certainly take a long time to accomplish the same task for Keynes. In the meantime perhaps we should be rather modest.

COMMENT

C. A. E. Goodhart

Allan Meltzer is extremely well qualified to give the main paper on this subject. Not only has he been a major contributor – both individually and with his colleague and earlier mentor, Karl Brunner – in the development of the analytical school known as Monetarism, but also he has recently produced a fresh and stimulating reinterpretation of Keynes's analytical and policy views in his paper in the *Journal of Economic Literature* of March 1981, which in turn provoked yet further papers and comments in the *JEL* of February 1983. Indeed, Allan now has full membership in the community of experts on the Economics of Keynes.[1]

Nevertheless, I am going to begin my comments by referring to a point which Allan does not mention, not perhaps surprisingly, since both Monetarists and Keynes himself in the *General Theory* seem blind to its importance. This concerns the supply of money. The point is that there is a contradiction, both in Monetarism and in the *General Theory*, between the *theoretical* treatment of the generation of the stock of money on the one side, and the *practical*, policy-oriented assessment of the actual conduct of monetary policy. Thus, Keynes in the *General Theory*, and Monetarists more generally, treat the money stock, for the purpose of theoretical exposition, as exogenously fixed, determined by Central Bank control of the high-powered monetary base, then related to the money stock through

---

[1] I make no claims myself to any similar expertise. Rather, I surmise that the organisers of the Conference chose me as discussant on the grounds that, as one of his few fellow Old Etonian economists, I would more intuitively appreciate the innate elements of Keynesian analysis. Has the battle of macro-economics also been won on the playing fields of Eton?

the familiar multiplier.[2] On the other hand, when considering the actual, practical conduct of monetary policy in the real world, both Keynes and the Monetarists have appreciated, correctly, that Central Banks in practice have almost always manipulated interest rates as their actual operational target. Indeed, this distinction is sharpened when one notes that in some of those periods when post-Keynesians are inclined to allow that Central Banks shifted more towards base control, e.g. in the U.S.A. between October 1979 and July 1982, Monetarists, e.g. Bill Poole,[3] quite frequently deny that there has been any such effective shift.

There is, however, clearly one important distinction between Keynes's own analysis and Monetarists in this respect, in that Keynes not only realised, when discussing practical political-economy, that Central Banks operated through controlling interest rates, but also felt that it was appropriate that they should do so. Allan Meltzer's half-suggestion[4] that Keynes favoured a 'monetary rule' is a bit mischievous, since when you turn to the page in question in the *General Theory*, it is quite clear in that context that Keynes was arguing for a determined and persistent policy to effect the level of long-term interest rates, and in no sense for a monetary rule relating to the rate of growth of the monetary aggregates themselves.

If the Central Banks are, as is usually recognized in practice, operating on interest rates directly, and not working through base control, then it follows that both the money stock and the monetary base are endogenously determined (and, indeed, that is a major criticism about actual policies which the Monetarists frequently make); but in that case the chain of causation does not run from base control to interest rates, but from interest rate manipulation to movements in the base. In no sense do movements in the base then control the stock of money; rather vice versa. Because of failure to appreciate analytically what was realised on a practical plane, money-supply determination has been mistaught, by mainstream Keynesians almost as much as by Monetarists, for decades. It was not until Tobin[5] that a proper analysis of money determination began to be developed, analyzing the equilibrium bank balance sheet within a profit-

---

[2] This subject has recently been highlighted and documented by Professor Basil Moore in his excellent paper on 'Keynes and the Endogeneity of the Money Stock' (City of London Polytechnic, mimeo, 1983). Moreover, the basic *IS/LM* framework appears to be predicated on the basis of money stock directly controlled by the Central Bank.

[3] 'Federal Reserve Operating Procedures', *Journal of Money, Credit and Banking* (November 1982).

[4] To be found on p. 69, n. 31, and in his earlier 1981 *JEL* paper in footnote 27 on page 51.

[5] 'Commercial Banks as Creators of "Money"', in *Banking and Monetary Studies*, ed. D. Carson (Irwin, Homewood, Ill., 1963).

maximizing framework, within which reserve ratios, and interest-rate controls, e.g. Regulation Q, were properly viewed as important constraints on banks' operational freedom – rather than as, formerly, key elements within a multiplier process.

More important for my present purpose, it was also not realised that the appreciation that it is interest rates, and not the money stock itself, that is actually policy-determined, torpedoes the attempt to express Monetarist analysis within an *IS/LM* framework, as, for example, Allan Meltzer sets out again here on pages 53 and 54. If:

$$C = f_1(Y/P, \rho)$$
$$I = f_2(\rho)$$
$$C + I = Y/P$$
$$r = \rho + \pi E$$
$$\pi E = E_t P_{t+1} - P_t$$
$$E_t P_{t+1} - P_t = (P_t - P_{t-1}) + b\left(\left(\frac{Y}{P}\right) - \left(\frac{Y}{P}\right)^*\right)$$

(where b is the normal level of real output, and r, the nominal level of interest rates, is determined by the Central Bank) then there is no room for monetary growth to have any direct influence on output, or prices, except via the single transmission route by means of the effect of interest rates on expenditures. In so far as the demand-for-money function, and velocity, are stable in such a model, so that movements in Y and M are closely correlated, this must, by construction, be the result of reverse causation: in effect, monetary developments become an endogenous, vestigial effect – as they have, indeed, been modelled in most UK economic macro-models, until at least very recently, in which models the level of interest rates is typically given as policy-determined, and this is the sole route through which monetary factors influence the 'real' economy.

And this is, indeed, exactly the conclusion that many post-Keynesians accept. It is not, however, my own conclusion. My own view, instead, is that it is extremely bad tactics for Monetarists to try to express their own analysis within the confines of the standard *IS/LM* construct, rather like choosing to play a match on the opponents' ground. It is, of course, true that Milton Friedman did exactly this in his celebrated 1971 *Journal of Political Economy* article, which was then followed by the even-more celebrated 'Special Issue on Monetary Theory' in the *JPE* in 1972. Even so, the *IS/LM* framework forces monetary factors to effect expenditures solely through interest rates. When this latter route is examined empirically, by testing for the effects of changes in actual interest rates on various kinds of expenditures, it has generally been found to be quite weak. Friedman has tried to broaden the approach by appealing to a range of other, unobserved or unobservable, general interest-rate effects. Thus, he claims 'The crucial issue that corresponds to the distinction between the 'credit' [Keynesian] and 'monetary' [Monetarist] effects on monetary policy, is not whether changes in the stock of money operate through interest rates, but rather the range of interest rates considered. On the 'credit' view, monetary policy impinges on a narrow and well-defined range of capital assets and a correspondingly narrow range of associated expenditures . . . On the 'monetary' view, monetary policy impinges on a much broader range of capital assets and correspondingly broader range of associated expenditures.'[6]

But this has led detractors to accuse Friedman, in particular, and Monetarists, in general, of a 'black-box' approach, whereby monetary developments affect nominal expenditures directly in some ineffable, disembodied and mysterious manner. This is, I think, unfair. The argument can be put much more concretely. Consider, for example, actions which serve to increase the money supply, say, open market operations in which the Central Bank bids a higher price for bonds, or expenditures by the Government not matched by debt sales, or activation by a borrower of previously unused credit facilities. The immediate recipient of the money thus created, whether he be a seller of bonds, goods or assets, will accept the money, not because his demand for money has increased exactly in line, but because the receipt of money represents a necessary stepping-stone en route to achieving the final desired portfolio of all goods and assets. In the instant of receiving the extra money, the recipient is not in a state of final equilibrium, and the 'excess' holding of money effectively enters his/her individual expenditure functions at that point of time.

The basic distinction here, in terms of the history of thought, I believe, concerns the analysis of interest rates, whether these latter are seen as determined by liquidity preference, or by loanable funds, that is whether they are seen as determined in the market for money, or in the market for bonds. Unfortunately, the Monetarists have been handicapped in making this essential distinction as clear and transparent as it should have been by their tendency also to believe in perfect and rapidly clearing markets. In so far as these latter perfect markets existed, the monetary disequilibria described above would work their way through the system so quickly, so instantaneously, in *meta*-time, as David Laidler has put it, that it would

---

[6] Friedman and Meiselman, 'The Relative Stability of Monetary Velocity and the Investment Multiplier in the United States, 1897–1958', Research Study Two in *Stabilization Policies*, Prentice-Hall, 1964, page 217.

never actually be seen empirically in process.[7] Or, to put it another way, when the system is in full equilibrium, the liquidity preference and loanable funds approaches become equivalent, a conclusion that allowed an uncomfortable truce to be reached in that long and difficult debate.

It was never, however, a secure, nor a well-founded truce. Keynes himself was, of course, never handicapped, as the Monetarists have been, by a tendency to believe in perfect markets, and he had to battle on this front against several critics[8] rather desperately in order to defend his own belief in the superiority of the liquidity preference viewpoint. In particular, Keynes had to deal with problems of dynamics in the process of moving from one equilibrium position to another. Thus, if someone were to borrow for investment purposes, would not this have the effect of raising interest rates before the accelerator/multiplier process could start working, thereby crowding out other expenditures? This question caused Keynes serious problems, and he responded with various, not very convincing, theoretical adjustments (i.e. the finance motive for holding money) and also with responses on the practical level. Turning to the latter, Mr Lonie of Dundee University has directed my attention to a series of letters that Keynes wrote in 1939 to *The Times*,[9] in which Keynes argued that an increase in Government expenditures should be initially financed by monetary expansion, since it would only be gradually that the recipients of the money from such expenditures would apply their 'excess' money balances to buying bonds. But, as Dennis Robertson noted (*Lloyds Bank Review*, 1939), the ease with which such funds could 'be shepherded into the gilt-edged market remains a matter of examination in each particular case'. Instead, an increase in money holdings, whether obtained in the form of extra income, or from an asset sale, would be as likely to be spent in the purchase of other assets, real and financial, as well as, or rather than, Government Bonds. Keynes's concentration on a limited number of financial markets as providing the outlet for 'excess' money balances seems to me and, I believe, to Monetarists a weak link in Keynesian economics.

[7] In the development of this analysis, I have benefited greatly from reading David Laidler's papers on this subject, notably 'The "Buffer Stock" Approach to Monetary Economics', which he gave in April 1983 at the AUTE Conference in Oxford. I share and strongly support Laidler's analysis on this subject, on which I have also written a paper, which will be forthcoming in a book to be published later this year by Macmillans.

[8] As an ex-Trinity man myself, this is the point at which to acclaim the value and sense of Dennis Robertson's analysis.

[9] 'Crisis Finance – An Outline of Policy – II The Supply of Savings', *The Times*, Tuesday, 18 April 1939, and 'Borrowing by the State – II A Programme of Method', *The Times*, Tuesday, 25 July 1939, reprinted in J.M.K., xxi, pp. 513–18 and 557–64.

My limited reading both of Keynes, and of the various current expert commentators on the Economics of Keynes, notably Allan Meltzer, makes me believe that Keynes placed considerable weight, in assessing his own particular contribution, on the liquidity preference explanation of interest rates. I doubt, however, whether this strand of Keynesian thought can indeed properly bear such weight, and I reckon that those who follow Dennis Robertson, including in my view implicitly *all* Monetarists, have the better of this crucial argument.

What, however, I find much harder to grasp is exactly how much weight *theoretically* Keynes placed on non-clearing markets, notably the labour market, as a cause of unemployment. In this respect Allan Meltzer leaves me no less confused. Thus he states, on page 55, that 'Economists from Thornton... through Marshall... to Keynes (1936) relied on wage rigidity, at least in part, to explain the severity of persistence of unemployment during business cycles': yet in his earlier 1981 *JEL* paper he argues in several places, notably in the Conclusions on page 60, that Keynes did not stress money wage inflexibility, thus, 'Keynes did not emphasize either the inflexibility of money wages, or money illusions or absolute liquidity preference . . . when responding to critics or restating his argument.' Once again, there is the problem of distinguishing theory from practical policy. Thus at the practical level one can entirely accept Keynes's argument, restated by Allan on page 50 of his *JEL* paper, that, in the real world with its given institutions, 'A moderate reduction in money-wages may prove inadequate, whilst an immoderate reduction might shatter confidence even if it were practical'; while at the same time one can believe on the *theoretical plane* that, in a world of perfectly clearing markets, systematic unemployment would not, could not, occur, so that on this latter abstract plane price and wage rigidity are the ultimate cause of persistent unemployment. Frankly I look for enlightenment from others as to whether Keynes really believed that in a world of perfect clearing markets an unemployment equilibrium could be theoretically possible.

Allan Meltzer goes on to discuss the relationship between the new Rational Expectations approach and Keynes, and one can indeed speculate how Keynes might have reacted to it. No doubt he would have accepted some parts of it, as all of us have, for example the Lucas critique of macroeconomic models. But the man who accepted the speculative and fashionable content of short-term financial market expectations and who, with Shackle, also emphasized that longer-term major developments in the world, such as nuclear war, oil shocks, major changes in the political and social framework, cannot be placed within a simple probability calculus, would hardly accept that the decision-making process can be purely rational in the sense that most rational expectations theorists appear to require, e.g. that expectations would necessarily be unbiased predictors of outcomes. If, for example, we find in future years that fears of reviving inflation (owing possibly to political shifts in priorities) should prove groundless, so that long-term real rates now exceed future realised short-term rates systematically and over a long period, would that be any evidence of irrationality?

In this comment as discussant I have, I fear, been rather unfair to Allan Meltzer since my own paper is, perhaps, tangential to his own, rather than a direct commentary on it; an approach which I hope can be justified by its circulation prior to the Conference. So I should like to end by saying how interesting and stimulating I found Meltzer's discussion of the importance within Keynes's analysis of the need to reduce risk, particularly in financial markets, and the associated emphasis on public investment (since the risk to private investors may not be capable of reduction sufficiently in order to make the social returns from higher investment equal to the private returns). These were the main points which Allan emphasized, and they seem to me to be good points.

DISCUSSION

The discussion opened with a query concerning Dr. Goodhart's argument that when extra money is received, the recipient is not in a state of final equilibrium (p. 78). This was challenged in so far as a person who sold bonds to the authorities is concerned; for it is a swap of one asset for another, tempted by the higher price of the bond, but no substantial change had occurred in their economic position, unlike an unemployed person who has received a job as a result of a rise in government spending. There is a small capital gain but this is true for all bond holders and so the impact on spending is likely to resemble theirs for none of them have any more or any less reason to go in for extra spending. The lower rate of interest may affect their spending and that of other groups. The main route by which monetary policy affects the economy remains the rate of interest. Dr. Goodhart's attempt to defend the monetarists against the black box criticism seems unsuccessful.

The discussion then turned to an issue raised in the previous session on Lord Kaldor's paper concerning the trade cycle. It was pointed out that while Keynes himself did not develop a model, his theory could be used to do so, for example, Harrod's book in 1936, whereby he added the relation to the multiplier, and Kaldor's model in 1940 itself, which now may be reworked in terms of catastrophe theory mathematics! It was added that in

the post war Keynesian era of 25 years or so the cycle was virtually
eliminated.

Next, a query was raised as to whether the essential properties of money,
as set out by Keynes in Chapter 17, that it is not readily reproducible and
that liquid assets are not easily substitutable into durable assets which are,
are consistent with monetarism? A distinction was then made between
commodity money and credit money regimes and the impact of monetary
policy or an increase in the supply of money in them. While an increase in,
say, gold requires that there be some inducement for people to hold it, that
is to say, a fall in its price as money, there is no such inducement to hold
required in a credit money regime. As to the general question of changing
the money supply, it was pointed out that it was important to distinguish
between two kinds of methods for raising it. First, the banking system
provides money to the public by buying securities – this does not directly
affect expenditures but it does tend to raise the prices of substitutes for
money, e.g., dwellings, commodities where organized producers' markets
exist (the *General Theory* dealt badly with the question of equities and other
substitute commodities). Secondly, banks may lend to previously unsatis-
fied borrowers who as a result are able to invest or consume and so create
additional demand.

A seeming paradox was raised – why is there such an emphasis on
rational expectations in recent times when Keynes's analysis was based on
irrational expectations – if people were rational they would not invest! The
Conference was referred to a diagram on p. 25 of an article by Lord Kaldor
in the July 1983 issue of *Lloyds Bank Review* which showed fluctuations in
world commodity prices in relation to world industrial production. After
1971, the responsiveness was three times greater. It was asked, which of
these periods was characterized by rational expectations? Obviously they
cannot both be equally rational!

One commentator was puzzled by Professor Meltzer's emphasis on
Keynes's policy conclusion concerning the State's direction of private
investment (which he had never seen) for the commentator thought
Keynes's main recommendation was the use of monetary and fiscal policies
to influence the level of output. Professor Meltzer referred the commentator to the last chapter of the *General Theory*. Keynes emphasized that
there was often a need to adjust the money supply, that this was more
efficient and effective than trying to change the structure of wages. Keynes
was criticized for making a distinction between anticipated and unanticipated inflation. Professor Meltzer intervened to say 'That was what
Keynes said, I never said he was right'.

The discussion then turned to economic policy and the appropriate
environment. There is a common interest of all macroeconomists to

minimize uncertainty as a contribution to economic stability. The issue is whether a stable government policy itself – holding instruments constant – is the best contribution that can be made. It may be that a better job could be done by mobilizing the economic environment through a successful activist policy. There is, of course, an irreducible uncertainty associated with the valuation of durable goods and assets that live longer than people. As a postscript the point was raised whether all economic institutions and not just the government should be subject to a similar analysis. For example, who pays the Walrasian auctioneer and is there free entry to this profession?

Dr. Goodhart replied to the discussion directed to him by referring to a unique species, the King's College Keynesians. He argued that money was not equally substitutable with other assets such as houses, so that when you sell any asset you have a subsequent portfolio adjustment to make.

Professor Meltzer replied to the comments as follows:

Professors Matthews and Tobin had raised related issues about uncertainty and rules. One of the main policy implications of the type of rational expectations model discussed in his paper is that pure discretionary policy is generally inferior to a policy rule. A principal advantage of rules is that rules reduce costs of acquiring information and reduce uncertainty about current and future policies.

A policy rule may be complex or simple. Built-in budget stabilizers are a type of policy rule. None of the versions of monetarism that Professor Meltzer discussed, or knew, denies a role of this kind for government policy. The issue is whether government contributes to stability or increases instability.

Keynes was not opposed to rules. In the *General Theory* Keynes favours state direction of investment because he claimed (or perhaps hoped) that the state would reduce the volatility of investment and, thereby, reduce fluctuations in income and employment. This belief (or hope) was misguided.

There is very little in the *General Theory* about public works or counter-cyclical fiscal and monetary policy. Keynes certainly made proposals along these lines but to find these proposals, one must look more to his public statements and less to his theoretical work in and after the *General Theory*. As a policy adviser or public person, Keynes at times favoured activist policies that are not closely related – or are contrary – to the policy rules that he advocated in his theoretical work. It is the former which are the basis for many 'Keynesian' proposals.

Keynes the theorist who favoured institutional changes and policy rules to increase stability is much closer to the monetarists than to Keynes the public person. Both Keynes and the monetarists favour predictable, stable monetary policies. Monetarists emphasize the uncertainty produced by government policies and deny that activist monetary policies reduce variability and uncertainty. They favour constant growth of money to reduce the variability of GNP. Instrument stability is one possible way to reduce monetary variability. Monetarists typically favour stable growth of a monetary aggregate, not a stable value of a monetary instrument such as the monetary base or total reserves.

Dr. Goodhart directs much of his attention to the endogeneity of the money stock and intermediation. In association with Karl Brunner, Professor Meltzer had devoted much of his professional life to these issues, so that he had not often been called to account for neglecting them. He did not see major relevance for this issue in a comparison of Keynes and monetarism, however. The reason is that in both Keynes's theory and in the monetarist theories he considered, the economy is closed. Governments and central banks can control money, if they choose to do so.

In practice, many central banks, including those in the United States and the United Kingdom, do not *control* interest rates. Typically, they set short-term interest rate targets to achieve a desired path for money or GNP. Deviations from the prescribed path induce an adjustment of the interest rate targets. Interest-rate control is often a means of achieving a path for the monetary aggregates. Professor Meltzer believed that this method of *monetary control* increases the variability of money, prices and real output and creates an excess burden. The excess burden would not be changed if exactly the same path for money was achieved with money exogenous in the short-run. The issues about exogeneity and excess burden are not the same and are not closely related. The latter is important and neglected, and it is the latter that he wanted to emphasize.

It is not useful to treat expectations as non-ergodic, since that rules out any serious economic analysis of future states. He saw no benefits in this suggestion, and he did not believe it to be based on a proper reading of the *General Theory* or the *Treatise on Probability*.

The chart in Lord Kaldor's *Lloyds Bank Review* article which purported to show that expectations are irrational and that rational expectations are impossible is totally irrelevant for both purposes. The fact that the coefficients changed after price variability increased is consistent with statistical theory. Further, it is consistent with the famous Lucas critique of econometric policy evaluation, based on rational expectations. A change in regime – formation of an oil cartel or a change from fixed to floating exchange rates – changes the variances and covariances of variables and the coefficients of structural equations. Finally, rational expectations do not imply that people do not make errors. The claim is very different. People use information efficiently and act 'as if' the subjective probabilities on which they base their decisions are accurate representations of the actual distributions of the same events. If the variances of the distributions are relatively large, rationally expected outcomes can be very different from actual outcomes. Keynes, like the monetarists, was interested in variability.

3

Keynes and the international economic order

JOHN WILLIAMSON*

In the first memorandum he wrote on postwar currency policy in 1941, Keynes remarked that there had been only two periods of notable world prosperity, coinciding roughly with the reigns of Queens Elizabeth and Victoria (J.M.K., xxv, p. 21). To those we would now have to add a third, covering the first 20 years or so of the reign of Elizabeth II. Whether one looks at real growth, at employment levels, at cyclical stabilization, at the spread of development to the farthest corners of the globe, at the expansion of trade, at the emergence of foreign aid and the rebirth of an international capital market, at the absence of financial crises, or even at the lack of sharp movements in price levels, the period from the early 1950s to 1973 must be rated the greatest and most stable boom in world history. That period covered the flowering of the postwar international economic order of which Keynes was a principal architect.

By an 'international economic order' I understand a set of generally accepted rules and conventions regarding the proper way for countries to conduct those of their economic policies that have significant repercussions outside their own borders. Conversely, the lack of such an order is characterized by at most weak rules and light-hearted breaches of such rules as are supposed to exist, resulting in countries adopting policies with significant international repercussions entirely at their national discretion. Contemplation of the recent erosion of the General Agreement on Tariffs and Trade (GATT) and the manner of determination of recent U.S. monetary policy would suggest that on this definition we enjoy little more of an international economic order than the interwar period did. The two periods since an integrated world economy emerged in the nineteenth century that have been characterized by an international economic order

* The author acknowledges a wealth of extremely valuable comments on a previous draft from C. Fred Bergsten, Edward M. Bernstein, James R. Crotty, Sidney Dell, Rudiger Dornbusch, Sir Joseph Gold, Elizabeth Johnson, Donald E. Moggridge, L. S. Pressnell, and Walter S. Salant. The usual caveat applies.

are the gold-standard era and the Bretton Woods epoch, which happen almost to coincide with the Victorian and second Elizabethan ages of world prosperity.

The preceding discussion surely suggests two questions. First, to what extent can we attribute responsibility to Keynes for the design of the postwar international economic order? Second, is the empirical association between the existence of an international economic order and world prosperity causal, or is it as coincidental as the sex of the monarch of England? To the extent that Keynes is judged responsible for the design of the postwar international economic order and that order is judged responsible for the postwar boom, we are led to a third question: what can we learn from Keynes in seeking to reconstruct an international economic order? The paper is organized around those three questions.

KEYNES AND ESTABLISHMENT OF THE POSTWAR ORDER

The postwar international economic order (henceforth simply 'postwar order', for brevity) combined microeconomic liberalism with a commitment to active macroeconomic management. This 'neoclassical synthesis', as Paul Samuelson termed it, is embodied in the typical economic attitude of the centre of the political spectrum, where Keynes's loyalties always lay. Keynes himself endorsed it in the *General Theory* (J.M.K., VII, pp. 378–9):

> if our central controls succeed in establishing an aggregate volume of output corresponding to full employment as nearly as is practicable, the classical theory comes into its own again from this point onwards. If we suppose the volume of output to be given, i.e. to be determined by forces outside the classical scheme of thought, then there is no objection to be raised against the classical analysis of the manner in which private self-interest will determine what in particular is produced, in what proportions the factors of production will be combined to produce it, and how the value of the final product will be distributed between them. Again, if we have dealt otherwise with the problem of thrift, there is no objection to be raised against the modern classical theory as to the degree of consilience between private and public advantage in conditions of perfect and imperfect competition respectively.

Microeconomic liberalism

The microeconomic liberalism of the postwar order was embodied in what survived of the International Trade Organization, namely the GATT, and the requirement of current-account convertibility embodied in Article VIII of the International Monetary Fund (IMF). It was also reflected in the absence of any concerted international measures to limit the fluctuations in commodity prices. In due course a private international capital market revived, against the expectations and wishes of the postwar planners, and the triumph of microeconomic liberalism was complete.

Harrod (1951, ch. 13) pictures Keynes as having been sceptical of the possibility of creating a macroeconomic environment that would permit the restoration of microeconomic liberalism, but as an enthusiastic liberal once he was convinced that macro questions would be resolved satisfactorily. I have to say that some passages of Keynes's *Collected Writings*, particularly in Volume XXVI, give the impression that Harrod allowed his admiration for Keynes to distort his judgement.

Keynes had of course argued as a classical free trader in the 1920s, explicitly denying that protection could increase employment (J.M.K., XIX, p. 151). This was why his support for a revenue tariff in March 1931 created a sensation (J.M.K., IX, pp. 231–38), even though he was rather clearly advocating a second-best solution for increasing employment subject to the constraint of defending the sterling parity. Once the gold standard had been abandoned he was emphatic that the currency question, not protection, was the key to expanding employment (J.M.K., IX, p. 243), and in *The Means to Prosperity* he labelled tariffs a 'competitive' means of improving employment and called for the general removal of protection 'imposed to protect the foreign balance' (J.M.K., IX, pp. 352, 361). But this was also the period of 'National Self-sufficiency', with its call 'let goods be homespun' (J.M.K., XXI, p. 236). In the *General Theory* he argued that in normal circumstances of underemployment a mercantilist policy is nationally advantageous, although in the closing pages where he dreamed of converting all the world to Keynesianism he was willing to embrace free trade – the position attributed to him by Harrod in the 1940s. But in the discussions on postwar commercial policy he spoke of the advantages of using tariffs to manipulate the terms of trade, of being able to pass the costs of varying output on to foreigners, and of using quantitative controls to reconcile internal and external balance, in passages that presumably are sacred texts to New Cambridge (J.M.K., XXVI, pp. 284–9). He nevertheless generally supported James Meade at the crucial moments, finally acquiescing in his proposals for a Commercial Union in the fol'owing grumpy terms (J.M.K., XXVI, p. 284):

if all the other countries in the world agree to fall in with the stipulations of his Commercial Union (which, in my judgement, is extremely unlikely), we shall gain more on the swings than we shall lose on the roundabouts. That we shall lose something on the roundabouts is, in my judgement, indisputable. Nevertheless, I am ready to be persuaded not to oppose the scheme, on the ground that our discretion is only restricted if others also are conforming to a strict code, and that the latter, if by a miracle it does come about, may be to our very considerable advantage.

Keynes also opposed unrestricted current-account convertibility (not just freedom of capital movements). After Bretton Woods, he challenged Dennis Robertson's interpretation of the Fund's Article VIII.2 (J.M.K., XXVI, p. 118):

> As I understand this clause, it involves an obligation not to kill convertibility; but there is no obligation 'officiously to keep alive'; it is a prohibition against blocking where a current transaction is concerned. If a non-resident owner of sterling can find a purchaser for it in exchange for foreign currency within the permitted range of parity, then he may not be forbidden to sell his sterling; but there is no obligation under this clause actually to provide him with the foreign exchange he desires, whether his own or another country's.

There ensued a lengthy and exceedingly complex controversy between Keynes and Robertson (and subsequently between Keynes and the U.S. Treasury) about the correct interpretation of Article VIII.2 and its relation to Article VIII.4 (see Gold, 1981a, 1981b). In fact the IMF has always followed Robertson's interpretation, which has made Article VIII.2(a) the centre of the Fund's efforts to liberalize exchange restrictions. Keynes's attitude had been very different on an earlier occasion when he drew up a reasonably comprehensive set of proposals for international monetary reform. In *The Means to Prosperity* (1933), he had suggested that countries be required *inter alia* to abolish exchange restrictions as a condition for access to his proposed 'international note issue' (J.M.K., IX, p. 361). But even in 1945 Keynes was not an ideological autarch, for it was he who fought London to retain the commitment to sterling area current account convertibility as a *quid pro quo* for the postwar Loan (J.M.K., XXIV, p. 600).

In an article in the *Economic Journal* in 1938 Keynes proposed government subsidization of a series of buffer stocks of food and raw materials, arguing on a combination of strategic and stabilization grounds (J.M.K., XXI, pp. 456–70). He returned to the topic in 1942, with a plan for an independently managed international body holding buffer stocks of the main primary commodities in order to stabilize prices within a band of 20 per cent around a base value that could be adjusted gradually at a rate not normally exceeding 4 per cent per annum[1] (J.M.K., XXVII, pp. 115–20). In one of those bizarre events that seem to abound in agricultural policy, the Ministry of Agriculture and the Bank of England joined forces in denouncing the threat that such a laissez-faire approach posed to the development of British agriculture, so the plan languished (J.M.K., XXVII, pp. 110, 196). The outcome was a less open system for temperate products

---

[1] The figures changed in revised versions of the proposal. Keynes envisaged the buffer stocks being financed by his International Clearing Union.

and a less controlled system for tropical products than would have resulted from uniform implementation of Keynes's proposals.

While the war-time planning for the postwar order envisaged an open multilateral trading system, there was no similar intention to restore a private international capital market. That market had collapsed during the Great Depression, and it was generally taken for granted that it would not revive. The World Bank was created as a substitute for private capital flows, in order to secure a flow of real resources to war-devastated and less-developed countries. The IMF Articles imposed no obligation on member countries to liberalize capital transactions, and indeed specifically prohibited use of the Fund's resources to finance capital flight as opposed to a current-account deficit (Article VI.1a). In the event the international capital market revived spontaneously in the 1950s, and official policies slowly adjusted to acknowledge and ultimately to support microeconomic liberalism on capital as on current account. But that was not a feature of the postwar order that was anticipated or desired by Keynes (J.M.K., xxv, p. 185).

The above account indicates that Keynes was at best ambivalent about basing the postwar order on microeconomic liberalism. The proponents of the latter were, rather, the Americans with whom he negotiated and the outstandingly able group of economists with whom he worked in the British government – Marcus Fleming, Roy Harrod, James Meade, Lionel Robbins, and Dennis Robertson, all of whom remained faithful to the combination of microeconomic liberalism and macroeconomic management for which Keynes had laid the basis in the 1930s.

Macroeconomic management

Arrangements for macroeconomic management in the postwar world were largely implicit in the Articles of Agreement of the IMF. Those Articles were hammered out during the protracted Anglo-American negotiations of 1942–44 and the ensuing Bretton Woods conference of July 1944, in all of which Keynes was the leading British figure.

Keynes started thinking about the postwar monetary order even before the United States entered the war, for the first draft of his plan for an International Clearing Union was dated September 1941 (J.M.K., xxv, pp. 33–40). The Clearing Union he envisaged would have organized a multilateral clearing of the bilateral imbalances between central banks, through which all international payments would have been directed. Member countries would have been able to build up credit balances or draw on overdraft facilities with the Clearing Union, expressed in terms of a new international currency unit which he christened 'bancor'. Overdraft rights would have totalled some $26 billion and a substantial part of them would have been available unconditionally.[2] Countries would have been charged interest on the deviation of their bancor holdings from zero in either direction, so as to provide an incentive for surplus as well as deficit countries to seek adjustment. Each country would have declared a value for its currency in terms of bancor, and this value could have fluctuated within a 5 per cent band with the central rate adjusted via a crawl of up to 5 per cent per annum. This was by no means Keynes's first effort at devising a plan for reform of the international monetary system: its historical antecedents are described in an Appendix.

It is well known that, in almost every case where the initial views of Harry Dexter White differed from those of Keynes, the Fund's Articles ultimately reflected White's proposals, which was no doubt inevitable given the relative economic muscle of the United States and Britain. The crucial differences between the two Plans seem to me to have been the following.

(1) Keynes envisaged generalization and perpetuation of the wartime British centralization of exchange transactions through central banks, whereas White envisaged the restoration of competitive exchange markets in which central banks would limit their role to residual intervention designed to influence the exchange rate.[3] (This provides another example of Keynes's abandonment of microeconomic liberalism.)

(2) Keynes proposed to create a new reserve asset, bancor, whereas White's plan posited maintenance of the gold-exchange standard reinforced by a Stabilization Fund (which became the IMF). It is true that at one stage the White Plan contained 'unitas', but these were merely the Fund's accounting unit (which in the event became the gold dollar of 1 July 1944).

(3) Keynes proposed to charge interest on excessive credit bancor balances so as to promote symmetrical adjustment pressures. Initial versions of the White Plan contained no similar provision, but in December 1942 the Americans inserted the 'scarce currency clause' into their plan, thereby giving Sir Roy Harrod (1951, pp. 544–5) the most memorable train journey of his life. It is not clear to what extent the scarce currency clause was inspired by a desire to meet British wishes for a guarantee of symmetry in adjustment pressures (as opposed to a technical concern that the Fund might otherwise be placed in the position of promising to provide a

[2] The amount of liquidity proposed was modified from one draft to the next, as traced by Moggridge (1983).

[3] For an elaboration of this point, see Gold (1981a) and Williamson (1981a).

currency that it did not have[4]), but it was so interpreted by the British. In the event the clause has never been applied.

(4) The White Plan provided for the fund to hold accounts at national central banks and to be able to initiate transactions that would have affected internal economic conditions in member countries. The British insisted on Fund 'passivity', which was accepted (Harrod, 1951, pp. 562–3; Blum, 1967, p. 266).

(5) The Keynes Plan involved access to overdraft rights of the order of $26 billion, in which the potential U.S. liability could have amounted to as much as $23 billion. (In terms of present arrangements, the nearest equivalent would be a once-off SDR allocation of over SDR 720 billion[5] with no acceptance limit!) The White Plan embodied conditional access to a pool of currencies that might have totalled $5.2 billion, toward which the United States would have contributed some $3.2 billion.[6] The Bretton Woods compromise retained the U.S. contribution of $3.2 billion but expanded the Fund to $8.8 billion. At that time Keynes, and most non-American delegates, believed that the United States had withdrawn its opposition to a large element of automaticity in drawings (Dell, 1981). It seems, however, that U.S. acquiescence in the wording of Article v.3 at Bretton Woods was a tactical move designed to avoid direct confrontation with a united opposition, and in due course the United States insisted that the Fund adopt a set of policies involving high conditionality for all except very limited drawings and a fixed period for repayment.

The postwar order involved restoration of competitive exchange markets, perpetuation of the gold-exchange standard without creation of any new reserve asset[7] (till 1969), no effective adjustment pressures on surplus countries, and conditional access to modest quantities of credit. In other words, Keynes had little more success in selling his wartime macroeconomic innovations than his wartime microeconomic illiberalism. The puzzle this poses is why he nonetheless worked unsparingly to achieve the Bretton Woods agreement and to ensure that it commanded support in Britain.

---

[4] The concern arose because there was at one stage a presumption that one would need (for example) Canadian dollars to settle a deficit with Canada.

[5] GWP in nominal dollars has multiplied at least 20 times since 1945, and the original Fund members now have less than two-thirds of the quotas: $26 \times 20 \times 1.5 = 780$, and SDR $1 \approx \$1.08$.

[6] The United States did, however, expect to make large loans – like the postwar Loan to Britain, and loans to the World Bank – through other channels. The Keynes Plan would have substituted for some of these, since it was originally envisaged as the main mechanism for postwar reconstruction.

[7] Unless one were to count Reserve Positions in the Fund as such.

Before exploring solutions to that puzzle, however, it is worth turning aside to look at the basic principles of macroeconomic policy that Keynes had developed in his prewar career.

The first major statement of his views on macroeconomic policy appeared in the *Tract*, in 1923. Keynes adopted the position that monetary policy should be directed at the maintenance of internal price stability, rather than at the establishment or maintenance of a particular exchange rate or gold par. (That position made him a hard-money man in the circumstances of the time, which is inconsistent with his 1930s views only at the most superficial level.) While that position is one that was already guiding the policies of the Federal Reserve Board, it was heresy in Europe. The British Establishment – Treasury, Bank of England, Cunliffe Committee, bankers, even Labour politicians – took it as axiomatic that sterling must be restored to its prewar par value, and to that end espoused deflation (in the sense of policies that would cut prices). Keynes remarked on the state of Continental opinion in an article in the *Manchester Guardian Commercial* in December 1922 (J.M.K., xviii, p. 77):

When I visited Berlin lately to discuss the stabilization of the mark, I found an influential authority arguing that it would be a wise policy to raise the value of the mark to thirty times the value ruling at that time. A restoration of their currencies to the pre-war par is still the declared official policy of the French and Belgian governments. I hear that Signor Mussolini has threatened to double the present value of the Italian lira – a fearful threat indeed if it could be carried out.

When in 1922 Keynes expressed his belief that monetary economics had recently taken one of the 'biggest jumps forward ever achieved in economic science' (J.M.K., xix, p. 160), I take it that he was referring not just to the groping steps towards monetary dynamics or the introduction of the bank deposit multiplier into money supply theory, but that he had in mind above all the parallel efforts of Irving Fisher and himself to establish the principle that monetary policy should be directed to the pursuit of what James Meade (1951) subsequently christened 'internal balance'.

The Keynes of the *Tract* interpreted internal balance as price stability. His writings of the early 1920s admitted the legitimacy of departing from that goal only when inflation was necessary for fiscal reasons to erode the real value of the public debt, or when a fixed exchange rate had to be treated as a constraint which imposed a need to deflate to improve competitiveness.[8] But as the 1920s progressed he became increasingly concerned with unemployment, and by the time of the *Treatise* his policy prescriptions

[8] It is interesting to note that Keynes analysed the question of competitiveness primarily in terms of the relative price of tradables in terms of nontradables, an insight that we nowadays customarily attribute to the Australians (J.M.K., xix, pp. 373–4).

reflected that (though the supporting citations were to the *Treatise* and look distinctly incongruous in retrospect). In due course (J.M.K., XIII, p. 343) the theory adopted the premise that in the relevant range the wage level would be reasonably stable and variations in aggregate demand would be reflected in quantities rather than prices. Internal balance therefore became identified with a full employment target, and state control of investment – subsequently transmuted into fiscal policy – became a second instrument for achieving it. He thus arrived at the basic Keynesian policy stance: advocacy of the active use of monetary and fiscal policy in pursuit of a full employment target.

Keynes's views on exchange-rate policy were a corollary of his conviction that primacy should be accorded to the pursuit of internal balance. At the time of the Genoa conference he was working his way toward the identification of internal balance with price stability. While still recommending restoration of the Gold Standard, he sought to avoid countries' embarking on large deflations to achieve that goal, and therefore urged that currencies be stabilized at rates that reflected their current purchasing powers. He also advocated limited exchange-rate flexibility, in both forms that reemerged in the 1960s' debate on how to save the Bretton Woods system: a wider band and a crawling peg. His proposal of a 5 per cent band between the buying and selling prices of gold was intended to provide adequate incentive for speculators to take positions that would finance seasonal imbalances (J.M.K., XVIII, p. 365).

Even more interesting, at least to this author, is the fact that he conceived of a crawling peg.[9] He advocated this as an expedient that would allow countries that wished to restore their prewar gold pars to nurture that ambition but nonetheless gain the immediate benefit of stabilization (which he argued to be desirable mainly in order to reduce the amplitude of the seasonal swings necessary to induce speculative finance for seasonal imbalances). These are the terms in which he made what appears to be the first proposal for a crawling peg (J.M.K., XVII, p. 364):

But there would be little harm in a moderate concession to popular illusion . . . which would leave open the possibility of some degree of future appreciation. When, therefore, the rate of conversion between their notes and gold is fixed, let the state banks announce that they guarantee not to raise the price at which they will issue their notes against the delivery of gold by more than 6 per cent in any year (and proportionately for shorter periods). The possibility of slow action on these lines would permit the satisfaction of national prestige without inviting speculation or depressing enterprise. It would also make possible participation in a uniform

---

[9] I find that I have previously erred in attributing invention of the idea of the crawling peg to Harrod in 1933 (Williamson, 1981b, pp. 4–5).

scheme by those countries which, having a present depreciation of less than 20 per cent, are likely to attempt an ultimate restoration of the pre-war parity.

By the time of the *Tract* Keynes was advocating a managed exchange rate which could crawl as needed to support price stability (J.M.K., IV, p. 190):

> The Bank of England should have a buying and selling price for gold, just as it did before the war, and this price might remain unchanged for considerable periods, just as bank-rate does. But it would not be fixed or pegged once and for all, any more than bank-rate is fixed. The Bank's rate for gold would be announced every Thursday morning at the same time as its rate for discounting bills, with a difference between its buying and selling rates corresponding to the pre-war margin [nearly 1/6 of 1 per cent] . . . except that in order to obviate too frequent changes in the rate, the difference might be wider . . . say, $\frac{1}{2}$ to 1 per cent. A willingness on the part of the Bank to buy and to sell gold at rates fixed for the time being would keep the dollar-sterling exchange steady within corresponding limits, so that the exchange rate would not move with every breath of wind but only when the Bank had come to a considered judgement that a change was required for the sake of the stability of sterling prices.

In the *Treatise* Keynes spoke of a 2 per cent band and did not mention crawling, consistent with the policy he pursued through the whole period when Britain was on the gold standard of avoiding saying anything that might undermine confidence in the parity. But in 'Notes on the Currency Question' (J.M.K., XXI, pp. 16–28) in November 1931 he reverted to the proposals of the *Tract*, while in *The Means to Prosperity* he called for a 5 per cent band and parities which 'should be alterable, if circumstances were to require, just like bank rate – though by small degrees one would hope' (J.M.K., IX, p. 362), and during the World Economic Conference he proposed basing changes in the dollar/sterling rate on differential inflation (J.M.K., XXI, pp. 261–2).

In the early 1920s Keynes was an elasticity optimist (J.M.K., IV, p. 130), in striking contrast to the position he took up in the 1940s, most vividly illustrated in correspondence with Marcus Fleming (J.M.K., XXVI, pp. 287–303). To an elasticity optimist, the dominant external condition necessary to reconcile internal and external balance is an appropriate exchange rate. An elasticity pessimist, in contrast, regards the state of the world economy as far more critical. Hence it was quite natural for Keynes's growing doubts about the effectiveness of exchange-rate adjustment to be accompanied by increasing emphasis on the importance of securing a high level of demand in the rest of the world. This preoccupation first emerged during the Depression, and provided the central theme of *The Means to Prosperity* and the motivation for the proposal to issue gold-notes to support a concerted international expansion (J.M.K., IX, pp. 350–9) – perhaps the first such 'locomotive proposal' ever made, unless one counts his own more abstract proposal in the *Treatise* for a supranational central bank with the duty of seeking to abolish the credit cycle (J.M.K., vi, p. 354). One of the few passages in the *General Theory* to recognize that economies are not closed argues that in a world of chronic demand deficiency – such as he had then come to regard as the historical norm – mercantilist policies are rational, from a national perspective (J.M.K., vii, pp. 348–9):

> For in an economy subject to money contracts and customs more or less fixed over an appreciable period of time, where the quantity of the domestic circulation and the domestic rate of interest are primarily determined by the balance of payments . . . there is no orthodox means open to the authorities for countering unemployment at home except by struggling for an export surplus and an import of the monetary metal at the expense of their neighbours. Never in history was there a method devised of such efficacy for setting each country's advantage at variance with its neighbours' as the international gold (or, formerly, silver) standard. For it made domestic prosperity directly dependent on a competitive pursuit of markets and a competitive appetite for the precious metals . . . For when in their blind struggle for an escape, some countries have thrown off the obligations which had previously rendered impossible an autonomous rate of interest, these economists have taught that a restoration of the former shackles is a necessary first step to a general recovery.
> In truth the opposite holds good. It is the policy of an autonomous rate of interest, unimpeded by international preoccupations, and of a national investment programme directed to an optimum level of domestic employment which is twice blessed in the sense that it helps ourselves and our neighbours at the same time. And it is the simultaneous pursuit of these policies by all countries together which is capable of restoring economic health and strength internationally, whether we measure it by the level of domestic employment or by the volume of international trade.

At the time of the *General Theory*, therefore, Keynes was arguing that countries should actively manage monetary and investment policy in pursuit of internal balance, which was usually threatened by a deficiency of demand. The exchange rate should be chosen with a view to supporting domestic policy (or reconciling internal and external balance, in Meade's terminology). Universal adoption of such policies would be beneficial to all.

And that is pretty much the basis on which Bretton Woods was set up. There was a presumption that demand should be actively managed by fiscal and monetary policy, with the main dispute between Britain and the United States concerning not economic principles but the extent of international (IMF) involvement in determining the policies of individual countries. The United States adopted the internationalist/interventionist position, doubt-less encouraged by the presumption that it would be on the dispensing end of the advising process. Britain fought for national autonomy, presumably fearing that it would effectively be receiving rather than giving orders.

A second dispute initially concerned the relative probabilities attached to the postwar world exhibiting a deflationary rather than an inflationary bias, with the British dominated by the fear of renewed recession and the United States adopting a far more balanced view of the dangers. Edward Bernstein has provided me with the following account of discussions on this topic:

After the series of seven meetings at the U.S. Treasury between September 13 and October 6, 1943, Keynes gave a dinner at his apartment at the Statler Hotel for Edward Bernstein of the Treasury and Walter Gardner of the Federal Reserve. Mr. Thompson-McCausland of the Bank of England was also at this dinner. During the dinner Keynes said that the United States would want to impose exchange control after the war. Bernstein asked whether this would be because of a severe depression that would result in a flight from the dollar. Keynes said that was what he had in mind. Bernstein then said that he did not believe there would be a severe postwar depression because such depressions were caused by the interaction of wartime inflation and the gold standard. Bernstein had discussed this in an article in the *American Economic Review*, 'War and the Pattern of Business Cycles', September 1940. He argued that war exhausted the money-creating power of a gold standard system so that the growth of the money stock had to be restricted after the war. Moreover, the uneven inflation necessitated deflation in the countries that wanted to restore the gold standard at the historical parities. Furthermore, in some countries that established new par values, this was done on the basis of free market rates that had been depressed by capital flight, so that the rates were much below what were appropriate on the basis of relative prices and costs. Keynes wrote a note for the British Treasury reporting Bernstein's view. Lord [Eric] Roll told Bernstein that he had seen the note when he was at the Treasury.

In fact it seems from an earlier Treasury memo ('The Long-term Problem of Full Employment', J.M.K., XXVII, pp. 320–5) that Keynes was already in May 1943 anticipating a lengthy transitional phase, involving up to 5 years of excess demand and 10 years where stabilization policy would be unlikely to encounter severe difficulties in avoiding a slump. Keynes's willingness to become more relaxed about a chronic world demand deficiency, and more willing to accept that international pressures should be directed even-handedly against both inflation and deflation, was not, however, shared by all his compatriots.

The area in which the IMF Articles had to spell out some of these principles explicitly is in relation to exchange rates. Keynes and White agreed that short-run exchange-rate volatility serves no social function and should be suppressed, but that there needed to be sufficient long-run flexibility to enable the exchange rate to be chosen to fit the needs of the domestic economy rather than *vice versa*. The original version of the White Plan had the Fund fix the exchange rates at which it would deal (although a member able to find a willing partner would have been free to transact at another rate through another channel – see Horsefield, 1969, vol. III, p. 60). These rates could have been changed 'only when essential to correction of a fundamental disequilibrium', and only with the consent of four-fifths of member votes (*ibid.*, p. 43). The Keynes Plan required members to 'agree between themselves the initial values of their own currencies'. Subsequently the Governing Board would have had the right to *require* a country to change its exchange rate if its bancor debit or credit balance exceeded one-half of its quota, and a country could itself have devalued by up to 5 per cent unilaterally once, or by more with the permission of the Board (*ibid.*, pp. 22–4). The right to a once-over unilateral 5 per cent devaluation was the remnant of a proposal in previous drafts for a debtor country to have the right to a rate of depreciation 'not exceeding 5 per cent within any year' (J.M.K., xxv, p. 35), in accordance with Keynes's prewar sympathy for crawling noted above. There seems to be no explicit record of how the adjustable peg came to be substituted for crawling, but in replying to Harrod in December 1941 (when the draft still allowed regular changes of up to 5 per cent) Keynes wrote that 'it would often be preferable, if a change were necessary to make it by a single significant amount rather than by a series of small steps' (J.M.K., xxv, p. 97). He argued that changes as 'small' as 5 per cent would not provoke speculation because the transactions costs would swallow up the potential speculative profit (J.M.K., xxv, pp. 107–8). One reader of the first draft of this paper conjectured that his appointment as a Director of the Bank of England may have led him to absorb some of the Bank's attachment to 'stable rates'. So it seems that Keynes must bear much responsibility for the fateful switch from crawling to adjustable peg, which in my view made the breakdown of the Bretton Woods system inevitable once the assumption of low capital mobility (not to mention astronomical transactions costs!) was no longer satisfied (Williamson, 1977, ch. 2).

Thus the key issue in negotiating the exchange-rate provisions of the Articles was neither the policy assignment of the exchange rate nor the exchange-rate regime, but rather the mix of national and international control over the decision to change an exchange rate. Although the Keynes Plan had provided for the right of the Governing Board to order exchange-rate changes for countries with large debit or credit bancor balances, it also provided for a national initiative to propose devaluations that was lacking in the White Plan, and the British fought hard for national autonomy. The version finally agreed at Bretton Woods stipulated that a member country had the right to propose a change in its par value but only to correct a 'fundamental disequilibrium', and that (except for a change within 10 per cent of the initial par value) Fund concurrence was necessary, but that the Fund had to concur provided it was satisfied that the change was actually needed for that purpose. Despite unsympathetic academic comment over the years about the lack of a formal definition of the term 'fundamental disequilibrium', there has never been any doubt that this was intended to describe a situation where at the existing exchange rate a country cannot expect to generate a current account balance to match its underlying capital flow over the cycle as a whole without, on the one hand, depressing its output below internal balance or imposing trade controls for payments purposes, or, on the other hand, importing inflation. Keynes also succeeded in negotiating a fallback position, the so-called 'Catto clause' in deference to the Governor of the Bank of England, who first proposed what became Article IV.6. This allowed a country that changed its par value without the Fund's approval to suffer no more than ineligibility to borrow from the Fund.

The role of Keynes

I have argued above that the postwar order rejected both the microeconomic illiberalism and the specific wartime macroeconomic innovations that Keynes sought to endow it with. It embodied instead an intellectual position which Keynes had been instrumental in moulding in the interwar period and which by 1942 commanded something of a consensus, excluding Keynes himself, among those charged with postwar economic planning in both Britain and the United States. Yet despite the rejection of almost the entire range of his policy proposals, Keynes worked unceasingly to establish the Bretton Woods system. He constantly urged graceful concessions with a view to achieving agreement and maintaining the momentum toward cooperation. He fought hard to ensure acceptance of the Bretton Woods proposals in Britain (which certainly had the power at that time to torpedo the entire effort, a possibility that seems to have been judged sufficiently real to concern the U.S. Treasury – see Blum, 1967, p. 259). Why, to return to the puzzle posed above, did Keynes work unsparingly for an agreement that included almost none of the specific proposals that he had favoured?

There would seem to be three plausible answers to the puzzle: misapprehension as to the nature of the agreement, a lingering attachment to his earlier ideas, and conviction that an international order of some form was essential, perhaps especially to ensure that the United States did not withdraw into isolation once again.

The first possible explanation is that Keynes simply did not comprehend the extent to which his proposals were being rejected. He did not believe that Meade's proposals for trade liberalization would get far, and he was satisfied that in that event Britain could continue to employ whatever protectionist measures it judged expedient. He did not expect the private international capital market to revive. Plans for commodity price stabilization languished rather than being formally killed. Keynes thought that Britain would continue to centralize exchange transactions and did not realise the commitment to current-account convertibility till after Bretton Woods. Britain had won the scarce currency clause, and how was Keynes to know it would never be applied? He thought he had ensured that Fund credits would be unconditionally available within quite generous limits. It took time for him to realise the extent of the rejection of his proposals.

As that realisation dawned, he became increasingly bitter (Crotty, 1983). Lord Kahn (1976, pp. 28) reports how he finally, on the return journey from the Fund's first Meeting of the Board of Governors in Savannah, wrote a report so critical that it could have precipitated U.K. withdrawal from the IMF. No trace of that draft survives: he was persuaded to resume his public support of Bretton Woods. Clearly there must have been factors other than early misapprehensions that persuaded him to continue supporting Bretton Woods and all that went with it.

The second possible explanation of the puzzle is that he drew considerable reassurance from the extent to which the new institutions were based on the intellectual consensus fostered by his work in the interwar period. It is not even clear to what extent Keynes really had changed his position: one sometimes wonders whether his heresies were not intended to tease more than to convert. Even where U.S. proposals that he would have strongly favoured – such as the proposal to give a specific responsibility for anticyclical policy to the World Bank – were subsequently withdrawn, the mere fact that the authors of the Stabilization Fund were thinking in those terms must have helped convince him that these were allies to be supported in the wider struggle. Richard Gardner's classic study pictures a team in the U.S. Treasury which, while sceptical of the probability of a major postwar depression, was thoroughly 'Keynesian' (Gardner, 1969, pp. 90–1):

> In view of the strong creditor position of the United States, the White Plan might have been expected to make provision for one-sided adjustment by the debtor nations. But the Treasury planners were too thoroughly imbued with the expansionist philosophy to give their plan a deliberate deflationary bias. The Stabilization Fund seemed to envisage roughly comparable adjustments on the part of both creditors and debtors. In its original form it made a remarkably bold attempt to ensure that these adjustments were actually made. Members were obliged 'not to adopt any monetary banking measure promoting either serious inflation or serious deflation without the consent of a majority of member votes of the Fund'.

The third possible explanation is that Keynes was passionately convinced of the need for an international economic order of some form, and especially of having the country whose economy then dominated the world accept its international responsibilities. He had grown up taking for granted the economic order of free trade, the gold standard, convertibility and a world capital market centred in London – the liberal order that survived till 1914 – and he observed in retrospect how well it had worked (J.M.K., II, pp. 6–7). He witnessed the breakdown of economic order in Europe in the aftermath of World War I. He was traumatized by the irresponsibility of the Council of Four in disregarding the economic disorder of central Europe and indeed guaranteeing its perpetuation by the imposition of impossible reparations demands. He launched on a long, and initially intensely unpopular, crusade to scale down reparations to a level that Germany could afford to pay and a formula that would leave her with an incentive to increase output. He repeatedly expressed concern at the lack of U.S. responsibility, especially as regards the cancellation of war debts. He maintained a stream of proposals for reconstructing international monetary relations on a more orderly basis, from Genoa in 1922 to the *Treatise* in 1930 and *The Means to Prosperity* in 1933 to the International Clearing Union in 1942. And then all of a sudden he had the chance to help construct a new order based on what he had espoused for the twenty-year period when the United States had withdrawn into isolation and the world had lacked any agreed international economic order and had, perhaps partly in consequence, got embroiled in a new war. The price proved to be abandonment of a set of proposals that he had developed in the immediately preceding years. Pride of authorship might have led a lesser man to defend those proposals to the last ditch, but statesmanship dictated a strategic retreat. Keynes proved himself a statesman, perhaps aided by doubts in his own mind as to whether his latest ideas were better than his earlier ones, and the world got a new and liberal international economic order.

THE POSTWAR ORDER AND GLOBAL PROSPERITY

Was Keynes's statesmanship worthwhile? Was the international economic order a significant factor contributing to the unparalleled prosperity that the world enjoyed prior to the disintegration of the Bretton Woods system in 1968–73?

Few economists would challenge the view that trade liberalization was an important stimulant to growth, particularly in allowing developing countries to adopt strategies of export-led growth and thus generalizing world prosperity. Doubts about the benefits of rejecting commodity price stabilization would be more widespread, though the best professional evidence does not confirm the view that the world, or even the developing countries, have lost much for that reason (Newbery and Stiglitz, 1981). Foreign aid and World Bank lending are generally rated eminently worthwhile innovations. Despite doubts about the form of private lending raised by the debt crisis of 1982 and about the social productivity of many speculative capital movements, the general view would probably still be that the re-emergence of a private international capital market has contributed to world welfare. By and large, microeconomic liberalism has served the world well.

No-one doubts that the U.S. assumption of a leadership role was a crucial factor in the postwar prosperity. A more contentious question is whether the Bretton Woods system was a cosmetic adornment or an important element in sustaining the postwar boom. There were those who loved to parody the 1971 debate on exchange-rate adjustment as concerning the price at which the United States did not sell gold, and the substantive economic issues at stake in international monetary controversies have indeed often been less than transparent. But, the further we have left Bretton Woods behind, the more convinced I have become that the world lost something of value when it acquiesced in a nonsystem rather than opting to renovate Bretton Woods.

One major reason for dissatisfaction with the existing non-system is the size of the exchange-rate misalignments that are generated as a result of the lack of explicit or implicit monetary coordination. The term misalignment is currently used to mean almost[10] the same thing as fundamental disequilibrium used to – a real exchange rate that is not at a level calculated to generate an appropriate[11] current-account outcome over the cycle as a whole without the imposition of trade controls for payments purposes. All three of the major currencies that are not in the European Monetary System have suffered swings in their real effective exchange rates of over 30 per cent in recent years, which almost tautologically implies that they have experienced misalignments of over 15 per cent – probably more than any of them endured under Bretton Woods. The costs of misalignments (in contrast to those of short-run volatility, which can be contained through use of the forward market) include the following:

(1) Distortions to the time-stream of absorption, as analyzed by Hause (1966) and Johnson (1966), the latter under the misleading title 'the welfare cost of exchange rate stabilization'.

(2) Loss of output in tradables during periods of overvaluation.

(3) Adjustment costs in redeploying resources between the tradable and nontradable sectors.

---

[10] The only difference is that misalignment is defined relative to a constant real exchange rate while fundamental disequilibrium referred to a deviation of the nominal rate from equilibrium.

[11] The term 'appropriate' signifies a level needed to transfer the 'underlying' capital flow that reflects the real forces of thrift and productivity.

(4) Probably, though this is not statistically confirmed, upward ratcheting of the price level from a sequence of over- and under-valuations.

(5) Overstimulation of investment in the tradable sector during periods of undervaluation and destruction of capacity in that sector during periods of overvaluation. Perhaps, though this is based on anecdotal rather than statistical evidence, overall discouragement of investment from a sequence of misvaluations.

(6) Stimulation of protectionist pressures during periods of overvaluation, especially if that follows a period of artificial expansion of the tradable sector as a result of undervaluation (Bergsten and Williamson, 1982).

There are of course benefits to set beside those costs, namely the benefits of being able to follow a monetary policy unconstrained by exchange-rate considerations. Those who retain faith in the stabilizing properties of targeting monetary growth despite the discouraging experiences of the last decade will rate those costs highly. Some Keynesians may also believe that it is more important to retain interest-rate autonomy than an appropriate level of international competitiveness (and, in view of the quotation from the *General Theory* above, it is conceivable that Keynes would have agreed with them). The rest of us will surely conclude that monetary policy should at least in part be directed to limiting misalignments, and that the failure to do this in recent years is a failing of existing international monetary arrangements, which are instead based on the premise that floating liberates monetary policy for domestic purposes.

A second major reason for dissatisfaction with the existing situation is the lack of policy coordination. It is sometimes said that the problem with the world economy at the moment is not the 'international monetary system' but rather the domestic policies that countries pursue (e.g. Willett, 1983). This is a false antithesis: an international monetary system worthy of the name should constrain the domestic policies countries choose to pursue, with a view to imparting global consistency to the policies adopted by n countries where there are only $(n - 1)$ degrees of freedom. There exist a number of constraints that face the closed world economy that do not, by virtue of the latitude provided by the foreign sector, confront each nation individually. Thus absorption may exceed or fall short of output in an open economy, but it cannot do so for the world as a whole. An individual country may be able to decelerate inflation without much loss in real income by varying the fiscal–monetary mix so that its currency appreciates, but this is not an option for the (closed) world economy. Credit creation need not equal monetary expansion in a single country, but it does so for all countries together. Policy coordination, either explicit through consultation or implicit through (for example) all countries being influenced by the need to take account of their level of reserves, is intended to ensure that the policies adopted by the *n* individual countries sum to an outcome consistent with the global constraints.

Corden (1983) argues that the present market system of floating exchange rates and private capital markets provides a mechanism for policy coordination. For example, suppose that there were a collective world desire for current-account surpluses. This would lead to countries reducing their interest rates in an attempt to depreciate their currencies and so enlarge their current surpluses. But the decline in interest rates would raise the attractiveness of investing and lower that of saving, so that some countries' aims for current surpluses would be trimmed and other countries' target current-account deficits would be increased, till the inconsistency in targets was eliminated. That is, of course, one possible outcome. But another possible outcome, and a likely one in countries that target monetary growth or are concerned about inflation, is that it is fiscal rather than monetary policy that is adjusted in pursuit of the current-account target. In that event, world real income would fall. That fall would be magnified to the extent that other countries felt obliged to match the foreign fiscal contraction to avoid either larger budget deficits or larger trade deficits. Creditworthiness constraints may also impede some countries accepting larger current deficits in the prompt price adjustment portrayed by Corden. The key question is whether a world economy that relies on floating exchange rates and private capital markets to reconcile the uncoordinated policies will eliminate the target inconsistency through a classical price adjustment as portrayed by Corden, or through a Keynesian quantity adjustment (global recession). The usual presumption is that the classical mechanism will operate, if allowed to, in the long run, but that there may be significant output losses in the short run. Recent experience would hardly seem to provide empirical grounds for setting aside the presumption of major short-run costs.

In contrast to the lack of any constraint tending to coordinate policies *ex ante* under the Jamaica nonsystem, the Bretton Woods system did contain systemic constraints, they were broadly symmetrical (for Bretton Woods was not, as sometimes supposed, a dollar standard), and they did contribute to the spectacular performance of the world economy. Each country directed its fiscal–monetary policy at an objective of non-inflationary full employment, modified by the state of its balance of payments. So long as reserves were at a broadly appropriate level and essentially exogenous, the reserve constraint operated symmetrically: some countries were being nudged into expanding as others were being constrained into trimming demand. The world as a whole did not deviate significantly from full employment because of payments imbalances. Only in 1958 was there much of a synchronized world recession: otherwise there were national recessions usually caused by the need to curb payments deficits (e.g. France in 1959, U.S.A. in 1960, Britain and Canada in 1962, Italy in 1964, Germany in 1966, Japan every other year). Since the deficits stemmed largely from excess demand, they provided both an early warning that deflation was needed and a safety valve that prevented excess demand being translated into inflationary inertia. There was a lot more logic in stop–go than most of us recognized at the time (but see Triffin, 1960, pp. 82–3, for an honourable exception).

There were two reasons why the Bretton Woods system ultimately collapsed. First, misalignments developed due to differential inflation, thereby breaking the benign impact of payments imbalances on the thrust of demand management policy. (A deficit in a 'dilemma case' can be eliminated only by creation of a wasteful degree of unemployment, unless there is parallel action to eliminate the overvaluation.) Misalignments could not, however, be corrected in a crisis-free manner by the adjustable peg, because capital mobility had returned. Bretton Woods could have been renovated by adopting that limited flexibility which Keynes had urged when he was seeking to reform a world with mobile capital, but the persuasive powers of those of us who were convinced of the necessity of that reform proved inadequate to the occasion. Second, the reserve constraint on the United States was allowed to lapse, thus replacing the reasonably symmetrical constraints of the gold-exchange standard by an asymmetrical dollar standard that invited inflationary financing of the Vietnam War. The Bretton Woods system just might have been renovated by prompt adoption of some variant of the Triffin Plan (like the SDR scheme) in association with asset settlement, before the United States started to doubt whether its national honour was inextricably bound up with the price of gold. Admittedly one cannot feel great confidence that the United States would have respected any external constraint on its monetary policy that it found seriously irksome, but a simultaneous early move to the crawling peg might have kept the monetary constraint tolerable. But without limited flexibility, and with introduction of the SDR delayed until 1970, there was no hope of an orderly evolution of the Bretton Woods system.

We therefore moved to a world of national autonomy in monetary policy that generates vast misalignments, and attempts by countries to defend themselves against other countries' autonomous monetary policies that generate synchronized world booms and recessions – or at least synchronized recessions. The fact that the world has just suffered the deepest recession for a half century is not exogenous to the lack of constraint on U.S. monetary policy (McKinnon, 1982), any more than the outburst of global inflation in the early 1970s was exogenous to the degeneration of the

Bretton Woods system into a *de facto* dollar standard. One may doubt whether Keynes or anyone else had a particularly clear vision of how the arrangements agreed at Bretton Woods would prevent such disasters, but the fact is that such disasters were conspicuous by their absence.

KEYNES'S ECONOMICS AND THE QUEST FOR A NEW ORDER

I have argued that Keynes's interwar views on economic policy, much more than his wartime proposals, guided the design of the postwar international economic order. I have also argued that the resulting order had a greater positive impact on the postwar boom than has usually been conceded. Those conclusions naturally lead one to ask what we can hope to learn from Keynes's economics as regards the restoration of an international economic order worthy of the name.

One conclusion that might be drawn is that any renewed order should seek to restore that combination of microeconomic liberalism and macroeconomic management that served the world so well in the postwar era. There is at present no consensus on the desirability of moving in that direction. On the contrary, the Third World has demanded further encroachments on microeconomic liberalism in order to give effect to the eminently reasonable objective of securing a measure of international income redistribution. The First World replied not so much by proposing more liberal ways of achieving that objective[12] as by abandoning attempts at both national and international macroeconomic management. If a new order is to re-establish the neoclassical synthesis and go beyond it by building in a decent concern with distributional issues, there is a preliminary need to rebuild an intellectual consensus similar to that forged by Keynes in the interwar years.

Any restoration of an attempt at global macroeconomic management that goes beyond *ad hoc* policy consultation will demand essentially two elements, an agreed exchange-rate regime and agreed rules for monetary control. On the exchange-rate question, I believe we could profit enormously by rediscovering the prewar Keynes. Not for him the sterile debate between the impossible alternatives of completely fixed and freely floating exchange rates: he took it for granted that the interesting issues concerned the choice between intermediate regimes. He strongly favoured a managed exchange rate, not the silly pretence that markets know how to fix exchange rates and governments don't, when in reality a dominant concern of

---

[12] An objective which the First World more or less accepted when it agreed in the Committee of Twenty that 'promotion of the net flow of real resources to developing countries' should be a 'main feature' of the international monetary reform (IMF, 1974, p. 8).

markets is to figure out the policies that governments propose to follow. He believed the exchange rate should be adjusted if necessary to fit the domestic economy, rather than that the domestic economy should be distorted to fit some arbitrary exchange rate. In this he differed sharply from the doctrines that have resurfaced over the last twenty years and acquired the label of 'global monetarism'. He recognized the importance both of selecting an interest rate appropriate to domestic needs and of maintaining a level of competitiveness appropriate to the medium term. He advocated limited flexibility – a wide band to give some interest rate autonomy and an ability to finance seasonal payments fluctuations, and a crawling central rate to keep competitiveness in line – as the regime calculated best to reconcile interest rate and competitiveness considerations under conditions of high capital mobility such as we have today. He proposed that under conditions of substantial price-level uncertainty the crawl should be chosen to offset differential inflation (J.M.K., XXI, pp. 261–2). Subsequent writing has neglected much more of this wise counsel than it has added to it.

In contrast, I do not see that we have anything much to learn from Keynes on the issue of monetary control. The main preoccupation of his later years was to ease monetary constraints, reflecting his view of chronic lack of demand as the historical norm. Some of his eulogies of the miracles to be performed by applying 'the essential principle of banking' at the international level almost suggest that he had come to disbelieve in the existence of supply constraints.[13] In retrospect it is clear that Keynes was over-generalizing from a very special historical situation, and hence one has to be relieved that he largely failed to expand liquidity, for the postwar boom could surely not have been maintained for a quarter century without exploding into inflation had fiduciary reserves been provided as liberally as under the Keynes Plan. Neither would it be conceivable now to reintroduce monetary control by the old mechanism of Bretton Woods, where a limited stock of primary reserve assets provided a constraint on the feasible level of domestic money creation: the myth that gold renunciation will have cataclysmic consequences cannot be recreated by fiat. In my view any restoration of world monetary control will have to come by a completely different route, which owes more to monetarism than to Keynes, and seeks to control the domestic credit rather than the external component of the monetary base. (The leading proposal in this class is, of course, that of McKinnon, 1982.)

---

[13] For example: 'The substitution of a credit mechanism in place of hoarding would have repeated in the international field the same miracle already performed in the domestic field of turning a stone into bread' (J.M.K., XXV, p. 114).

At the moment there is no consensus on any of the critical issues needed to design a new international economic order: the combination of microeconomic liberalism and macroeconomic management, the principles of exchange-rate policy and monetary control, or the introduction of an element of international income redistribution. Without a fair measure of such consensus, there is no point in convening a 'second Bretton Woods conference', for there will be no chance of persuading countries to bind their own freedom of action in the expectation that they can benefit more by similar restraint on the part of others. There may, of course, be room for *ad hoc* agreements on specific issues. When asked recently to construct a list of monetary topics that would be worth seeking to negotiate, I suggested: *ad hoc* policy coordination (locomotives and all that), measures to curb exchange-rate misalignments, indexed long-term bonds issued by a consortium of developing countries, extension of the IMF's compensatory financing facility to cover (at least for a time) adverse exogenous payments shocks from any source, an emergency SDR allocation to aid financial reconstruction, and promotion of the SDR as a vehicle currency (Williamson, 1983). But such measures, while a good deal more ambitious than currently in favour in the North, would add up to much less than a new international economic order in the sense that the postwar order was – a framework that significantly constrains countries' policies in the general interest. It has to be said that the same is true of the catalogue of *ad hoc* proposals that constitute the program for a New International Economic Order. One may not be an uncritical admirer of all of Keynes's proposals for the postwar order, but one can nonetheless endorse his passionate belief in the need for having an order and recognize that the accomplishments of his statesmanship exceed the aspirations of the present day.

APPENDIX – THE ANTECEDENTS OF THE INTERNATIONAL CLEARING UNION

Harry Johnson (in Johnson and Johnson, 1978, ch. 8) once suggested that the origin of Bretton Woods could be traced back to *Indian Currency and Finance* (1913), on the grounds that Keynes had argued in favour of the gold-exchange standard and that the gold-exchange standard had been endorsed by Bretton Woods. I find this unconvincing, for two reasons. First, in *Indian Currency and Finance* Keynes was quite unambiguously concerned with exploring the rational policy for a single country that was sufficiently small to take systemic behavior as parametric, whereas at Bretton Woods he was designing the system. (Let it be added that Johnson is absolutely right to point out that Keynes developed in 1913 the seigniorage analysis that was rediscovered with some excitement in the late 1960s: see Mundell and Swoboda, 1969, ch. 5.) Second, in 1942 Keynes wanted to abolish the gold-exchange standard, and only acquiesced reluctantly in its perpetuation.

My own nominee for the title of first precursor of Bretton Woods is an ingenious scheme which he dreamed up in the course of the Paris peace conference in 1919. Economic organization in central Europe had collapsed in part because the new states were not sufficiently creditworthy to borrow and were incapable of exporting until they could import some inputs. Germany was supposedly going to pay them some reparations one day but was unable to start immediately, again largely because of a lack of imported inputs. Very well, said Keynes, let Germany and the other enemy states issue some bonds (and let the allies give a joint guarantee) and distribute these around the various claimants immediately, which could then resell the bonds to purchase the raw materials they needed to revive economic activity. The plan was vetoed by the U.S. Treasury (J.M.K., xvi, pp. 429–41).

In October 1919 Keynes attended a financial conference in Amsterdam, devoted mainly to mulling over the various proposals for international loans then on the table. It is recorded that among the ideas explored 'were a new international currency to be issued by a world bank', but there are no details of who initiated the idea or the form of the proposals (J.M.K., xvii, pp. 129–30).

Keynes's first detailed plan for international monetary reform appeared in an article in the *Manchester Guardian* published just before the Genoa conference in April 1922. He advocated stabilizing the European exchanges at levels appropriate to their existing price levels, and abandoning the efforts then in vogue to deflate price levels to permit the restoration of prewar parities. Countries were recommended to adopt a gold bullion standard and a 5 per cent band in terms of gold. A country determined to revert to its prewar parity, provided it had depreciated by no more than 20 per cent, might be allowed a crawling appreciation. The Federal Reserve system was urged to lend gold to assist stabilization efforts – an early swap proposal. Curiously, despite his enthusiastic support for withdrawing gold from circulation and centralizing it in the reserves of monetary authorities, neither his initial proposals nor his subsequent despatches from Genoa mentioned establishment of the gold-exchange standard, which has for many years been regarded as the principal economic accomplishment of the Genoa conference (J.M.K., xvii, ch. 16). Perhaps this reflects his concern at the time regarding the inflationary dangers of excess gold liquidity (J.M.K., vi, p. 157).

In volume ii of the *Treatise* Keynes urged the desirability of establishing a supranational authority charged with seeking to abolish the credit cycle and manage gold as a 'constitutional monarch', by varying its value so as to stabilise a 'crude' (60 commodity!) international tabular standard. He sketched two schemes, a supposedly practical one and an ideal one. The practical one would have convened a conference of central banks which would have called for the centralization of gold in central banks, a promise by all central banks that they would hold at least 50 per cent of their reserves in currency balances (either at other central banks or at the newly established Bank for International Settlements), an agreement that a committee of central banks could instruct participating countries to vary their legal reserve requirements by at least 20 per cent, and a 2 per cent band. The ideal scheme would have established a world central bank issuing deposits of SBM (supernational bank money) to its central-bank clients, would have abolished minimum reserve requirements (so as to release reserves for use in financing deficits), would have prohibited conversion of national monies into anything but SBM, and would again have involved a 2 per cent gold band. SBM would have been created by central banks depositing gold or borrowing from the supernational bank, or by the bank's open-market operations, which would have been conducted with a view to stabilizing prices and, particularly, to avoiding profit inflations or deflations (J.M.K., vi, ch. 38). The scheme bears a close resemblance to the Triffin Plan that sparked the debate on international monetary reform some 30 years later.

Keynes returned to the theme of international monetary reform and the need to create a new reserve asset in 'Notes on the Currency Question' (1931) and subsequently *The Means to Prosperity* (1933). This originated as a series of articles in *The Times* developing a set of proposals for the World Economic Conference in London. The aim of the conference was conceived as that of raising prices (Lucas was not the first to err in the direction of causality involved in the Phillips curve); Keynes had to emphasize that supply restriction was perverse, and that the need of the hour was for an increase in expenditure. For the world as a whole, that required an increase in 'loan-expenditure' (i.e., autonomous expenditure), whereas each country was individually trying to achieve a similar outcome through currency depreciation and protection. His policy proposals stemmed from this analysis: resumption of foreign lending and increased domestic spending by the strong financial centres, and creation of a new fiduciary reserve asset termed 'gold-notes' in order to facilitate simultaneous adoption of expansionary policies. The gold-notes would have been created according to quota rules[14] and issued against deposit of gold-

---

[14] Quotas were to be based on pre-depression gold holdings. Seven countries would have qualified for the maximum quota of $450 million: the present Big Five plus Spain and Argentina (J.M.K., ix, p. 360).

bonds (which reminds one of the SDR scheme) subject to conditions requiring countries to abolish trade and exchange restrictions, resume debt service, and maintain their exchange rate within a 5 per cent band around a gold par. The par could have been changed (gradually) but only to compensate for differential inflation or to promote adjustment. Gold-notes would have been accepted as equivalent to gold by all members and a large immediate issue was advocated to promote recovery from the depression (J.M.K., IX, part VI, ch. 1).

REFERENCES

Bergsten, C. Fred and John Williamson (1983), 'Exchange Rates and Trade Policy', in W. R. Cline, ed., *Trade Policy in the 1980s* (Washington, Institute for International Economics).

Blum, John Morton (1967), *From the Morgenthau Diaries: Years of War, 1941–1945* (Boston: Houghton Mifflin).

Corden, W. Max (1983), 'Is There an Important Role for an International Reserve Asset such as the SDR?', paper presented to the IMF Conference on 'International Money, Credit, and the SDR'.

Crotty, James R. (1983), 'On Keynes and Capital Flight', *Journal of Economic Literature*, March.

Dell, Sidney (1981), *On Being Grandmotherly: The Evolution of IMF Conditionality* (Princeton, N.J.: Essays in International Finance No. 144).

Gardner, Richard N. (1956), *Sterling–Dollar Diplomacy* (London: Oxford University Press).

Gold, Sir Joseph (1981a), 'Keynes and the Articles of the Fund', *Finance and Development*, September 1981.

(1981b), *The Multilateral System of Payments*, IMF Occasional Paper No. 6.

Harrod, Roy F. (1951), *The Life of John Maynard Keynes* (New York: Harcourt, Brace and Co.).

Hause, John C. (1966), 'The Welfare Costs of Disequilibrium Exchange Rates', *Journal of Political Economy*, June.

Horsefield, J. Keith (1969), *The International Monetary Fund 1945–1965* (Washington: International Monetary Fund).

IMF (1974), *International Monetary Reform: Documents of the Committee of Twenty* (Washington: IMF).

J.M.K., I–XXX, *The Collected Writings of John Maynard Keynes* (London: Macmillan, for the Royal Economic Society).

Johnson, Harry G. (1966), 'The Welfare Costs of Exchange Rate Stabilization', *Journal of Political Economy*, October.

Johnson, Elizabeth S., and Harry G. Johnson (1978), *The Shadow of Keynes* (Oxford: Basil Blackwell).

Kahn, Lord (1976), 'Historical Origins of the International Monetary Fund', in A. P. Thirlwall, ed., *Keynes and International Monetary Relations* (London: Macmillan).

McKinnon, Ronald I. (1982), 'Currency Substitution and Instability in the World Dollar Standard', *American Economic Review*, June.

Meade, James E. (1951) *The Theory of International Economic Policy: Vol. I, The Balance of Payments* (London: Oxford University Press).

Moggridge, Donald E. (1983), 'Keynes and the International Monetary System, 1909–1946', paper presented to the History of Economics Society meeting at Charlottesville.

Mundell, Robert A. and Alexander K. Swoboda, eds. (1969), *Monetary Problems of the International Economy* (Chicago: University of Chicago Press).

Newbery, David M. G., and Joseph E. Stiglitz (1981), *The Theory of Commodity Price Stabilization* (Oxford: Clarendon Press).

Triffin, Robert (1960), *Gold and the Dollar Crisis* (New Haven: Yale University Press).

Willett, Thomas D. (1983), 'The Functioning of the Present Financial System: Strengths and Weaknesses', paper presented to the IMF conference on 'International Money, Credit and the SDR'.

Williamson, John (1977), *The Failure of World Monetary Reform, 1971–74* (London: Nelson).

(1981a), review of *The Collected Works of John Maynard Keynes*, vols. xxv and xxvi, in the *Economic Journal*, June.

(1981b), *Exchange Rate Rules: The Theory, Performance and Prospects of the Crawling Peg* (London: Macmillan).

(1983), 'International Monetary Reform: An Agenda for the 1980s', paper written for the Commonwealth Secretariat, London.

COMMENT

R. Dornbusch

Williamson's paper copes thoroughly and in a stimulating and imaginative way with the difficult assignment of assessing Keynes's contribution to the successes of postwar international order. He does so by posing three questions: To what extent was Keynes responsible for the *liberal* international postwar order, to what extent was that order in turn responsible for the prosperity of the 1950–73 period, and what can be learnt from that experience in rebuilding the economic order?

Williamson is entirely right to place the unrivalled economic performance of the postwar period at the centre of his essay. Keynes's chief interest was macroeconomic performance and in that perspective the growth achievement of the 1950–73 period stands out in this century.

In commenting on Williamson's paper I will single out four issues of disagreement. They happen to coincide, I believe, with areas where Williamson wished Keynes or the world were different from what they actually are. I start with the question of Keynes as a liberal, and then turn to exchange rate issues, Bretton Woods and monetary policy in the non-system.

Table 1 *Real per capita growth in the major industrial countries*

1870–1913	1913–50	1950–73	1973–80
1.6%	1.1%	3.6%	1.8%

Source: A. Maddison *Economic Growth in the West*, Norton, N.Y. 1964 and OECD, *Historical Statistics*.

Keynes as a laissez-faire liberal Williamson shows quite clearly that Keynes cannot be credited with contributions towards the liberal features of the postwar order. I am doubtful, however, of the remaining claims. Was Keynes a liberal in any area, though perhaps not at Bretton Woods? Keynes's case for free trade in his 1923 campaign speech for the Liberal Party is a striking piece of economic liberalism, even to the point of straining the case, but after 1930 there is little evidence of either liberalism or internationalism. Keynes, above all, was oriented toward practical policies that would provoke employment and prosperity, prove politically acceptable and economically advantageous for Britain. He was a Marshallian economist doing macroeconomics. In my reading his liberalism was much less a matter of principle than a belief that messing around in some areas might prove poor politics.

Williamson notes that in 1931, having just advocated a tariff, Keynes turns around (upon the suspension of gold) to make a point of the currency question, not protection, being the issue. But surely Keynes continues to say 'when the currency question has been settled, then we can return to protection and to our other domestic issues with a solid basis to go upon'. Perhaps Keynes was really saying this: if our competitive depreciation sticks we won't need a tariff; if other countries match sterling we will need protection. Keynes as a liberal, except by party affiliation, is an unusual picture. Above all I see him as an interventionist, spending his life identifying troubles in the economic system and schemes for solving the problem in a politic way. His own qualification of the liberal position is well characterized by the following notes for a speech organized by the Liberal Summer (sic) School in December 1923:

We are traditionally the party of laissez-faire. But just as the economists led the party into this policy, so I hope they may lead them out again. It is not true that individuals acting separately in their own economic interest always produce the best result. (J.M.K., xix, i, p. 158)

We do not really know about Keynes as a liberal because most of his professional life Keynes spent on the problems of achieving higher employment and macrostability.

Bretton Woods The postwar, pre-1973 international economic order which was part, if not the cause, of the growth achievement is portrayed by Williamson as 'combining microeconomic liberalism with a commitment to macroeconomic management . . . the neoclassical synthesis . . . at the centre of the political spectrum where Keynes's loyalties always lay'. Certainly it is correct that active Keynesian macroeconomic management was an essential part of the prosperity. It was essential in stretching out the high-growth and full employment experience of the 1950s. After the boost from reconstruction, aid and European payments discrimination growth might have petered out in the late 1950s. That it was in fact continued quite unexpectedly for another ten years we owe primarily to the Kennedy–Johnson administration's expansion.

I find it surprising that Williamson should credit the Bretton Woods system with the benefits of high growth in the 1950–73 period and to charge the poor performance of the 1970s to the absence of an economic order. Surely the 1960s, for the world economy, worked exactly in the manner Keynes would have hoped – dollar overvaluation without adverse effects on the world economy because under the dollar standard the U.S. was willing to sustain an aggressive demand expansion without ultimate, effective regard to external liabilities or trend inflation. The U.S., in contrast with Keynes's fears at Bretton Woods, was super-Keynesian – I think here of 1962–67 – and that gave the world economy an extra ten years of above-normal growth.

Contrary to Williamson I do not believe that the Bretton Woods system contained effective, systemic constraints that were broadly symmetrical. If the U.S. had abided by such constraints we might never have seen the expansion of the 1960s. On the contrary, the asymmetry of the constraints made the U.S. set the expansionist tone and forced the more conservative countries into higher rates of nominal *and* real expansion than they otherwise might have seen. Germany or Japan, for example, have had the same rates of inflation between 1960 and 1973 as they had between 1973 and 1980. Of course, in the second period their growth rates were much lower than they had been before.

Exchange rates If Keynes had no part in shaping the liberal features of the postwar order, how influential were his open economy, macroeconomic ideas? Williamson singles out three areas: specific proposals in the Bretton Woods negotiations, monetary policy for internal balance and the crawling peg. I am completely unpersuaded by the argument that Keynes in April 1922 was even remotely considering a Williamson-style crawling peg or, for that matter, attached any lasting significance to his passing remark in 1922.

Keynes *was* concerned that in the U.K. and in France the threat of a return to gold at the prewar par was exerting a severely deflationary effect. He was drawing attention to the 'peso problem' induced by ambiguity in official policy. The cure was to immediately fix exchange rates and, should there be political problems in doing so, leave the door just a little bit open (the 'concession to popular illusion') by allowing a return to the prewar par, making up a 20 per cent overvaluation, over a period of at least three years and thus at only a very small speed. There is nothing in the proposal that gears exchange rate movements to prices, the external balance or anything for that matter. In fact, the proposal's only purpose is to remove objections to an immediate fixing at rates that are not deflationary. There is no evidence that Keynes attached lasting interest to his proposal. In December 1922 in his follow-up piece 'The Stabilization of the European Exchanges – II' he summarizes his early proposal in a footnote:

In this article I suggested as a basis for discussion certain rates at which the leading exchanges might be stabilized, providing a margin of 5 per cent between the fixed rate at which notes would be redeemed and those at which they would be issued. (J.M.K., xviii, p. 70)

There is no mention here of the possibility for gradual appreciation that had appeared in the earlier paper, confirming the belief that Keynes was interested above all in fixing rates. Indeed, in the article Williamson quotes Keynes had noted:

If, however, the gold values of the currencies are fixed at a low figure in the first instance, should this low figure be final and permanent or merely a beginning with subsequent improvement in view? It would be wiser to make it final. (J.M.K., xvii, p. 363)

In Keynes's position on fixed rates there is an interesting ambiguity. He makes a point that rates should be fixed to limit the large within-year fluctuations of 15 to 25 per cent in *nominal* exchange rates. But at the same time he argues for a 5 per cent margin to give speculators a large enough 'turn' to provide smoothing services and thus as a protection against gold withdrawals. But why tolerate that much exchange rate variability? The central bank could finance easily seasonal movements, particularly when they are understood to be seasonal and thus assume some of the private exchange risk which is the reason for the large required turn. Williamson is right, I believe, in arguing that Keynes, faced with the choice, preferred domestic control over interest rates to narrower exchange rate fluctuations.

I stray from the topic of international order for a moment to Keynes's contributions to understanding the linkage between internal public debt problems, inflation and exchange rate issues. What was to him Central Europe and France clearly applies today to Latin America. The question of how the domestic debt burden will come to disappear and the consequences for exchange rates are altogether topical. (See J.M.K., IV, pp. 53–60.)

But one of his proposals looks particularly interesting after the experiments in Chile and Argentina. In a section entitled 'Exchange Demoralization' he notes:

> If seasonal pressure is a reason why even a fairly healthy currency requires a policy of definite stabilization, there is an equally strong reason for endeavouring to fix, at however low a level, a very sick currency. (J.M.K., XVIII, pp. 81–2)

Such a policy stands in the way of a loss of confidence which, if it happened, would lead to adverse speculation:

> When this process sets in seriously a currency system is in great danger, and depreciation may proceed at a tremendous rate, quite independently of the increase in the volume of the circulation . . . When, taught by past losses and excusably struggling for self-preservation, a whole population becomes a 'bear' of its own currency, the psychological obstacles to a remedy are almost insuperable (*op. cit.* pp. 82–3).

Monetary policy and the non-system Williamson documents well Keynes's move from Victorian concepts of monetary policy – defending the exchange rate – to an internal balance target. In notes for a 1923 speech already quoted above we find Keynes's comments on the new scope of monetary policy to mitigate the short period 'instability of the standard of value':

Progress of scientific investigation since the War.
Hawtrey, Harvard Cambridge everywhere
One of the biggest jumps forward ever achieved in economic science
Although widely bruited, not yet taken in detail outside limited scientific circles
Ups and downs of trade long existing back to 18th century
Various theories   Sun spots   Colds in the head
Now recognized as mainly monetary
The diagnosis is almost complete
Now even if gold was stable over long periods, it cannot deal with short periods
For the cure for short period fluctuation depends on being able rapidly to expand or
Contract the volume of money (J.M.K., XIX, I, pp. 160–1).

This shift of emphasis from a policy geared toward long-run price level stability (or whatever trends gold dictates) to short-term stabilization of aggregate demand is one of the lasting contributions of Keynesian economics. Up to the early 1970s the mainstream of the profession recognized the switch as decisive progress and it was an essential part of the dollar standard. Today it is viewed by many as problematic and as the source of our systemic inflation problem. Suggestions are seriously advanced and even implemented to try and re-establish monetary rules in order to regain the presumption of a stable long-run price *level*.

Williamson attaches much importance, in a new international order, to co-ordinated monetary policies based on domestic credit rules. Indeed, his main charge is that the present system fails in the international macroeconomic area because:

> The rest of us will surely conclude that monetary policy should at least in part be directed to limiting misalignments, and the failure to do this in recent years is a failing of existing international monetary arrangements (p. 104).

The U.S. move to tight money, and the prospective fiscal expansion, are certainly the reasons for the severe changes in real exchange rates. But it is also the case that the move toward monetary restraint was entirely appropriate if inflation was to be stopped. Furthermore, the severity of the world recession is in good part due to the excessive coordination of monetary policies following 1981.

The problem, however, is not tight money policy but the failure to accompany the shift in monetary policy by a decisive use of wage controls and other measures of incomes policy. In the absence of incomes policies, and very much as a second-best policy, interest equalization taxes would have been appropriate. Faced with our present situation Keynes might well have repeated his 1923 line:

> The more troublous the times, the worse does a laissez-faire system work. I believe the times are likely to remain troublous for a generation and that the magnification of the evils of monetary instability which we have suffered in the past 5 years are likely to continue unless we do something about it. (J.M.K., xix, i, p. 160.)

Out present non-system has been criticized because it has allowed large exchange rate volatility and persistent misalignments. I do not see our problem in that way. I believe the problem is above all our inability to cope with inflation through decisive controls. That inability in turn makes us fall back on pure monetary restraint (very inappropriately combined with long-term fiscal expansion that raises long real rates) throughout the world economy.

There is now a world-wide perception of overvaluation – overvaluation of wages relative to prices. Surely the dollar is seen to be high, but there are few countries that would seek real appreciation to restore balance. On the contrary, beggar thy neighbor mentality is pervasive and animates proposals for wage freezes as non-inflationary means to create employment. In these conditions shaping international systems based on monetary co-ordination and exchange rate rules is by no means a priority and indeed may poorly serve the purposes of recovery. The priority surely is to revive the world economy by co-ordinating internationally *fiscal* policies – more shortrun stimulus in Europe, less long-run expansion in the U.S. – and by solving the debt problem through medium-term restructuring at sensible real interest rates. Long-term real interest rates must be brought down to sustain the incipient recovery and to promote resumption of investment and trend productivity growth. At the same time there is a need for a rapid resumption of demand. None of this provides much of a role for monetary policy co-ordination or exchange rate agreements.

COMMENT

Sidney Dell[1]

In the short time available to a discussant, it may be more useful to add certain elements to John Williamson's excellent paper than to take issue with it, except perhaps on the characterization of the Bretton Woods period, and on the allegedly inflationary potential of the Keynes Plan.

As the performance of the world economy deteriorates and international economic problems become more and more intractable there is a tendency to look back to the Bretton Woods period with nostalgia. Yet it is not clear that that period was as rosy as it is now often described. Much depends on the standard of comparison used. There cannot be any doubt that the 1950s and 1960s were incomparably better than the 1930s in terms of both the level and stability of economic activity and employment. Even here one might comment that the more successful performance of the Bretton Woods period owed more to the automatic fiscal stabilizers than to deliberate macroeconomic management, which was frequently wrong-headed or perverse.[2]

But if the standard is the fulfilment of economic potential, the assessment would have to be less favourable. Richard Ruggles has demonstrated that from 1945 to 1975 the United States 'has not achieved full employment except under the pressure of war demand' and that continuous growth was not sustainable. The record showed that during that period there had been ten years of recession, twelve years of recovery and seven years under the influence of wartime pressures. Recoveries were so short-lived that a new recession was always just around the corner and under these conditions long-term growth was reduced to a level considerably below its potential.[3]

---

[1] The views expressed in this paper are those of the author and not necessarily those of the United Nations Secretariat.

[2] See, for example, the assessment by E. Cary Brown of U.S. fiscal policy in the 1950s in *Postwar Economic Trends*, ed. Ralph E. Freeman, New York, 1960.

[3] Richard Ruggles, 'Economic Growth in the United States: Its Behavior and Measurement', Studies prepared for the use of the Joint Economic Committee, Congress of the United States, Volume 2, 10 November 1970.

Nor can one overlook the continuing polarization of the world economy as between the less developed and more developed countries – with 70 per cent of the world's population living in the former group of countries and only 30 per cent in the latter. The economic gains of the 1950s and 1960s were unequally distributed. Per capita growth in developing countries lagged behind that of developed countries, and the share of the former group of countries in world trade declined drastically – from 31 per cent in 1950 to 18 per cent in 1970 (or from 24 per cent to 11 per cent if major petroleum exporters are excluded).

If we are talking of world order we cannot limit ourselves to relations among the Group of Ten, or Seven, or Five, as if the relative importance of the components of the world economy could be measured by weighted voting power in the Bretton Woods institutions. Any assessment of the international economic order should look to the future rather than to the past. One of the most important characteristics of a healthy world order would be that it would facilitate the realization of the full potential of all countries.

It is true that the less developed countries themselves did not always make the most effective use of their resources and opportunities, any more than the developed countries did. But the external environment was hostile in a number of ways to the development efforts of the former group of countries. One major defect of the international system was that tremendous fluctuations in commodity prices continued throughout the period and another was the gross imbalance in the distribution of adjustment burdens between rich and poor countries.

Keynes was fully alive to the danger that these past shortcomings of the world economy would continue in future, and the remedies that he proposed for them are as relevant today as at the time that he put them forward. He proposed the creation of an international body to stabilize the prices of the main traded commodities by means of a system of buffer stocks financed through an international monetary agency that was the subject of a separate proposal. There is no doubt that if his buffer stock scheme had been adopted, the experience of the postwar period would have been quite different for the Third World's primary commodity exporters.[4] Moreover, as Lord Kaldor has pointed out, the buffer stock scheme, by providing a stimulus to primary production and incomes and hence to the demand for industrial goods would lead ultimately to a situation in which the pace of industrial growth would be stepped up to the limits set by the supply of primary commodities instead of the latter being limited by the growth of demand from the world's industrial centres.[5]

[4] J.M.K., xxvii, pp. 115–20.

[5] *Economic Journal*, March 1983, p. 210.

Keynes considered that basic prices for commodities set by the international body responsible for management of his commodity scheme should take into account 'the requirements of a suitable standard of life for the majority of producers concerned'. A minority of producers with low standards of life must not, he said, be allowed to depress the international price of any staple commodity for all producers alike. 'The desire to maintain more adequate standards of living for primary producers has been the mainspring of the movement towards commodity regulation schemes in recent years, and this is a purpose which the buffer stock controls must be prepared to take over.'[6]

What, then, if producers with depressed living standards exerted a downward pressure on prices, thereby facing the control with the dilemma of either accumulating excessive stocks or allow the basic price to fall below the level that would allow reasonable standards for producers generally? 'Restriction schemes should be regarded in such a case as a last resort . . . some "protective" measures must be held in reserve as a proper defence of standards of life for other producers.'[7]

Subsequently, in a document prepared for circulation to the War Cabinet on The International Regulation of Primary Products, Keynes came close to attempting a definition of a 'just price', which, however, he called 'a reasonable international economic price':

In fixing this price, the Executive shall have primary regard to the level which would provide the average (not marginal) producers of, say, two-thirds or three-quarters of the exporting countries, weighted according to their standard tonnages, with a standard of life in reasonable relation to the general standards of the country in which they live, and, where these standards have been low, shall err in the generous direction with a view to their gradual improvement.[8]

If thinking of this kind had prevailed in international approaches to the commodity problem after the war, one of the most important divisive forces in the world economy could have been neutralized or perhaps even overcome.

On the distribution of the burden of adjustment Keynes was equally incisive. He summed up the historical experience of the functioning of the adjustment process as follows:

It is characteristic of a freely convertible international standard that it throws the main burden of adjustment on the country which is in the *debtor* position on the international balance of payments . . . Thus it has been an inherent characteristic of the automatic international metallic currency (apart from special circumstances) to

---

[6] J.M.K., xxvii, p. 123.

[7] *Ibid.*, p. 124.

[8] *Ibid.*, p. 190.

force adjustments in the direction most disruptive of social order, and to throw the burden on the countries least able to support it, making the poor poorer.

As Keynes pointed out, the process of adjustment is compulsory for the debtor and voluntary for the creditor. Moreover, most of the means of adjustment open to the debtor country are apt to have adverse effects on its terms of trade, and in the case of the poorer countries – exporting mainly primary products – the adverse price effects may be large enough to offset, or more than offset, any favourable movement in trade volumes.

Keynes concluded

that the architects of a successful international system must be guided by these lessons. The object of the new system must be to require the chief initiative from the creditor countries, whilst maintaining enough discipline in the debtor countries to prevent them from exploiting the new ease allowed them in living profligately beyond their means.[9]

Coupled with these ideas was the suggestion that the management of the new international monetary institution should be 'genuinely international without preponderant power of veto or enforcement to any country or group; and the rights and privileges of the smaller countries must be safeguarded'.[10]

Still another proposal of great relevance to today's concerns was that

we need a means of reassurance to a troubled world, by which any country whose own affairs are conducted with due prudence is relieved of anxiety for causes which are not of its own making, concerning its ability to meet its international liabilities; and which will, therefore, make unnecessary those methods of restriction and discrimination which countries have adopted hitherto, not on their merits, but as measures of self-protection from disruptive outside forces.[11]

The idea that a clear distinction should be drawn between cases of balance-of-payments difficulty depending on whether the causes of such difficulty are, or are not, of the country's 'own making' is a particularly significant one that the industrial countries have consistently rejected as a governing principle for IMF programmes. The Fund gives partial recognition to the principle in the context of the Compensatory Financing Facility, which, however, deals only with cases of balance-of-payments difficulty attributable to export shortfalls (or cereal import coverages) that are beyond one country's control and are expected to be temporary in nature.

[9] J.M.K., xxv, pp. 27, 29, 30.

[10] Proposals for an International Clearing Union, *The International Monetary Fund, 1945–1965*, Vol. iii, ed. J. Keith Horsefield, International Monetary Fund, Washington, D.C. 1969, p. 20.

[11] *Ibid.*, p. 21.

But the Fund does not otherwise accept Keynes's approach to the question of responsibility for external imbalance. The argument used against this approach is that

Despite its intuitive appeal, this proposal essentially addresses the wrong question. The necessity for adjustment policies depends not on the geographic origin of the imbalance but rather on its nature, on whether or not the imbalance is temporary and self-reversing in a reasonable period of time. If the imbalance is not transient, then whether or not its causes were within the control of the authorities (assuming that this can even be determined with sufficient accuracy) is of secondary importance.[12]

On this reasoning, the question whether a deficit country's difficulties are of its 'own making' is irrelevant from the standpoint of the adjustment burden to be borne. Even if a country were the victim of beggar-my-neighbour policies, the burden of adjustment on that country would be exactly the same as if it had brought its troubles upon itself by its own actions.

Any basic deficiency in the international monetary system or in the management of the dominant economies will generally tend to be reflected in balance-of-payments deficits of the weaker countries at the margin. At such times it is all too easy to point the finger at the weak countries and forget about general problems of the system and any mismanagement by the major industrial powers. There are always things that one can criticize in a weak or poor country – the balance struck between agriculture and industry, the structure of incentives, the inadequacy of resource mobilization, the neglect of exports and so forth. At any particular time, the balance-of-payments problem may be due, fundamentally, to quite different causes of external origin, but it can always be attributed to one or more of the domestic failings.

Although, in terms of amount, Third World debt is highly concentrated at the present time, from 1980 to 1982 no less than forty developing countries were compelled to undertake multilateral debt renegotiation. Of these, twenty cases occurred in 1982 alone; the number of such renegotiations in the second half of the 1970s had averaged only four per year. While some, or perhaps even all, of these countries may have made mistakes in their general economic policies or in the management of their external debt, it was unprecedented in the post-war period for so many countries to be seeking debt relief at the same time. The only possible explanation for this generalized debt crisis was the world recession brought about as a result of the particular policies adopted by the industrial

---

[12] Bahram Nowzad, *The IMF and its Critics*, Essays in International Finance, No. 146, International Finance Section, Princeton University, December 1981, p. 16.

countries in attempting to deal with inflation. It was this factor, for example, that led to the collapse of commodity prices (and hence of the earnings of commodity exporters) to their lowest level in real terms since the Great Depression. Moreover, it was the emphasis on monetary restriction in the policies of the industrial countries that drove up interest rates and hence the debt service obligations on the floating rate loans of the debtor countries. To these factors should be added the rapid spread, under the influence of the self-same recession, of discriminatory import restrictions directed against the Third World.

In a rational world such as Keynes envisaged, the remedy for balance-of-payments difficulties caused by recession in the industrial countries would be a programme of economic recovery in these countries, accompanied by appropriate balance-of-payments support to deficit countries during the period of transition to more prosperous times. It would likewise be the responsibility of the countries imposing import restrictions to adopt remedies for the consequential difficulties for other countries.

Traditionally, of course, deficits caused by cyclical fluctuations in the import demand of other countries, and which were therefore expected to last a relatively short time, could be regarded as 'temporary and self-reversing' as indicated above, and in these circumstances it was recognized that short-term deficit financing without adjustment would be appropriate. But under current conditions, where recession has become chronic, it is impossible to distinguish between a reversible and a non-reversible deficit. Are deficits that are due to the collapse of commodity prices reversible or non-reversible? There cannot be any doubt that commodity prices will recover sooner or later, but this consideration is not deemed relevant by the conventional wisdom in assessing the adjustment obligations of commodity exporting countries seeking balance-of-payments support, except in so far as they qualify for compensatory financing. In 1982 the aggregate export shortfall experienced by capital-importing developing countries, estimated on the basis of the IMF formula for compensatory financing, was $16 billion. Net drawings on the Compensatory Financing Facility, however, amounted to only $1.5 billion.[13]

If the determination of responsibility for balance-of-payments disequilibrium is considered irrelevant in prescribing adjustment obligations, it is the victims who must bear the cost of having been victimized. Not only must they endure the injuries inflicted, albeit unintentionally, by the economically dominant countries – through contraction of import demand, discriminatory import restrictions, and excessive monetary retrenchment (with its interest rate consequences) – but they must also

[13] United Nations, *World Economic Survey 1983*, ch. 11.

shoulder the entire burden of correcting the imbalances caused by the same injuries. The fact that the injuries, other than protectionism, are not deliberate does not make them any less real. The industrial countries and the international banking community require, in return for debt relief on a short leash, that the debtor countries bear the brunt of the burden of adjustment.

Keynes would not have condoned this shifting of the burden of adjustment almost exclusively to the deficit countries. Nor would he have accepted a one-sided imposing of conditions on these countries. He was strongly opposed to the U.S. idea that the IMF should have wide discretionary and policing powers over member countries. He considered that the Fund's initiative and discretion should be limited 'to cases where the rules and purposes of the institution are in risk of infringement'. The Fund should, he felt, be 'entirely passive in all normal circumstances, the right of initiative being reserved to the central banks of the member countries'.[14]

This does not mean that he thought that all drawings on the Fund should be automatic. His own proposal for an International Clearing Union set out certain requirements, including devaluation if necessary, for cases in which the debit balances of member countries exceeded half of their quotas.

His principal concern was that

if countries are to be given sufficient confidence they must be able to rely in all normal circumstances on drawing a substantial part of their quota without policing or facing unforeseen obstacles. Indeed, we have been inclined to think, on second thoughts, that the Clearing Union may have been too strict on this, though this was actually balanced under the Clearing Union by the much greater size of the quotas. If the Clearing Union provisions were applied to the lower quotas now contemplated, we gravely doubt whether those concerned, particularly some of the smaller countries, would feel adequate confidence.[15]

The case made by Keynes in 1943 for giving countries a reasonable degree of freedom of action in their economic management applies *a fortiori* to the situation in 1983. While IMF quotas corresponded to about 16 per cent of the world imports in the late 1940s, the proportion had fallen to about 4 per cent in 1983. Thus the Fund is far less well equipped than it was even in Keynes's time to perform the functions that he envisaged. Until recently it was thought that the deficiency of the Fund in this regard did not matter since balance-of-payments support was also available from commercial banks – which was not the case in Keynes's time. But the multiple debt crises of 1982–83 have prompted second thoughts on this matter, and

[14] J.M.K., xxv, p. 404.

[15] From Keynes's letter to Jacob Viner of 17 October 1943, J.M.K., xxv, p. 333.

if the commercial banks continue to limit their new lending, as seems likely, there is no choice but to restore the role of the Fund, especially for those countries that have in any case had little access to balance-of-payments financing from these banks. In that event, the need for establishing a proper balance between the high-conditional and low-conditional resources of the Fund will be all the more pressing.[16]

Keynes's own solution to the problem of symmetry in international monetary obligations was to require strict enforcement of the 'banking principle' at the international level. This objective was to be realized by providing, through the Clearing Union, 'that a country finding itself in a creditor position *against the rest of the world as a whole* should enter into an obligation to dispose of this credit balance and not allow it meanwhile to exercise a contractionist pressure against the world economy'.[17] In other words, the financial resources remaining unused by a creditor country should be lent, through the Clearing Union, to finance the deficits of other countries. The maximum liability assumed by a creditor country would lie within its own control:

No more is asked of it than that it should hold in bancor such surplus of its favourable balance of payments as it does not itself choose to employ in any other way, and only for so long as it does not so choose.[18]

Lord Balogh was critical of the idea that an International Clearing Union would automatically remove the deflationary pressure exerted by creditor countries. There was, he pointed out, no assurance of a compensating increase in the effective demand of other countries unless special steps were taken to this end.[19] Keynes was no doubt aware of these considerations, but in the context of the Clearing Union he was not writing and speaking only for himself. He had to carry his official colleagues with him, and retain also some prospect of convincing the Americans; the latter were more concerned about the possibility of inflation than of depression. He may well have felt, moreover, that for some time after the war there would be no lack of demand in the potentially deficit countries, and that the real question was whether there would be sufficient finance for the needs of these countries.

---

[16] For an account of Keynes's unsuccessful efforts to limit the doctrine of conditionality, see Sidney Dell, *On Being Grandmotherly: The Evolution of IMF Conditionality*, Essays in International Finance, No. 144, International Finance Section, Princeton University, October 1981.

[17] J.M.K., xxv, p. 47.

[18] J. K. Horsefield, *op. cit.*, p. 26.

[19] *The Economics of Full Employment*, Institute of Statistics, Oxford, 1944, pp. 159–60.

Williamson is at the opposite pole from Balogh. He voices astonishment at the size of the overdraft rights proposed under the Keynes Plan and expresses relief that Keynes largely failed to expand liquidity 'for the postwar boom could surely not have been maintained for a quarter century without exploding into inflation had fiduciary reserves been provided as liberally as under the Keynes Plan'. Williamson provides no evidence for the existence of such a simple relationship between international reserves and inflation, and even if a statistical association could be demonstrated, this would prove nothing about the direction of causality. There is in any case no means of determining the ideal relationship between reserves and world trade, if indeed such a concept has any meaning. In 1937 the ratio of world reserves to world imports was about five times as high as in 1913, and $2\frac{1}{2}$ times as high as in 1928.[20] Yet reserves in 1913 were generally considered to be adequate,[21] while in 1937 what a Williamson of the day would undoubtedly have regarded as a liquidity explosion was accompanied by high unemployment, with a steep recession in the following year: world industrial production shrank by one third from mid-1937 to mid-1938.

We may conclude that in dealing both with commodity instability and with the problem of symmetry between the adjustment obligations of countries, Keynes was profoundly influenced by considerations of equity as well as of logic, and by a concept of world order in which a better future for the poorer members of the international community was an indispensable element. Many of the ideas that he developed along these lines during the war years remain highly relevant today, four decades later.

DISCUSSION

Reference was made to the old hat or, rather, the bread and butter nature of Keynesian stabilization policies to students of Professor Dornbusch's vintage and to how this bread and butter has now been withdrawn from the supermarket. There is a fundamental difference in Keynesian theory between national and international questions. Students in the 1960s were taught that we could model the economy, diagnose the state of effective demand and devise appropriate fiscal interventions. This was the position

[20] The ratio of world reserves to world imports, excluding socialist countries, was 21% in 1913, 42% in 1928 and 101% in 1937. See International Reserves and Liquidity, Study by the Staff of the International Monetary Fund, J. Keith Horsefield, *op. cit.*, p. 360.

[21] *Ibid.*, p. 405.

until the early 1970s when Keynesian policies were undermined because the government could not maintain balance of payments equilibrium. If we had not had balance of payments problems we would not have found the problems of inflation so insuperable.

Keynesian policies are not as useful in the international arena because, first, there is no international institution which is analogous to the national government. National economies are merely clients of the international banking system and there is no agency capable of fiscal and demand management at this level. Secondly, we have no model of demand levels and fiscal policy which is empirically testable. As a result we have had a number of partial explanations of our recent experience of growth and then stagnation. We need to develop methods for which Keynes did *not* leave the foundations, in order to be able to analyse the international economy, that is to say, we need an empirical macro model for the whole world.

The first point, that there is no international institution comparable to a national government, led to an historical reflection. Not only was there an intellectual consensus at the time that something like Bretton Woods should be established, there was also a major power willing to and interested in supporting the system – the United States was to Bretton Woods what the United Kingdom had been to the Gold Standard. But if there is no such strong and willing leader available, as seems to be the case today, an intellectual consensus, even if one were to be attained, is likely to be ineffectual.

The conference was then reminded that Keynesianism gave out in America when the Republican administrations came in, and the Keynesians in the economics profession lost the most precious thing they could have, the young, precisely at the point when there was liberation from the balance of payments constraint at the policy level. Throughout the dying decade of Bretton Woods in the 1960s the balance of payments constraint was biting, yet by good luck the 1960s worked out very well in the Keynesian fashion. But it was precisely after President Nixon in 1971 delivered us from the 'slavery' of Bretton Woods, that the Keynesian behaviour equations gave out and there had to be both a change of paradigms and a change in our ways of describing them. (During the war Keynes said that politics is the science of plausible lies and Professor Samuelson once quipped to Abba Lerner 'But you know, Abba, they have to be plausible'.)

The discussion then took up the theme: was Keynes a liberal in international economics? Keynes had advocated tariffs at a particular time in the 1930s because he was interested in end results, not in dogmas. With a depressed world economy it was not possible to deliver to potential exporting countries the theoretical fruits of free trade. Therefore he argued instead for temporary protection, so that expansionary policies could be followed domestically, in the hope that, collectively, these would lead to a greater quantum of trade in the world as a whole than would have been possible with free trade policies in the same situation. It was pointed out as further evidence that Keynes was not an absolutely convinced free trader, that Keynes had said that if he had to choose between exchange rate fluctuations and protection he would choose the latter because it reduced uncertainty and did not turn the terms of trade against the domestic economy. It was also pointed out that even if Keynes were in favour of tariffs that was not a reason to support them. How, for example, do the participants see a world system of tariffs operating? Arguments not opinions are what we should be interested in.

Professor Meade then commented as follows:

First, he was not a Keynes scholar, he had not read any of the volumes of collected works, and he read the *General Theory* in 1936 and had not read it since. So we were to realise that he was talking from memory, that memory is always wrong so that most of what he has to say would be false! Nevertheless, it would be useful for him to give an impression of Keynes's attitude to liberalism, particularly in international affairs in the years 1940–46, when Professor Meade worked very closely with Keynes on these subjects. While Professor Meade did not go to Bretton Woods, he was present at a number of the negotiations with Harry White and he discussed all these matters with Keynes a great deal.

In 1941, on a visit to the United States, Keynes told the American officials that the United Kingdom would be in a very perilous economic position after the war ended, that the balance of payments position would be appalling and that some form of controls would be needed if the United Kingdom were to be able to preserve any decent standards at all. Keynes himself believed for a long time that after the war there could be a repetition of the 1930s, that the United States probably would have a slump which they would not control and, therefore, that the United Kingdom must be free to protect itself and not have to deflate. Keynes started from this position when he discussed his views with those who, like Professor Meade, believed in the neoclassical synthesis and argued that surely something better could be built. Keynes believed this to be utopian but he nevertheless started to draft a plan. Then his magic worked on himself and, as ever, on others and he came to believe in his own plan very strongly.

There can be no question whatever that throughout this period and probably throughout his life, Keynes was concerned with macroeconomic conditions, with getting able people to design policies which would expand or maintain high levels of activity. He thought that this was infinitely more important than the free allocation of resources. At the same time, he was a man who believed in the freedom of the human spirit, so that he did not believe in an economy that had to be excessively controlled, but in one in which there was the necessary intervention in order to obtain a high level of activity.

People sometimes forget that Keynes was not only a very great economist, he was also a wise statesman and during the war he was in the most extraordinary position in that, while neither a Civil Servant nor a minister, he was in Whitehall and he dominated it. Keynes was not just an economist writing a memo on whether we should have a crawling peg or not, he was somebody who believed passionately in building a new, decent, liberal and effective international order which was based on conditions which would allow prosperity and expansion to be. If things are looked at in this way and if the atmosphere of the time and the fear of what was going to happen are remembered, then Professor Meade thought that Professor Williamson was a little off target. For the IMF did allow internal balance to be the top priority and the exchange rate within limits to be subject to this priority. It is true that article 7 was never used but it was an achievement to write down that creditor countries as well as debtor countries have an obligation to take on some of the strains of adjustment. Professor Williamson used exactly the right phrase in saying that Keynes was 'grumpy' about GATT and all that. Nevertheless, the point that Professor Meade was making is that while Keynes was not working for the micro liberal part of the synthesis, he was not opposing it, he was saying that if you can get the rest to work you may do quite a bit of good by getting it in as well. But he needed to erect safeguards to make sure that the most basic macro economic objectives were achieved. Keynes was a man of immense liberalities, absolutely devoted to building an international order of a broadly liberal kind.

It was then pointed out that the current liquidity crisis, so reminiscent of 1929–33, has intensified interest in Keynes's last phase. His return, as far as international trade and payments were concerned, to the pre-war neo-classical orthodoxy, has become a matter of controversy. The new orthodoxy started by denying that cost inflation was conceivable. They asserted that the old theoretical basis remained valid and that crises were due to excessive borrowing and could be dealt with by orthodox methods.

In the earlier debates on Bretton Woods there had been warnings against the United Kingdom joining a nondiscriminatory trade and payments area and abolishing controls, when it was still lacking in strength. The view that sufficiently stable relations existed between the volume of liquidity and output to allow management of the economy by global methods alone was discounted. Moreover, it was felt to be essential to bring the volume of the available reserves into a proper relationship with the increasing need for them.

The liquidity created by Bretton Woods was very much smaller than Keynes's original proposals. There was a risk then of being overwhelmed and of the United Kingdom being forced to accept unemployment as a policy measure. Yet Keynes defended fiercely the truncated end result of Bretton Woods.

Hardly three years after the United Kingdom acceded to the IMF and accepted the 'liberal' rules of the game, the American loan was greatly reduced while the resources of the IMF were frozen. The IMF in fact was not activated until the Suez Crisis in 1956. A major European crash was averted only through Marshall Aid which in fact was a multiple of that implied by Bretton Woods. The Americans moreover under Marshall Aid permitted the discrimination and protection essential to the restoration of European industry.

The successors of Keynes in the Treasury were free traders and did not understand the mechanisms of the IMF which exposed countries to U.S. pressures. Hence the dominance of the pre-Second World War economics was restored among the policy makers – civil servants, politicians and bankers – no doubt aided by the desire of the economics profession to present a united front. This was evident also in Keynes's posthumously published article.

Discussion next turned to the long-term importance of the step which was all too lightly taken by President Nixon in August 1971 in cutting any *formal* link between the dollar and gold. At the time this was not regarded as important because in practice the dollar was not convertible into gold. Nevertheless, it was of great importance for world commodity markets, the efficient functioning of which requires inelastic expectations associated with a belief in 'normal' prices. Keynes has shown that only if there is a strong belief that prices will eventually return to their 'normal' levels can markets function without intolerable price fluctuations. For, then, markets will be willing to release stocks in the face of excess demand and absorb them if there is excess supply, i.e., to act against the market as a whole and so to stabilize prices. Following President Nixon's action there was an immense and purely speculative rise in prices, first in gold and then in other commodity prices, and fluctuations in them have since then been very much greater than previously.

It was therefore a pity that Professor Williamson dismissed so curtly the idea of buffer stocks. Keynes himself, as we now know, regarded the creation of international buffer stocks of utmost importance, a cause which he fought for unsuccessfully, as the British Cabinet turned it down.

(Professor Meade said that when this item came on the Cabinet Agenda, Churchill, who was preoccupied with aspects of the war itself, took little notice and was heard to ask afterwards, 'What's all this about Butter Scotch?') Keynes believed in the establishment of an international agency separate from the IMF, with finance linked to Bancor (SDRs), which would hold commodities and so create something akin to an international commodity standard. Such an institution was needed for the control of inflation in the world as a whole, to dampen down the inflationary impact of relatively small shifts in supplies on world economic activity. If commodity prices could be stabilized – their lack of stability is the biggest stumbling block to a return to a situation something like that which prevailed before 1973 – national problems of wage induced inflation would become much less pressing and could more easily be dealt with.

Professor Williamson replied to the comments as follows:

The correct criteria for deciding on policy attitudes is not whether or not Keynes was in favour of them. Nevertheless, it is an interesting question to try to find out what his position was. Professor Williamson felt, after the reading he had done and listening to the discussion, that Keynes was not a doctrinaire free trader, that he saw a second best case for tariffs when exchange rate policy was constrained as it had been in 1930–31. On the question whether his first best policy would dispense with tariffs, Professor Williamson thought that it would. Certainly that was the version he had obtained from Harrod's biography, and Professor Williamson held to it, even though he had to admit that there were portions of volumes 25 and 26 which read as though they had been written by Wynne Godley.

Professor Williamson agreed with the point made in the discussion that the system worked best when there was a major country which in effect not only policed the system but also felt itself to be bound by the rules, so that it would follow the same policies at appropriate times. The United States did just that when the Bretton Woods system was working, but by the late 1960s and early 1970s – Professor Williamson thought that the critical point was probably the abolition of the gold pool in 1968 and the lack of an attempt to put an alternative mechanism in its place – this was no longer the case. The question which is posed for the future is whether we can negotiate a set of rules which can be policed by the nations cooperatively, now that we clearly are not going to have a world dominated by a single power as it was in 1945 when half of the world gross product was produced by the United States.

Professor Williamson reaffirmed his faith in basic 'Keynesian' policies, viz, that overall demand should be expanded when it is deficient and contracted when it is in excess. It was the failure in the late 1960s and early 1970s of many economists who called themselves Keynesians to accept this rather than to call for expanding demand whatever the circumstances, which helped to discredit Keynesianism. Economists would not face up to the fact that there *was* such a thing as the natural rate of unemployment when the evidence first came in and consequently we were insufficiently disciplined in our macroeconomic policies.

Finally Professor Williamson mentioned that in the *Tract* and especially in *The Means to Prosperity* Keynes argued for adjustments of exchange rates by small steps to their ultimate parities in order to avoid speculative movements in the exchanges themselves.

4

Keynes and the management of real national income and expenditure*

WYNNE GODLEY

Introduction

How did Keynes think the economy worked? Any time between 1950 and 1970 I would have confidently attributed to Keynes, as preeminently important, the following views about economic policy:

(a) Real demand, output and employment are determined via a multiplier process by the fiscal and monetary operations of the government and by foreign trade performance.

(b) Inflation, though influenced by the pressure of demand, is largely indeterminate in terms of economic variables and therefore, if it is to be controlled, requires some kind of direct political intervention.

(c) Fiscal and monetary policies in any one country are potentially subject to important external constraints.

While there is reasonable support for these views about economic policy in Keynes's writings,[1] there is no warrant for them at all in the *General Theory*. Indeed it is strange, seeing how commonly the view is attributed to Keynes that fiscal policy is crucial to real output determination, that the *General Theory* is concerned with an economy in which neither a government nor for that matter a foreign sector exist at all.[2]

Notwithstanding this I still think, not only that the propositions can be correctly attributed to Keynes, but that they are, themselves, essentially

---

* I am greatly indebted to Francis Cripps for extensive help in the preparation of this paper which in any case draws heavily on the book *Macroeconomics* which we have coauthored.

　　I am also grateful for help from Kenneth Coutts, Nicky Kaldor, Hashem Pesaran and David Vines.

[1] See for instance 'Can Lloyd George do it' and 'The means to prosperity', *Collected Writings* Vol. IX and a large number of documents in Vol. XXVI, particularly 'Bretton Woods & After'.

[2] It is true that there are a few passages in the *General Theory* (see e.g. pp. 119 and 120) where Keynes makes statements about what would happen if the government undertook public works and if there were 'leaks' out of the income expenditure system into imports. But these processes were no part of the core theory he proposed.

correct. I have however been forced to the conclusion that Keynes was a long way from achieving a coherent theoretical basis for maintaining them, and largely for this reason, his ideas have proved very vulnerable to the attacks from many different directions to which they have been subjected, particularly in the last fifteen years.

My purpose in this paper is to describe some modifications which have, in my view, to be made to Keynesian theory if it is to provide a sound underpinning for Keynesian policies.

The paper concentrates on proposition (a) – or rather proposition (a) as it would apply in a closed economy.

For convenience of exposition I shall deploy various models in terms of adjustments to stationary equilibria. These models could all be readily adapted to represent continuous change (for example an economy in a state of steady growth) by supposing that the economic system is always undergoing a series of overlapping adjustments caused by changes in the models' exogenous variables in successive periods.

I first deploy a model which resembles Keynes's model in the *General Theory* in that it represents a closed economy with no government expenditure or taxation. But whereas in Keynes's core model aggregate income brings the flow of the savings into equality with investment, in mine the income flow equalizes the demand for financial assets with the stock of debts. There are several advantages to be derived from starting off from the assumption of stock equilibrium as governing a corresponding flow equilibrium; in particular, we have a model which, although extremely simple, is comprehensive in the sense that all flow variables have explicit counterparts in stock variables. I go on to demonstrate the conditions under which all the processes postulated in this model (the creation of debts and assets as well as income and expenditure flows) are 'inflation neutral'. The conclusions *at this stage* have a somewhat 'monetarist' flavour since the nominal income flow is shown to be a function of the nominal stock of financial assets and the real income flow a function of the real stock of such assets; in this model control over the creation of debts and assets has a potentially crucial role in stabilizing the income flow (both nominal and real).

The second main section of the paper introduces fiscal policy, which radically alters the properties of the system.

It has been well known, particularly since the work of Christ and Ott & Ott[3] in the mid sixties, that once we allow for existence of a fiscal system,

[3] C. A. Christ, 'A short-run aggregate demand model of the interdependence and effects of monetary and fiscal policies with Keynesian and Classical interest elasticities'. American Economic Association, Papers and Proceedings of the 79th Annual Meeting, 1966. *American Economic Review*. D. J. Ott and A. F. Ott, 'Budget balance and equilibrium income', *Journal of Finance*, Vol. 20, March 1965.

full stock equilibrium is only achieved when the government's budget is balanced – i.e. when the flow of taxes to the government (net of interest payments) is equal to the flow of government expenditure. This condition for equilibrium of stocks can be described in terms of flow variables alone, since it is fulfilled when aggregate income is equal to government expenditure divided by the average tax rate.

In the 'crowding out' literature which succeeded the work of Christ and Ott & Ott fiscal policy and monetary policy (the latter defined in terms of the creation of monetary aggregates) were treated as independently determined, leaving an endogenous rate of interest to reconcile any combination of the two. The analytic solution of the dynamic processes consequent on changing policy became extremely complex and the results were contingent on the values of whole families of elasticities and lags which would have to be estimated econometrically.

In the model proposed here monetary policy is initially defined in terms of the maintenance of a given pattern of interest rates. The explicit stock/flow framework, while not inconsistent with *IS-LM* analysis, facilitates a transparent representation of the interaction of fiscal and monetary policy in determining the evolution of the system as a sequential process in historical time.

The first task will be to show how one condition for stock equilibrium when there is a fiscal system (that government expenditure equals its income) will only be fulfilled when the other condition (that stocks of financial assets are in a desired relationship to flows of disposable income) is fulfilled at the same time. I shall demonstrate, standing the usual 'crowding out' argument on its head, that under certain conditions the fiscal system makes government debt accommodate (i.e. change to whatever extent is necessary for assets to be created or destroyed on the required scale) in contrast to the usual story where the debt created by government expenditure displaces private loan financed expenditure. In addition the existence of norms for private assets and debt relative to disposable income pins down the delay involved in the system's responses to fiscal policy. We shall thereby indicate how large will be the mean lag in the response of aggregate income to changes in government expenditure, given the tax rate.

Most of the rest of the paper will be concerned with implications of this model in various circumstances.

First I show the consequences of adopting an active monetary policy involving changes in interest rates. Monetary policy, it will be argued, has a large effect on the structure of portfolios – the composition of financial assets and liabilities – and may also have a significant effect on asset and debt/income norms. But the fact that full stock/flow equilibrium is only consistent with an aggregate income flow which is equal to government expenditure divided by the average tax rate (net of interest payments) implies that monetary policy as distinct from fiscal policy can only have temporary effects on the size of the national income flow.[4]

A similar line of reasoning leads to the conclusion that even if changes occur in the valuation of existing assets (in particular the stock market valuation of equities) and these have a significant effect on private expenditure relative to income, the fiscal system will rapidly restore the national income flow to what it otherwise would have been. In other words the effect on expenditure of spontaneous changes in the value of financial assets will be fully offset, through the operation of the fiscal system, in the same way as in the case of adjustments consequent upon changes in monetary policy.

In the final section of the main exposition I deal with the translation of all nominal stock and flow processes into real terms. To put it crudely, I explore the conditions under which real income and expenditure have a life of their own irrespective of the rate of inflation.

So long as real fiscal policy is defined consistently, I shall show that real national income is determined by real fiscal policy in just the same way as nominal national income is determined by money-denominated fiscal policy, subject only to simple assumptions about the inflation neutrality of private asset and debt norms.

At the end of the paper the suggestion is made that discussion of the interaction between fiscal and monetary policy, including particularly the vexed question of crowding out, has been bedevilled by the misleading assumption made by Keynes concerning the exogeneity of the stock of money. The analogue to this, in more recent times, resides in the assumption that it is sensible to set targets for monetary aggregates independently of the stance of fiscal policy.

A STOCK EQUILIBRIUM MODEL OF A CLOSED CREDIT MONEY ECONOMY WITH NO FISCAL SYSTEM

We start with the balance sheet of the commercial banking system as a whole[5]

$$D \equiv FA \tag{1}$$

---

[4] Except if it induces changes in government expenditure or the average tax rate, e.g., when a target is adopted for the size of the *ex post* budget deficit measured in nominal terms.

[5] This world is a logical abstraction. Historically banks have always had to hold reserves usually in the form of gold or deposits with a central bank. We ignore banks' own equity in the identity (1) since it is not logically required and would only complicate matters.

where

> D = Total bank loans outstanding at the end of each period
> FA = Total financial assets held by the non bank sector at the end of each period.

Next the national income flow identity for a closed economy with no fiscal system is

$$Y \equiv E \equiv PE + \varDelta I \qquad (2)$$

where

> Y = national income (before inventory valuation adjustments)
> E = aggregate expenditure
> PE = (private) final expenditure
> I = inventories valued at cost at the end of each period.

All variables are defined in nominal terms assuming, to begin with, that there is no inflation.

Next postulate as a behavioural hypothesis that inventories are wholly financed by bank loans

$$D = I \qquad (3)$$

This assumption gives us a clear though not a unique rationale for the existence of credit since only if (3) is true will profits (gross of interest and depreciation) become fully realizable to entrepreneurs as a cash flow. It is assumed that loans for the finance of inventories are made by commercial banks, and it must be the case that the assets created as a counterpart of this loan finance arise in the first place as a means of payment; the inventories being built up by entrepreneurs are nothing other than income paid to suppliers or to employees who expect to receive money as their reward.

We now have a spring welling from the ground. The act of credit creation simultaneously generates financial assets and also an injection of income, all of equal size.

As we have

$$\varDelta FA \equiv \varDelta D = \varDelta I \qquad (4)$$

we can substitute (4) into (2) to obtain

$$Y \equiv PE + \varDelta FA \qquad (5)$$

The aggregate income flow is equal to final expenditure plus the change in financial assets. The expression could readily be adapted to accommodate the assumption that inventories are not wholly loan financed or that loans finance the acquisition of tangible assets other than inventories;

PE would simply have to be redefined to exclude any such loan financed expenditures.

I have set up a system where, up to this point, there is only one financial asset – credit money – and loans are only made to finance expenditure, not the acquisition of financial assets. As will be pointed out later on there are, in real life, portfolio adjustments of a speculative or other nature between money, other financial assets and debt. At the moment credit money is considered to be net of all financial intermediation i.e. there can be no speculative demand for money. The symbol *FA* has been used even at this stage so that the model can be adapted as easily as possible when the representation of the financial system is more comprehensive.

We come next to the important hypothesis, central in one version or another to all *IS-LM* analysis as to all monetarist theory, that stocks of financial assets will tend to some norm relative to flows of income; this may be represented formally as

$$FA^* = \alpha Y \tag{6}$$

where the star implies a norm.

Equation (6) is not intended to exclude the possibility that α changes with the rate of interest or that it changes through time spontaneously. But, as will later become clear, the postulate of an asset/income norm enables so much to be explained with so little that it serves as a very powerful organizing principle even if the norm has a time trend or is moderately unstable.

It is well known that (6) implies a long run marginal propensity to spend out of income equal to one. It does not however seem to have been generally realised that it has a logical implication not only for the scale but also for the dynamics of the response of expenditure to income. In particular it implies that the mean lag in the response of expenditure behind income is necessarily equal to α; and that this mean lag is entirely independent of the asset adjustment process itself.[6]

The proof of this, at least when the adjustment process is linear, is as follows.

If

$$FA^* = \alpha Y \tag{6}$$

[6] Alan Spiro got close to this result ('Wealth and the consumption function', *J.P.E.*, 1962) but he seems to have made the error of supposing that nominal income, expenditure and the change in the value of assets can all be meaningfully divided by one price index (see equation 17 below). Perhaps for this reason he did not draw any conclusion about the mean lag in the response of expenditure to income. It may help the reader if he or she bears in mind that, with financial assets appropriately defined to equal the cumulative difference

and

$$FA = \sum_{i=0}^{n} \alpha_i Y_{t-i} \tag{7}$$

with

$$PE \equiv Y - \Delta FA \tag{5}$$

we can solve for

$$PE = \sum_{i=0}^{n+1} \beta_i Y_{t-i} \tag{8}$$

where

$\beta_0 = 1 - \alpha_0$.

$\beta_i = \alpha_{i-1} - \alpha_i \qquad i = 1, \ldots, n$

$\beta_{n+1} = \alpha_n$

Now the mean[7] distributed lag of expenditure after income is defined as:

$$
\begin{aligned}
l &= \sum_{i=0}^{n+1} i\beta_i \\
&= 0.\beta_0 + \sum_{i=1}^{n} (i\beta_i) + (n+1)\beta_{n+1} \\
&= \sum_{i=0}^{n} \alpha_i = \alpha
\end{aligned}
\tag{9}
$$

The fact that the α_i always have precise implications for the β_i closes down some options which might seem plausible unless explicit consideration is given simultaneously to stock and flow adjustment processes. For instance, if people were to anticipate higher future income levels by raising their expenditure in advance of an increase in income this necessarily implies that the prospect of higher income has initially caused them to change their stocks of assets *away* from the equilibrium level. When eventually they restore assets towards the normal level, as our basic premise implies will happen, expenditure must then be lower relative to income after the initial burst than it otherwise would be.

We can now put together an 'animal spirits' model of aggregate income

between private (not personal) disposable income and expenditure, the value of α both in the U.S. and in the U.K. has for years been equal to between 1 and $1\frac{1}{2}$ years' flow of disposable private income.

[7] The significance of the mean lag theorem would be reduced if any of the β_i turned out to be substantially negative.

determination by taking inventory accumulation as exogenous and assuming for simplicity the asset adjustment process

$$\Delta FA = \varphi(FA^* - FA_{-1}) \tag{10}$$

This model has a 'disequilibrium' solution for the aggregate income flow in any period of time

$$Y = (\Delta I + \varphi FA_{-1})/\alpha\varphi \tag{11}$$

as well as a full stationary 'equilibrium' when $\Delta I = \Delta FA = 0$ and

$$Y = Y^* = FA/\alpha = I/\alpha \tag{12}$$

The dynamics of this system are closely pinned down. First, as we have seen, the lag of PE in response to Y has a mean equal to α. Second, the response of the entire system to I is virtually instantaneous for as soon as I settles down (ΔI zero) there can be no change in Y notwithstanding that final expenditure lags behind Y. Under the adjustment process assumed in (10) it immediately follows from (11) that whenever I is zero, Y must be in a full steady state (12).[8]

It has been possible to generate exceptionally simple results with inventory accumulation taken as exogenous. With a feedback from income to inventory accumulation the whole system could obviously be highly unstable. In such an economy there would be an onus on the banking system to control the rate at which credit was created. Control over the rate of expansion of credit would be both the necessary and the sufficient condition for stable evolution of the economy. Unless there were quantitative controls over the expansion of credit the only way for the authorities to achieve a stable evolution of the economy would be to operate an active monetary policy taking the form of controlling, and if necessary changing, interest rates.

Next let us assume that, for whatever reason, inflation occurs, perhaps at high and unstable rates. The following paragraphs lay down the conditions under which such inflation makes no difference whatever to the real values of stock and flow variables in the model. If these conditions were nearly or completely fulfilled we would have a useful theory of the determination of real demand and output as a process having, so to speak, a life of its own irrespective of the rate of inflation.

---

[8] This result follows from the specific nature of the adjustment process assumed. Alternative assumptions could produce fluctuations after I has fallen to zero but these will be small unless the adjustment process is quite drastically different. Virtually instantaneous equilibrium is achieved because effects of changes in ΔI and those of disequilibrium in holdings of financial assets ($FA^* - FA_{-1}$) are mutually offsetting. The result also depends on the stability condition that $\varphi < 1$.

We must first set out accounting conditions for translating nominal stocks and flows into real stocks and flows when there is inflation. The crucial adjustment is that which has to be made to private disposable income to allow for inflation gains and losses on money-denominated liabilities and assets including inventories. We have to make these adjustments if we are to preserve identities (4) and (5) in real terms.

Using lower case letters to denote real values we seek to ensure that

$$\Delta fa \equiv \Delta d = \Delta i \tag{13}$$

and

$$y = pe + \Delta fa \tag{14}$$

A simple approach is to deflate final expenditures by their own price index in the same period

$$pe \equiv PE/p \tag{15}$$

and deflate all end-period stock variables by the same index:

$$d \equiv D/p, \, fa \equiv FA/p, \, i \equiv I/p \tag{16}$$

Note that changes in real assets and debts are equal to deflated changes in nominal values *less* an adjustment for loss of purchasing power. For example

$$\Delta fa \equiv fa - fa_{-1}$$
$$\equiv FA/p - FA_{-1}/p_{-1}$$
$$\equiv (\Delta FA - \%p.FA_{-1})/p \tag{17}$$

where $\%p$ is the rate of inflation – i.e.

$$\%p \equiv p/p_{-1} - 1 \tag{18}$$

To preserve the budget constraint

$$y \equiv pe + \Delta fa \tag{14}$$

we need to measure real income with a corresponding adjustment – i.e.

$$y \equiv (Y - \%p.FA_{-1})/p \tag{19}$$

Equations (5), (10) and (19) imply that real private expenditure is given by

$$pe = (1 - \alpha\varphi)y + \varphi fa_{-1} + \left\{1 - \varphi(1 + \alpha)\right\} \%p.FA_{-1}/p \tag{20}$$

The conditions under which inflation makes no difference to real solutions of the model are as follows.

We must now take *real* inventory accumulation as exogenous, implying that the nominal value of inventories varies with inflation – i.e.

$$I = p.i \qquad (21)$$

We only have to make the assumption that the proportion of inventories which is financed by bank loans is constant (a special case of which is that they are 100% loan financed) for the entire stock of debt and therefore of financial assets to rise in proportion to the price level.

We thus have a simple condition for the inflation neutrality of the debt and asset creation process.

Under what conditions will the evolution of final expenditure in real terms be the same irrespective of the inflation rate?

The conditions are, first, that the asset/income norm (α) should be inflation neutral. Second, the asset adjustment process

$$\Delta FA = \varphi(FA^* - FA_{-1}) \qquad (10)$$

must be such that φ takes on the specific value of $1/(1 + \alpha)$ since this makes the final term in (20) equal to zero. If φ takes this value it follows that

$$FA = \frac{\alpha}{1 + \alpha}(Y + FA_{-1}) \qquad (22)$$

and

$$PE = \frac{1}{1 + \alpha}(Y + FA_{-1}) \qquad (22a)$$

so that in each and every period

$$PE = FA/\alpha \qquad (23)$$

implying also that

$$pe = fa/\alpha \qquad (24)$$

Indeed if we now define

$$fa^* \equiv \alpha.y \qquad (25)$$

it will be found that

$$\Delta fa \equiv \varphi(fa^* - fa_{-1}) \qquad (26)$$

So the asset adjustment process expressed in terms of real variables will be formally identical to the same process expressed in terms of nominal variables.

We then have disequilibrium and equilibrium solutions for real income which are the analogues of (11) and (12):

$$y = \frac{\Delta i(1+\alpha)}{\alpha} + \frac{fa_{-1}}{\alpha} \tag{27}$$

$$y^* = fa/\alpha = i/\alpha \tag{28}$$

The above conditions are sufficient for inflation-neutrality of the solution for aggregate real income in and out of equilibrium, conditional on real inventory accumulation. More elaborate conditions would be needed for inflation neutrality of the *distribution* of real income.[9]

How far are we now from Keynes's model? It too was a model of a closed, monetary economy without a fiscal system. But whereas in the Keynesian model the aggregate income flow brought savings and investment into equivalence through a multiplier process, in our model the same multiplier process brings about equality between the creation of credit (ΔD) and the demand for financial assets as a function of income. Keynes treated the money stock as exogenous. In our model a stock of financial assets (FA) is endogenous though at this stage logically equivalent to private loans outstanding (D). Keynes's model was an exercise in comparative statics. Our model yields a sequential solution in historical time with intrinsic dynamic properties. Keynes's savings/investment model gave explicit consideration to flow variables alone thereby ignoring an important aspect of the nature of economic adjustment processes. The Keynesian equilibria (the outcome of multiplier processes) are essentially short run. In long run equilibrium the stock of assets is constant and the rate of net investment is zero. Our model, once set in motion, does not need to be 'driven' by investment at all. Once money and income have been created by loan financed expenditure the circular flow of income and expenditure is self perpetuating by virtue of (12) even when inventory accumulation and all other loan expenditure is zero.

Finally, Keynes sidestepped the effect of inflation on the solution of the system by denominating output in terms of wage units thereby leaving a huge number of awkward questions unanswered. Our model is at least potentially inflation neutral. If the conditions for inflation neutrality are completely or nearly fulfilled we shall have a model of real expenditure and output determination which is in no way dependent on how wages or prices are determined – whether or not they are 'sticky' and so on. And while we have powerful 'real balance effects' which taken by themselves would reduce real expenditure when inflation accelerates, our generous 'spring' causes the supply of assets to fully offset such negative effects.

[9] What is necessary is that real interest rates are held constant and that profits are a constant mark up on the sum of historic costs and interest charges. See Godley & Cripps, *op. cit.*, Appendix to Chapter 10.

FISCAL AND MONETARY POLICY

The traditional textbook enlargement of the Keynesian savings/investment model simply added government expenditure as an exogenous variable to investment; and it added taxation as a 'leak' additional to savings. When the economy was 'opened' exports were added to the exogenous variables and imports to the leaks. The inclusion of the government and foreign trade sectors thus made no fundamental difference to the model. By contrast the introduction of a fiscal system into our model transforms the whole way in which it works.

As in the initial deployment of our previous model the fiscal model below describes nominal values but it is again assumed, to begin with, that there is no inflation. I shall also assume, initially, that monetary policy is completely passive in the sense that interest rates are fixed.

Starting again with the balance sheet identity, we now have that total financial assets held by the non-bank private sector are equal to the sum of government and private debt

$$FA \equiv GD + PD \qquad (29)$$

where

GD = government debt
PD = private debt

Next we enlarge the national income flow identity to include government expenditure

$$Y \equiv G + PE + \Delta I \qquad (30)$$

where

G = government expenditure.

We also have a flow of taxes and a flow of funds identity

$$G - T \equiv Y - T - PE - \Delta I \qquad (31)$$

where

T = the tax yield net of interest payments by the government.

Next we postulate that the government collars a share of national income net of whatever interest it pays on its debt

$$T = YG = \theta Y \qquad (32)$$

where YG is government net income and θ is not a parameter but a policy variable.

We now assume not only that there is no inflation but that with interest rates constant there are no independent policy targets for monetary aggregates.

We finally assume that inventories or, less specifically, the total of private debt associated with loan financed expenditure tends to some norm relative to disposable income

$$I^* = PD^* = \gamma(1 - \theta)Y \qquad (33)$$

This equation can be interpreted to mean that the coefficient which links inventories to income will depend on the mean production period.

Now consider the solution of the whole system. As is well known, full stock equilibrium requires that the tax flow (net of interest payments) is equal to government expenditure. This implies

$$Y^* = G/\theta \qquad (34)$$

where the star means a warranted or equilibrium rate of flow.

But we also know that full stock equilibrium is characterized by the analogue of (12)

$$Y^*(1 - \theta) = FA/\alpha \qquad (35)$$

How are these two aspects of full stock equilibrium reconciled? The answer is quite clear as soon as we rewrite equation (35) substituting debts for assets using the balance sheet identity (29)

$$Y^* = (GD + PD)/\alpha(1 - \theta) \qquad (36)$$

Since the government is operating a fiscal system, public debt must adjust to whatever level satisfies the condition that

$$GD + PD = FA^* = \alpha(1 - \theta)Y \qquad (37)$$

This implies GD has to adjust both to changes in Y^* and to changes in PD. How do the adjustments take place?

Given the fiscal stance (G/θ), so long as aggregate income exceeds its warranted level $(Y > Y^*)$ the tax yield must be such that the government's income exceeds its expenditure so that government debt is falling; if income is below the warranted level $(Y < Y^*)$ the government's income is less than its expenditure so government debt is rising. Either way Y will converge towards Y^*, accompanied by changes in government debt until it reaches whatever level exactly satisfies the stock equilibrium condition (35).

The dynamics of the response of aggregate income to fiscal stance are largely pinned down by the stock flow norms. We have the material to infer not only how large *but also how rapid* must be the response of the entire system to changes in fiscal policy subject to two conditions.

Just as we were able to prove that the existence of a norm for the stock of assets relative to the disposable income flow would imply a long run marginal propensity to spend out of income equal to one and a mean lag in the response of expenditure to income equal to α, we can now show[10] that the existence of norms for stocks of financial assets and private debt relative to disposable income (α and γ) necessarily implies not only that the whole national income flow (Y) has a unit response to the government's fiscal stance (defined as G/θ) but also that the mean lag of this response (l') is given by the expression

$$l' = (\alpha - \gamma)(1 - \theta)/\theta \tag{38}$$

The speed of response is clearly very sensitive to the size of the government's operations. If θ were zero the mean lag of the response would be infinite because income would rise for ever as a consequence of a stable stream of public expenditure. If, at the other extreme $\theta = 1$, the whole response would be instantaneous (the lag zero) but confined in scale to the flow of government expenditure itself (since $Y = G/\theta$).

The mean lag in the response of aggregate income to changes in fiscal stance is independent of the adjustment processes by which stocks of assets and debt adjust. The mean lag depends on the existence of asset and debt norms α and γ alone, together with θ.

I note parenthetically that if the economy is an open one the warranted national income flow is given by the expression

$$Y^* = (G + X)/(\theta + \mu) \tag{39}$$

where X is exports and μ is the proportion of income flowing abroad in the form of imports and current transfers. The balance sheet identity for an open economy is

$$FA \equiv PD + GD + OD \tag{40}$$

where $\bar{O}D$ is cumulative net foreign investment valued at cost. By analogy with the closed economy model we can infer that the mean lag of the unit response to fiscal stance and trade performance (defined as X/μ) is given by

$$l'' = (\alpha - \gamma)(1 - \theta)/(\theta + \mu) \tag{41}$$

while it is government debt in combination with net lending by foreigners which adjusts, whatever the size of private debt, so as simultaneously to satisfy the balance sheet identity (40) and the condition for full stock flow equilibrium (35).

This digression has been made so that we can make an approximate

---

[10] See Godley & Cripps, *op. cit.*, p. 123 for a simple geometrical proof.

evaluation of the mean lag in the response of national income to exogenous stimuli in real life economies.

U.K. and U.S. data relating to financial assets[11] and liabilities, the government and international trade accounts together with various income flows suggest that the mean lag is around one year in the U.K. and a little more in the U.S., the difference arising mainly because the U.K. is a more open economy (i.e. μ is higher over here). In other words the mean lag of the response of the national income flow to changes in fiscal policy (or trade performance) is so short that it would make this model of income determination highly relevant for short term forecasting and policy determination. This is contrary to the assumption of Blinder & Solow[12] that the response of a closed economy to G/θ would be so long drawn out that the concept is not any use for short run analysis. The mean lag is also so short that the distribution of the lag about the mean is unlikely to make much difference to the way the whole model is solved.

In theory the possibility exists that the process could be unstable. This could happen if the propensity of the system to generate private debt exceeded the asset income norm (i.e. if $\alpha < \gamma$). Such a situation would imply that there was no government debt and no net private financial assets. In any case, if a substantial proportion of the national income goes into taxes and imports, this alone may be sufficient to ensure stability. Except on absurdly extreme assumptions, a modern fiscal system will quickly be able to gobble up any excessive or unruly private debt creation. The fiscal system is thus an automatic 'stock stabilizer' which (so long as θ and μ at the margin are large – say 0.4–0.6 as in most modern economies) is much more powerful than the 'flow' stabilizer it has always been acknowledged to be.

Active monetary policy

Our conclusion so far is that the fiscal system automatically adjusts the stock of financial assets to the level desired by the private sector at the income level determined by fiscal policy. Is there anything left for monetary policy to do?

---

[11] For the formula to hold good, financial assets *FA* must be defined as the cumulative difference between private disposable income and total private expenditure (other than that financed by loans). *FA* is therefore roughly equal to a broad definition of the money stock plus government bonds held by the non bank private sector valued at cost. *FA* thus does *not* comprise all financial wealth. The values of α and γ are not of course the same as the *ex post* asset and debt/income ratios though it is easy to demonstrate that they are not very different from them.

[12] A. S. Blinder and R. M. Solow, 'Analytical Foundations of Fiscal Policy', p. 49, *The Economics of Public Finance*, Brookings.

Whatever the institutions, instruments and objectives of monetary policy nothing can alter the balance sheet identity

$$FA \equiv PD + GD \qquad (29)$$

Without giving here any close characterization of institutions, etc., it seems uncontroversial to say that the operation of monetary policy as distinct from fiscal policy at least has the effect of changing the structure of private financial portfolios; that is, it can change the non-bank private sector's allocation of its total financial stocks between the different assets – bonds, various kinds of money, etc., and perhaps change borrowing for financial purposes. But can it do more; in particular can it alter the aggregate income expenditure flow?

In the present section I shall assume that the economy is closed, that assets and liabilities are all valued at cost, that there are no independent targets for monetary aggregates but that monetary policy is conducted by controlling interest rates.

There are only two ways that monetary policy can impinge on the national income flow[13] namely by altering α and γ, the asset and private debt, to income norms. It is not in my view particularly plausible that α will be interest sensitive – why should the level of interest rates affect the speed with which income gets spent? On the other hand interest rates are very likely to alter debt to income norms if only because higher interest rates imply that a given quantity of debt increases the proportion of income paid in interest.

But we know in any case that any effect of changes in α or γ will be transient because the national income moves towards G/θ with a very short time lag and any effects on the aggregate income flow from changes in asset and debt norms will rapidly be neutralized since *whenever* $Y > Y^*$ government debt must be falling.

This general statement holds good even if institutions develop so as to cause a substantial and prolonged change in private debt (e.g. mortgages) relative to disposable income. Here, as with policy induced changes in financial norms, the fiscal system, if there is a high marginal tax rate, will operate in such a way as nearly to neutralise the effect on the aggregate income flow even while the change in norms is taking place and, as the counterpart to this,[14] private debt will progressively displace public debt as a share of national income.[15]

---

[13] So long as we continue to assume that the government predetermines its own expenditure and its share of national income.

[14] Except in the improbable case that loan financed expenditure is rising at an accelerating rate in relation to income.

[15] Benjamin Friedman, 'Debt and Economic Activity in the United States', in B. Friedman

Even though I am not going to go in detail into monetary mechanisms it is worth drawing attention to the fact that the commercial banks' role, apart from creating credit to finance certain kinds of expenditure, is to mediate the non-bank private sector's portfolio choice, given the income flows and the central authorities' funding policy.

The point can be illustrated by decomposing the stock of financial assets

$$FA \equiv BD + BP - PDF \tag{42}$$

where

FA = financial assets
BD = bank deposits
BP = bonds held by the non bank private sector valued at issue price
PDF = private debt to banks incurred for the purchase of financial assets.

Thus if we now assume that the government buys and sells bonds in the open market and requires commercial banks to hold a proportion of its assets in the form of reserves, the government's financial operations are defined by

$$G - \theta Y \equiv \varDelta RA + \varDelta B \tag{43}$$

where

RA = reserve assets of banks
B = total bonds outstanding valued at cost

The non-bank private sector's financial operations (netting out transactions within that sector) are given by

$$(1 - \theta)Y - PE - \varDelta I \equiv \varDelta BD + \varDelta BP - \varDelta PD - \varDelta PDF \tag{44}$$

The flow of funds identity makes the r.h.s. of (43) and (44) identical and implies the commercial banks' balance sheet

$$\varDelta BD \equiv \varDelta RA + \varDelta BB + (\varDelta PD + \varDelta PDF) \tag{45}$$

where BB is bonds held by the banks valued at cost.

The total of financial assets and the allocation of them by the non-bank private sector between various categories of money and bonds less debts is all, in principle, endogenous to the model, being determined by fiscal stance and net sales of securities by the government, all treated as exogenous.

(ed.), *The Changing Roles of Debt and Equity in Financing U.S. Capital Formation*, Chicago U.P. (1982) has been drawing attention for some time to the fact that in a large number of countries changes in the structure of what he calls 'non financial' debt ($PD + GD$ in our terminology) have occurred without much change in its total relative to national income. This is just what we would expect to find if our main line of argument is correct.

Wealth, equity and capital gains

The model so far has ignored capital gains and losses (other than the inflation loss on holding financial assets) and tangible wealth, assuming financial assets to be valued at their issue price.

The inclusion of all assets, tangible as well as financial, in the model greatly increases the stock of wealth relative to the disposable income flow. The fact that capital gains and losses occur (for whatever reason) may make a great deal of difference to the spending behaviour of individuals; and it may well make a significant difference to the relationship between the disposable income and expenditure of the whole private sector.

When, however, we consider the economy as a whole and so long as we continue to postulate a substantial fiscal system, changes in wealth, because of capital gains or for any other reason, may make very little difference to the aggregate income flow.

For instance suppose that private wealth, W, includes fixed tangible assets, K, as well as financial assets FA (as before, financial assets comprise government debt GD and private debt PD on account of inventories I). We may now write

$$W \equiv FA + K \equiv GD + PD + K \equiv GD + I + K \qquad (46)$$

Heroically ignoring problems associated with the distribution of wealth within the private sector, we might assume, in harmony with the life cycle theorists, that the desired stock of wealth rises with income. Thus

$$W^* = \alpha_w (1 - \theta) Y \qquad (47)$$

Changes in financial assets FA are still governed by the flow of funds identity

$$(1 - \theta)Y - PE - \Delta I \equiv G - \theta Y \qquad (48)$$

whose stock counterpart remains

$$FA \equiv PD + GD \equiv I + GD \qquad (49)$$

Changes in the value of fixed tangible assets, K, may arise through net investment expenditure (part of PE) or through changed expectations giving rise to capital gains.

Let us first note that only if the ratio of financial assets to total wealth changes does this generalization make any difference at all. For so long as FA/W is constant, there will be no operational difference between a model with $W^* = \alpha_w (1 - \theta) Y$ and one with $FA^* = \alpha(1 - \theta) Y$.

However, the ratio FA/W will not always be constant. What happens when it changes? We may start from a steady state with Y given by G/θ and with consistent stocks of tangible and financial assets. Now suppose there is a rise in the value of fixed tangible assets K (e.g. part of PE is temporarily diverted from consumption to net investment in fixed assets)[16] while desired wealth W^* remains unchanged. The rise in actual wealth W relative to desired wealth will start to generate additional private expenditure and the aggregate income flow will rise. It follows that government revenue θY will now exceed expenditure G and therefore government debt will fall. A new steady state will eventually be established where Y once again is exactly equal to G/θ. In the new steady state total wealth is unchanged, private debt and inventories are the same too, and therefore the rise in value of fixed tangible assets must have been matched by an equal reduction in financial assets and government debt. Using primes to denote values of these variables in the new steady state, comparison of the old and new balance sheet yields

$$FA' - FA = GD' - GD = -(K' - K) \tag{50}$$

So long as monetary policy accommodates, the fiscal system will ensure that the aggregate income flow and the stock of wealth are in the long run invariant with respect to changes in components of private wealth (K or I) whether generated by capital gains or by real investment. Perturbations of the income and tax flow will always adjust GD so as to offset the changes in K or I.

How large changes in the ratio of tangible private wealth to income are, and how they affect demand for financial assets, are of course questions for empirical investigation. What we have just examined is a case in which fixed tangible assets are substitutes for financial assets. If this were not the case in practice, changes in K/Y would provoke even less disturbance to the stock/flow system.

Inflation neutrality

On pp. 143–145 above the conditions for the full inflation neutrality of real national income determination in an economy with no fiscal system were set out, conditional on real inventory accumulation. These conditions were that real inventory accumulation, the proportion of inventories financed by loans, the asset income norm and the adjustment of financial assets towards the norm were all inflation neutral.

When there is a fiscal system the analysis of inflation neutrality requires a definition of the real fiscal stance such that in stable equilibrium the flow of the government's real expenditure is equal to its net receipts of real income and the real government debt is constant.

---

[16] Monetary policy here is assumed to be accommodating (i.e. interest rates are fixed).

The fiscal stance will be inflation neutral provided, first, that real government expenditure is not changed in response to changes in inflation. That is

$$G = g \cdot p \tag{51}$$

where real government expenditure is a policy variable.

The second condition for the inflation neutrality of fiscal stance is that the government's share of national income compensates for any erosion in the value of its debt through inflation. This condition will be met either if nominal interest rates are fully adjusted so as to keep real interest rates constant when inflation varies; or alternatively if tax rates are altered in such a way that sufficient assets are shunted out through the fiscal system to compensate for the inflationary erosion.[17]

We thus define the real fiscal stance as g/θ' where the prime suffix indicates that an adjustment has been made to compensate holders of financial assets for inflation. So in stable equilibrium

$$y = y^* = g/\theta' \tag{52}$$

and no change is occurring in the real stock of the private sector's financial assets taken as a whole.[18]

The remaining conditions for inflation neutrality are the same as before plus, in addition, that the normal ratio of debt to income (γ) and also the adjustment process of debt towards its norm are inflation neutral.

How strong are these assumptions?

That α, the normal ratio of financial assets to disposable income, should be invariant to inflation seems quite a weak and uncontroversial assumption, at least in the absence of hyperinflation.

The inflation neutrality of γ, the normal ratio of debt to disposable income, is somewhat more problematic. The volume of inventories relative to real income will be nearly inflation neutral since as already mentioned this ratio equals the mean production period; it is also plausible that a more or less constant proportion of the cost of inventories will be borrowed. The ratio of other kinds of private debt (e.g. mortgages and consumer credit) to the disposable income flow will probably take some time to adjust as old

---

[17] Though as in our first model this will not fulfil the condition for inflation neutrality of the distribution of income and wealth. For this, as before, real interest rates must be constant and equity profits must be in a constant ratio to the sum of historic costs and current interest payments.

[18] Taking real government expenditure and real inventory accumulation as exogenous the disequilibrium solution for real income is

$$\left(1 + \frac{\theta}{\alpha}\right) . y = \left(1 + \frac{1}{\alpha}\right)(g + \Delta i) + \frac{fa_{-1}}{\alpha}$$

contracts get paid off but I can see no reason to suppose that it will not eventually do so and this is confirmed by preliminary consideration of U.K. data.

So far as the adjustment processes both of assets and debt towards their norms are concerned, I hope to show shortly that in each case these are indeed close to being inflation neutral in the U.K. and in the U.S. However the mean lag theorem (p. 141 above) holds as well for real as for money processes. That is to say, the existence of norms alone is sufficient to establish the mean lag of the response of the entire system independently from the nature of these adjustment processes; provided α and γ are inflation neutral it follows logically that there will be a one for one response of real national income (y) to the real fiscal stance (g/θ') with a mean lag equal to $(\alpha - \gamma)(1 - \theta)/\theta$. As this can be evaluated at $1-1\frac{1}{2}$ years in the U.K. and the U.S. we may conclude that the asset and debt adjustment processes will probably not gravely qualify the proposition that real national income is completely determined with a short lag by real fiscal stance[19] irrespective of the inflation rate.

Fiscal and monetary policy: the 'crowding out' issue

We now have a slightly new perspective on the 'crowding out' discussion. It has been demonstrated above that fiscal policy under the assumptions so far made must work in such a way that fiscal stance uniquely determines the aggregate income flow

$$Y = Y^* = G/\theta$$

and simultaneously precisely satisfies the private sector's demand for financial assets irrespective of what happens to private debt

$$FA = FA^* = Y(1 - \theta)/\alpha$$

The conventional crowding out discussion is essentially concerned with what happens if monetary policy is conducted so as to predetermine the path of FA or some component of FA (say M_1 or M_3) independently of fiscal stance.

There is one extreme case which is easy to analyse. This is where a target has been set for the total stock of financial assets held by the non-bank private sector. Suppose such a target to be inconsistent with the evolution of financial assets as implied by the fiscal stance. We have demonstrated that, given fiscal stance, the fiscal system will ensure that, whatever happens to private debt, public debt will make up the difference to keep financial

---

[19] And foreign trade performance.

assets in total on track. Monetary policy will only therefore be able to achieve *its* target by an *accelerating* rate of change in private debt. Interest rates must explode and the system as a whole must crash.

Less extreme cases where the aim of monetary policy is to control the growth of some particular sub-category of financial assets, or of the reserve assets of the banking system itself, are somewhat more complicated and less determinate. If the target is such that a class of assets is targeted to change at a rate different from the rate of change in all financial assets which is implied by the fiscal stance, then obviously the monetary authorities must be changing individual interest rates in such a way as progressively to alter the portfolio composition of the private sector's assets. It is unclear whether and, if so, at what stage a catastrophic conflict between monetary and fiscal policy will emerge if targetry is confined to only one class of assets; much will depend on the ingenuity of bankers and the flexibility of banking institutions.

I would like to be able to dismiss the discussion of the outcome of various degrees of inconsistency of fiscal and monetary policy as arbitrary and artificial. Unfortunately this is not possible so long as governments are prepared to attempt inconsistent policies (maybe without realizing they are doing so) or so long as there are countries such as the U.S. where fiscal and monetary policy are put into the hands of separate and independent authorities.

Concluding observations

I conclude with the observations first that an economy can only be sensibly and safely run if fiscal and monetary policy are formulated in a mutually consistent way. Second that the common analysis of the effects of fiscal policy on alternative assumptions about the degree to which monetary policy is 'accommodating' is tendentious. One could quite equally well analyse the effects of monetary policy on alternative assumptions about how accommodating fiscal policy was. Finally, since any non-catastrophic monetary policy can only alter the portfolio composition of the private sector and its asset and debt income norms, real fiscal policy must be left with pride of place. This is because, as I have explained at length, real fiscal policy will determine real demand and output with a short time lag nearly irrespective of those asset and debt norms.

In order that the conditions for inflation neutrality should be fully met, it is necessary to assume that there are no constraints on real growth from the 'supply side'. In my view such constraints relate quite simply to limitations on the speed at which supply can adapt to demand rather than the existence of some exogenous resource endowment which sets an upper limit to real income. Of course at any one time the size of the labour force and the physical output capacity is given by the outcome of past history. In relation to that an excessive rate of growth of real demand will take such forms as rising external deficits, accelerating inflation or the absence of goods or services for sale at any price. Indeed a balance of payments constraint[20] could exist which would prevent real output from rising enough to reach full employment of labour and, still less, of physical output capacity. But such constraints (whether coming from the side of labour supply or physical capacity) are essentially of a frictional or short term character. Over a longer period sustained expansion of real demand in any particular economy will attract the necessary labour and generate the necessary accumulation of physical and human capital. Hence in my view the sustained expansion of real demand is the necessary and sufficient condition for expansion of real output on any scale whatever in the long run.[21]

COMMENT

E. Malinvaud

At this time of confusion it is pleasing to read such an undisturbed restatement of the theory that aggregate demand alone determines income, it is also interesting to consider the additions that follow when strict consistency requirements between stocks and flows are introduced into this theory. Indeed, the two main claims of Wynne Godley seem to be conveyed in the two following particularly strong sentences: 'the sustained expansion of real demand is the necessary and sufficient condition for expansion of real output on any scale whatever in the long run' (p. 157) and, starting from the assumption of no supply constraint and introducing stock–flow norms: 'the national income moves towards G/θ with a very short time lag' (p. 150).

This discussion will concentrate on each one of these two claims. Since most of the paper elaborates arguments for the second one, this will be

[20] I shall not go into remedies here but point out that Keynes was very emphatic that protection was likely to be the most effective and least inflationary way of removing such a constraint. See e.g. J.M.K., XXVI. pp. 287 & 288: 'I am not one of the "most economists" who believe . . . that disequilibrium ought, so far as possible, to be corrected by movements in the rate of exchange rather than by controls over commodity trade. There is, first of all, to the contrary the simple-minded argument that, after all, restriction of imports does do the trick, whereas movements in the rate of exchange do not necessarily do so.'

[21] I have let this sentence stand as a true record of the conference proceedings. But many people have pointed out that in this form it is vacuous. Is the long run 5 or 2000 years?

taken up at first before going to the broader issues raised by knowing whether demand analysis alone suffices for deciding about the 'management of real national income'.

The core of the analysis is contained in the model presented at the beginning of the second part of the paper and in the mean lag property that is there proved (pp. 146–49). I should like to argue that the model is more restrictive than the author seems to believe and that, before drawing strong conclusions from it about the impact of fiscal and monetary policies, we ought to proceed to serious econometric studies.

I hasten to state that this model is interesting and stimulates reflexion. The main assumption for the validity of the mean lag theorem may be formulated as 'all incomes are eventually spent and nothing else', or alternatively 'the long run marginal propensity to spend is equal to one'. When a few other assumptions, to be discussed later, are added, a kind of multiplier–accelerator relationship of income determination is derived; it has the special feature that aggregate demand contains three parts: government demand G_t, disposable income $(1 - \theta) Y_t$ and a linear function of successive first differences of income $Y_{t-\tau+1} - Y_{t-\tau}$. If G_t remains constant and equal to G, the long run solution for Y_t is of course G/θ. Moreover, the mean lag for the adaptation of Y_t to a change in G only depends on θ and on two long run stock–flow ratios α and γ, the exact formula being given by equation (38). This last result is interesting because it shows independence of the mean lag with respect to the exact pattern of income spending by economic agents.

A more precise scrutiny of the model requires that attention be given to three equations, which I interpret as follows:

– equation (33): desired inventories amounts to a fixed proportion γ of disposable income;

– equation (35): desired private financial wealth is a fixed proportion α of disposable income;

– equation (5): financial wealth increase is equal to savings minus fixed investment.

Four features deserve attention.

In the first place, the stock–flow ratios α and γ are taken to be fixed. This has something to do with the rather negative view expressed in the paper about the potential role of monetary policy. The author is right when he finds it clarifying for his exposition to first assume the interest rate to be fixed and only later to discuss the role of interest movements. But we need not follow him when he says on page 150 that it is 'not particularly plausible that α be interest sensitive' and we wonder why interest sensitiveness of γ is not discussed.

In the second place, there is no room in the model for exogenous shifts besides those due to fiscal policy (G and θ). This feature is probably not meant to be significant. But one does not see how changes in business prospects, for instance, will be introduced in the model: will they concern only the time profiles of income spending by economic agents?

In the third place, equation (15) does not allow for capital gains or losses. They are discussed on pages 152 and 153, whose conclusion is not very clear to me. On the one hand, we are told that capital gains 'can make very little difference to the aggregate income flow'; on the other hand it is explained later that people may 'spend "out of" capital gains'. Considering how large capital gains and losses have been in France during the last thirty years (on industrial capital, on real estates as well as on stock market assets), I consider they cannot be neglected in any study stressing stocks–flows consistency.

In the fourth place, this is a quite aggregated model and one may wonder whether no difficulty results from the fact that wealth is much more unequally distributed than income. Full linearity of the model and fixed income shares would permit an easy aggregation that would maintain the validity of the mean lag theorem, so far as I can see. But I should not have thought these hypotheses to be easily made in Cambridge.

A last comment about the theory concerns the importance of the consideration given to the mean lag. This would be an interesting measure of the adjustment time if, once disturbed, the income path would monotonically converge to its new equilibrium (this is well recognized by the author, notably in his book coauthored by F. Cripps). But the existence of such a pattern cannot be proved by purely theoretical arguments. Indeed, as I said, the model is a kind of multiplier–accelerator which can very well generate cycles and even lack of convergence.

As the preceding remarks may already reveal, I am suspicious when I see the author's claim that he needs no econometrics in order to establish that fiscal policy is powerful and requires only a very short time lag (this claim is mostly implicit in the paper but appears *a contrario* on page 137 where the weakness of a previous theoretical effort is said to be that 'results were contingent on the values of whole families of elasticities and lags which would have to be estimated econometrically'). The issue of knowing what role should be granted to econometric research for the study of economic policies must certainly be faced in this Keynes Centenary Conference. It is a good opportunity to raise it here.

Actually, Wynne Godley does not completely neglect statistics. He needs to substantiate his statement of a short mean lag and makes reference to U.K. and U.S. data on page 149. We may even infer from page 155 that he intends to go more fully in the future into the quantitative problems raised by his theory.

But what is written in the paper (or in the book for that matter) is not sufficient in this respect. The application of a simplified formal model to an actual economy can always be made in various ways and the author should be much more explicit in presenting his estimates. A careful reader of my comments may for instance see that I did not give to the model exactly the same interpretation as does the author, who stresses the role of financial assets. He may also wonder about such things as how actually to translate the hypothesis according to which the *value* of government expenditures and the *rate* of government receipts are the exogenous variables of fiscal policy.

Taken literally, the model makes the one year mean lag estimate incredible. Indeed it is associated with the large multiplier $1/\theta$ (or $1/(\theta + \mu)$ for an open economy). Such estimates contradict a very large number of econometric results about dynamic multipliers, which have been systematically found much smaller, at least for the initial years. (This has something to do with the presence of supply constraints, a subject to which I shall turn attention in a minute; but even multipliers in value are much smaller.)

Moreover, estimation of the mean lag does not complete what ought to be done with the data. A more thorough test of the model is required, for instance with respect to interest insensitiveness of the stock–flow ratios. Estimates of the adjustment time profiles are also necessary if we want to check monotone convergence to the long term solution. This means a good deal of econometric work. I suspect that it will eventually turn out to be similar to what is currently done by others, except that it will be more careful in the treatment of stock–flow relationships and will use more systematically data on assets, two features that will be most welcome.

Let me now take some distance from the paper and argue that, notwithstanding Wynne Godley's last sentence, supply analysis has a role to play, on a par with demand analysis, for the study of appropriate economic policies. One should not, of course, dismiss demand analysis, that also plays an essential role in any case and that usually provides fairly reliable prediction of short term consequences, as long as it is based on good econometric knowledge. But recent history and the present concerns of our fellow citizens remind us that economic policies should not be judged only by their immediate impacts.

One must first note that situations in which supply constraints would be negligible are exceptional. In France for instance the proportion of industrial firms reporting that they would not produce more if they had more orders did not decrease below 15 per cent during the past twenty years, except in 1975 and 1981. Supply constraints need not be predominant for playing a role; one can easily see that, even when they concern a small part of the economy, they substantially reduce the multiplier.[1] Properly taking this fact into account already requires some supply analysis intended to detect the trend in the frequency and nature of supply constraints.

Moreover this trend cannot be assumed independent of economic policies, which willingly or not react on participation rates of the labour force, on labour mobility, on business profitability, hence on the stimulus to enterprise, on equipment building or scrapping, and the like. Supply analysis therefore cannot be viewed as an addendum, to be considered at the end of a study in order marginally to revise its conclusions or simply to split value changes into volume and price changes; it must be incorporated within the central body of any economic policy evaluation that pretends to go beyond short term consequences.

Needless to say, this requires that particular consideration be given to investment. I do not know whether advocates of pure demand analysis will like the way in which Godley mixes fixed investment with consumption within an aggregate disposable income the time profile of whose spending does not much matter; but supply analysis certainly requires the traditional distinction.

Investment can be inappropriate in each one of its two dimensions. It may not provide enough capital widening, resulting in too slow a growth of productive capacities, hence in a worsening of equipment constraints that bar expansionary measures. Alternatively it may be too capital deepening, unduly compressing the demand for labour.

Of course, such imbalances in the investment process sooner or later generate corrective changes in the price system. For instance, if demand is pressing too hard on capacities, output price will increase, profitability will go up, which will stimulate capital widening investment. I can well imagine that some neoclassical economists would then prove what I may call 'Godley's law' referring to the last sentence of his paper: 'Demand creates its own supply'. (If Wynne Godley accepts such a proof, I wonder whether his price theory should not be revised; if he does not, I wonder what alternative proof he has to offer.)

But the problem is precisely that, in some circumstances, the corrective changes may be to a large extent ineffective. For instance if wages are indexed to the price level, if productivity increases are slow, and if profitability is very low, the economy may be sunk in a supply depression against which demand expansion is powerless. It may be that such an

---

[1] See for instance E. Malinvaud, 'Macroeconomic rationing of employment', in E. Malinvaud and J.-P. Fitoussi, eds., *Unemployment in Western Countries*, Macmillan, London 1980.

extreme situation has never been experienced by any country; but I believe that something of it was present in some countries and at some times, which I shall not mention in order for my comments to remain on the suitable theoretical tone.

One should be careful not to associate demand analysis with demand management and oppose both of them to an alternative package made of supply analysis and supply management (whatever that may be). Any policy measure must on the contrary be evaluated in all its consequences and this requires supply as well as demand analysis, one of the difficulties of this combined evaluation being that supply consequences are usually more slow to appear than demand consequences.[2] This is why 'providing a sound underpinning for Keynesian policies', the aim selected on page 136 by Wynne Godley, requires more than I find in the paper.

At the end of these comments, on this occasion, and remembering the title of the paper, I am expected to say something about the relation between the theory being presented and Keynes's thinking. I must confess that I feel quite diffident about it; so much has been said on 'what Keynes really thought'; by lack of time and interest I was not able to check my own ideas on this issue by extensive and scrupulous examination of the works of our great economist; on the contrary people around here have the benefit of both the oral tradition and the familiarity with the *Collected Writings*.

I shall, however, raise in this respect a question which seems worth considering today. Confronted with the whole range of criticism that recently attacked Keynesian theory, do we not find better answers in the original works of Keynes than in the present paper? Do not we have to explain, as Keynes had to do in the thirties, why the price system, left alone, does not prevent the appearance and development of macroeconomic disequilibria? Should not we stress again the importance and real nature of entrepreneurial expectations, which, faced with given real wages and real interest rates, affect so much the growth of supply as well as of demand?

COMMENT

Robert M. Solow

The topic assigned for this session is 'The Application of Keynesian Economics Today'. I take that phrase to pose an implicit question: Is Keynesian economics relevant for analyzing today's economy? From

---

[2] This is the main theme discussed in some of my recent work, for instance, in 'Wages and unemployment', *Economic Journal*, March 1982.

which follows yet another question: Is a Keynesian economic policy appropriate in today's economy? To ask such questions, even implicitly, already suggests the existence of a residual doubt.

It must be admitted that the confidence of Keynesian economics and Keynesian economists has been eroded in the past 15 years. In Britain, the battle for the hearts and minds of the masses appears to have been lost, although these things have a way of turning around. In the United States, we bastard Keynesians – to use a term of endearment that originated right here in Cambridge – have more life left in us, perhaps a result of hybrid vigor, but we too have lost ground.

It is important, in discussing all this, to distinguish between the intellectual and the political fortunes of economic doctrine. There is a tendency to mix the two. The intellectual opponents of Keynesian economics claim explicitly or tacitly that the electoral victories of Reagan and Thatcher are somehow evidence of the truth of the monetarist or of the new-classical approach to macroeconomic theory. (They then have the problem of dissociating themselves from the awful results of the economic policy committed in their name. There are well-known ploys for that, occasionally used by us good guys too.) Reciprocally, the political right in both countries claims that its policy choices follow from the truth of monetarism or new-classicism. It is well to treat both claims critically.

The intellectual attack on Keynesian economics came first from the old monetarism and more recently from the new classical economics. Each of these is the topic of a separate session at this conference, so I ought not discuss them as alternative analytical schemes. But I am entitled to discuss what happened out in the world that offered them the opportunity to undermine Keynesian views.

The reciprocal question is more complex. The world did not really abandon the use of countercyclical fiscal and monetary policy because it was convinced by Robert Lucas that only unanticipated monetary policy can affect real output, or by Robert Barro that debt finance and tax finance of public expenditure are equivalent in a world of rational agents with effectively infinite life, during no part of which they will expect to be liquidity-constrained or employment-constrained as they operate in perfect capital markets. Only academic economists could actually believe those stories. The political world abandoned compensatory policy for less refined reasons. Actually it is too simple to say merely that the political world has abandoned compensatory policy. In the U.K. it only seems to have abandoned expansionary policy. And in the U.S. something stranger has happened: we are prepared to have expansionary fiscal policy provided we call it something else and offset it, or more than offset it, by contractionary monetary policy. (It is also possible to make contractionary monetary

policy look like expansionary fiscal policy; it is only necessary to create a
deep recession, run up a big interest bill on the public debt, and then point
with alarm at the government's budget deficit.)

What is certainly clear is that neither government is now prepared to
follow the Keynesian policy prescription. Neither is the Democratic
opposition in the U.S. for that matter. I cannot speak about the U.K. if
only because there does not appear to be an opposition. Why are
Keynesian policies so unpopular? Is it for reasons that tell a convincing
story of the failure of Keynesian macroeconomic theory? I might as well
state my own answer at the outset. Keynes's main insights into the way a
modern capitalist economy works seem to me to have been fundamentally
right. Nothing has happened to contradict them. There are, however,
important gaps in Keynesian macroeconomic theory. Some of them have
been or are being filled, but others have not yet been tackled successfully.
Correspondingly, there are aspects of contemporary economic life for
which Keynesian economics has no ready theory and problems for which it
has no ready policy. That should not be unexpected in an evolving
economy. So much the better for our students. But I see precious little in
fact or in theory to lend credibility to either the old or the new monetarism.

Let me be more precise. Perhaps the largest theoretical gap in the model
of the *General Theory* was its relative neglect of stock concepts, stock
equilibrium, and stock–flow relations. It may have been a necessary
simplification for Keynes to slice time so thin that the stock of capital
goods, for instance, can be treated as constant even while net investment is
systematically positive or negative. But those slices soon add up to a slab,
across which stock differences are perceptible. Besides, it is important to get
the flow-relationships right; and since flow-behavior is often related to
stocks, empirical models cannot be restricted to the shortest of short runs.

Workers in the Keynesian tradition have, of course, done a lot to fix this
defect. This is where Wynne Godley's paper fits in. He follows the life-
cycle theorists (Modigliani–Ando for example) in deriving a private
expenditure-function from target-wealth considerations, although his
definitions are different. They are designed to allow him to exploit the
interesting restrictions that the stock adjustment mechanism places on the
lag-relations among flows, at least in the linear case. These are new results,
so far as I know, and useful ones. It is, however, a problem for Godley that
he needs to define 'aggregate financial assets' as the sum of all past
differences between disposable income and private expenditure, a total
unaffected by capital gains and losses on existing assets. The problem is
that it is not clear why anyone should wish to achieve and maintain a fixed
ratio of *this* total to disposable income.

A striking aspect of Godley's approach is that it takes seriously the notion that one of the equilibrium conditions in a stationary economy is a balanced-budget requirement that stabilizes the public debt. 'Taking it seriously' means he holds that the effective multiplier for government purchases is the reciprocal of the marginal tax rate, and that the process works itself out quickly. I have two comments. The lag needs to be studied empirically. The dynamics may be oscillatory and/or unstable. In any case, aggregate income will not be related to autonomous spending by a distributed lag all of whose weights are positive. So the mean lag is simply not informative. Secondly, if nominal income is growing, the appropriate equilibrium condition calls not for a balanced budget but for a deficit big enough to keep the debt growing in proportion to income, the proportion determined by portfolio considerations. In a growing economy, the corresponding supermultiplier seems to be smaller than the reciprocal of the marginal tax rate, the more so the larger the growth rate and the larger the target ratio of debt to income. All this would be worth further investigation.

I have some sympathy with Godley's analytical device of getting monetary policy out of the way by assuming it to be permissive in the sense that the central bank holds the interest rate constant. But one can hardly stop there, for both practical and analytical reasons. The modern economy generates a wide – and changing – menu of financial assets that are imperfect substitutes for one another on both the supply side and the demand side. There are as many interest rates as assets. A completed Keynesian model must certainly contain a lot of portfolio theory; it will have to model asset exchanges as thoroughly as exchanges of goods and services. This vein has been most thoroughly mined by Tobin, as summarized in his Nobel lecture 'Money and Finance in the Macroeconomic Process'. I would hope Godley could follow suit. Keynes would certainly have found extension in this direction congenial, though no doubt he would have done it his own way. He thought the capital market was the stage on which a lot of the economic drama – and farce – was played out, and would have been unhappy to see the *General Theory* embodied in a model whose only assets were base money and bank deposits.

A second deficiency in the *General Theory* was the casualness of its microeconomic basis. Keynes seems to have been content to think of the goods market as more or less competitive. Most of us would think of the natural habitat of the Keynesian system as being a network of generally monopolistically competitive and occasionally oligopolistic markets, in which prices do not simply trace out the intersections of supply and demand curves. Instead they reflect a complicated mix of conventional behavior, strategic behavior, and guesswork. I imagine Keynes would have been agreeable. He certainly made no effort to cling to the competitive assumption in view of the Dunlop–Tarshis–Ruggles evidence that real and money wages did not move in systematically opposite directions in the business cycle. Even now we are far from having a satisfactory micro-account of the goods markets in recession. We do have some interesting stories plus the more refined 'French' – Bénassy, Drèze, Malinvaud – model of general 'equilibrium' with binding quantity signals.

Still on the micro-side Keynes paid more attention to the labor market. This was probably the right instinct at a time when nominal prices were collapsing so much faster than money wages that real wages rose in the main capitalist countries in the face of soaring unemployment rates. The fragmentary insights of the *General Theory* were enough to permit Keynes to get on with his main business, but they are not an adequate model of the labor market. Theoretical and empirical study of labor markets goes on all the time, some with macroeconomics in mind and some without it, some in the Keynesian tradition and some outside it. The current favorite among macro-theorists appears to be the model of optimal wage-employment contracts with asymmetric information. I confess I lack enthusiasm for this story; its assumptions and its conclusions seem far-fetched. (Merely as an example of one, I cite the asymmetry itself: if that were an important source of disadvantage to workers, they would put more pressure on public companies for verified disclosure. As an example of the other, I cite the model's urge to equalize the welfare of employed and unemployed workers.)

Partly as a result of Keynes's understandable casualness about microeconomics, the *General Theory* does not provide an adequate theory of inflation. Godley imputes to Keynes the belief that the rate of inflation is more or less exogenous or arbitrary. I don't recognize that view as Keynesian, but even if it were I would think it unsatisfactory. Whatever was the case in 1936, today Keynesian economics needs an endogenous theory of inflation. As I read the *General Theory* it offers some warrant for the rather simple view that I picked up in my youth: that changes in nominal spending work themselves out almost entirely on real output and employment if they occur in an economy operating short of a reasonably well-defined 'full-employment' level, and almost entirely on the price level if there is already a non-negative 'inflationary gap'. I think the vast literature on the Phillips curve and its variants should be taken as an attempt to improve on this simple notion. Although there are variations in concept, most contributors argue that the division of any nominal impulse between real output and prices depends fairly smoothly on the state of the labor market (or the average state of labor markets) with the impulse being transmitted to goods via costs and margins. The third step in this elaboration, stimulated by the inflation of the 1970s and by the monetarist critique, is to give considerably more weight to expectations about the price level in the determination of the inflation rate. Here we come back to the element of truth in Godley's remark. If expectations about the price level are 'largely indeterminate in terms of economic variables' then so is, to that extent, the rate of inflation. At the other extreme is the hypothesis of rational expectations. There is a lot of room in between. Keynes would certainly have rejected rational expectations; he regarded the economy as pretty opaque to most of the participants, and I think he was right. But that is not the same thing as a belief in the arbitrariness of expectations. At a minimum, something must depend on the source of the impulse: an overnight monetary reform is not the same thing as a complicated combined act of debt-management and open-market operations, and still less is it the same thing as a bond-financed rearmament program. Something more depends on the propaganda to which the economy is currently subject.

I describe these as gaps in Keynesian macroeconomic theory in the same spirit in which someone might have – and no doubt did – point out, on the centenary of Darwin's birth, that there remained gaps in the fundamentally valid theory of evolution by natural selection. Keynes's great advance was to see (a) that the year-to-year path of the economy does not trace out a locus of Walrasian general equilibria; (b) that the specific functioning (or malfunctioning) of the labor and capital markets allows the economy to be pulled about by pointless fluctuations in real aggregate demand or can allow it to get trapped in a bad 'bootstrap equilibrium'; and (c) that conscious fiscal and monetary policy might smooth these fluctuations in the short run and raise their average level in the longer run, or dislodge the economy from a persistent slump. In these respects Godley's paper is directly in the Keynesian tradition.

This is not an appropriate occasion to discuss issues of current policy. But there is room for a concluding comment on 'the application of Keynesian economics today'. Is the standard sort of Keynesian policy prescription relevant now?

One must first ask if real wages are too high, if much of the current high unemployment in Europe and North America is 'classical unemployment'. In the U.S. the answer is simple: No. Real compensation per hour in the first quarter of 1983 was no higher than it had been in 1976 and only one per cent higher than in 1973. (Productivity is five or six per cent higher.) The question is more delicate in Europe, where real wages did not fall after the first oil shock. Nevertheless, a recent survey by Basevi, Blanchard, Buiter, Dornbusch, and Layard makes a strong case that even if the rise in EEC unemployment through 1980 were to be ascribed to excessively high real wages in the face of rising materials prices and sluggish productivity, the further large increase in 1981 and 1982 (a doubling in Germany and nearly that in the U.K.) is accounted for by a shortfall in real aggregate demand. Let me accept that conclusion.

Then why is there not more pressure in the main countries for the traditional remedy of expansionary fiscal and monetary policy, with the mix chosen on compositional grounds? (Godley could allow this role for monetary policy if he were to include endogenously determined investment in private expenditure.) I think there are two reasons for this. One is purely political: what Mr Reagan and Mrs Thatcher share is not so much a set of real economic ideas as a belief that the lives of its members is none of society's business, and that the proper role of government is to get out of the way of, if it cannot actively support, the rich and powerful. The second reason is the directly relevant one: it is the widespread fear that real economic expansion will be accompanied by a revival of inflation. Included under that heading is a worry about entrenched rigidity in the labor market and elsewhere, which makes inflation easy to start and hard to stop.

I conclude that what Keynesian economics needs today is a convincing analysis of the mechanism by which expansion turns too soon into inflation, if it does, and a convincing policy to defuse the threat if and when it occurs. It may be a market or a non-market policy, or some mixture of the two. It seems unlikely that straightforward demand-oriented policy will suffice.

To say this is implicitly to disagree with Godley's very last, very strong, remark. It may have been necessary in 1936 to insist on the central importance of fluctuating real aggregate demand in explaining the movements of output and employment. That does not entail the belief, in 1983, that considerations emanating from wage behavior, potential output, and supply price have nothing to do with the way the economy reacts to injections and subtractions of aggregate demand. The experience of the past few years, including the deceleration of inflation during the prolonged recession, only underlines the reality of these interactions. The import of capital and labor can hardly be a realistic evasion of the problem.

DISCUSSION

Professor Godley opened the session with a statement of which the following is a summary:

I would first like to say something which is more directly related to the official topic for discussion this morning. The world economy is in a dangerous state of distress. I think it is important at this conference that we should square up to this. It would be nice if we could reach some sense of agreement as to whether there is anything to be done. And about whether Keynes's teaching helps us.

I completely agree with Solow's comments (on page 164) that 'Keynes's main insights into the way a modern capitalist economy works seem [to him] to have been fundamentally right. Nothing has happened to contradict them'. To this I would add that in my view the basis for the conduct of macroeconomic policy during the 50s and 60s was also fundamentally right. I deny that the problems of the 70s and 80s are the result of policies in the 50s and 60s, except possibly in a very indirect sense. The fact that high inflation has become such a feature, and such a difficult policy problem, does not prove anything either way since it was always recognized that inflation might greatly accelerate.

Perhaps I should here give my grounds for attributing certain views about inflation to Keynes, since these have been called in question by Professor Solow and others. What I had in mind in particular were letters written in 1944 and 1945 and quoted by Professor Moggridge in his *Life of Keynes*, p. 130. 'The task of keeping efficiency-wages reasonably stable (I am sure that they will creep up steadily in spite of our best efforts) is a political rather than an economic problem.' In these circumstances, says Professor Moggridge, Keynes seems to have acted as he noted in a comment on the Australian Full Employment White Paper: 'One is also, simply because one knows no solution, inclined to turn a blind eye to the wages problem in a full employment economy.' (Letters dated December 1944 and June 1945.) If Keynes and the Keynesian policy makers in the post war period did not know how to reconcile inflation with full employment, it is becoming increasingly clear that no one else knows how to do this at an acceptable cost either.

I also share Professor Solow's uncomprehending distress about losing 'the battle for the hearts and minds of the masses' at least in England and at least for the time being. Even more distressing to me is the view expressed I think, quite correctly, by Professor Leijonhufvud that 'Keynesian economics is losing the battles for the best young talent in economics.' If this is so it will of course profoundly influence the advice given to governments for years to come and the way the next generation of students is taught.

I think the state of confusion and division within the profession has been a significant cause of what has happened to the world economy and economic policy. We could have been influential if we had been united. As it is we have been brought into disrepute with the public and also – not at all the same point – the confusion has made it possible for politicians to find some kind of academic support for any dangerous or crazy policy they fancy.

Coming to the conference papers, I naturally agree with Professor Solow when he says 'Perhaps the largest theoretical gap in the model of the *General Theory* was its relative neglect of stock concepts, stock equilibrium, and stock–flow relations.' So, my first objective in this paper is to make a contribution to this particular gap in Keynesian theory. The central idea of the paper is to unify stock and flow processes at the heart of macroeconomic theory – the trick being invariably, from the simplest case onwards, to consider the asset and income creation processes simultaneously – i.e. as different aspects of the same process. This will make the creation of financial assets, including money, endogenous.

Another thing I tried to do in this paper – and it is something which neither of my commentators has taken up but to which I attach the greatest importance – is *to outline a theory of the determination of real expenditure and real output in a monetary economy*. The *first* part of the analysis is concerned purely with inflation accounting – that is, how to construct a full and consistent set of stock and flow accounts denominated in real terms, something on which in general not enough work has been done. The *other part* lays down the conditions under which the same processes which describe the determination of money income and expenditure would also describe the determination of *real* expenditure and output *regardless of the rate of inflation*.

Professor Malinvaud might justifiably have criticised me in this context as in relation to my framework for the analysis of nominal income because I have insinuated in a purely theoretical paper that the conditions for full inflation neutrality are nearly fulfilled in practice or at least that only weak assumptions need to be made. In fact all I am formally entitled to claim is that the conditions for inflation neutrality are *few*.

I want to make two points to finish up with.

First, I do not want to leave the impression that because I do not believe anyone understands inflation or what to do about it that I think it is unimportant. Indeed *if* it is true that there is a unique NAIRU, that really is the end of the discussion of macroeconomic policy. At present I happen *not* to believe it and that there is no evidence for it. And I am prepared to express the value judgement that moderately higher inflation rates are an acceptable price to pay for lower unemployment. *But I do not accept that it is a foregone conclusion that inflation rates will be higher if unemployment is lower.*

Finally I do not want to leave the impression that I think an individual country, particularly the U.K., can operate a fiscal policy to secure full employment on its own regardless of what is happening in the rest of the world. It may sound hopelessly idealistic and unrealistic today but I do not see any way out of the present world depression which does not involve a very elaborate new kind of international cooperation.

Professor Solow commented on Professor Godley's paper as follows:

He had been feeling guilty about his written contribution because it said very little about Wynne Godley as it was mostly on the current state of Keynesian economics. (Professor Solow noted that Professor Godley too was feeling a little guilty about writing a paper on Godley's economics and that he had had to make amends by talking about Keynes. As a general proposition it is not love but guilt that makes the world go round.)

The first point is about stock–flow relations. Lord Kaldor had mentioned the day before Keynes's habit of stopping short at short period analysis. Professor Solow agreed: it is important to get the stock relationship right and he approved very much of Professor Godley's efforts to do this. The most distinctive contribution in Professor Godley's paper is the proposition about the mean lag of real income flow behind the flow of real expenditure. The fiscal stance of the government is measured, as Professor Malinvaud pointed out, by real or, for that matter, nominal government spending divided by the marginal tax rate. The Godley analysis of the mean lag works (as he says quite clearly) only with a rather unusual definition of the stocks in question. For example, the public debt must be defined as the accumulation of the budget deficit – capital gains and losses are excluded. Why should the public wish to maintain a fixed target ratio of that stock to the current flow of after tax income? Professor Godley does say something about this towards the end of his paper. He could have added that his definition lends itself to the behavioural analysis that he wished to make. Moreover, in the model the steady state level of income is simply determined by G/θ and if in fact it is true that it is wealth with capital gains and losses included that is proportional to income, the model is still determined, for it turns out that any capital gains or losses that occur must by some process displace budget deficits from the wealth total. This, however, calls into question the mean lag propositions in the dynamic processes away from the steady state; they can be violated in very complicated ways even though the steady state propositions still hold.

Professor Godley took seriously the proposition that the operative multiplier for government purchases was the reciprocal of the marginal tax rate in any model in which a balanced budget is a condition for steady state equilibrium. He shows that the dynamics of the process involved entails that in a very specific sense the average lag of income behind the fiscal stance is measured by the wealth–income ratio; he estimates the lag to be very short so that the multiplier process not only holds in some hypothetical steady state but ought to be observable also in the data in hand. If you work out, as Professor Solow had done, the generating function for the full model which is discussed on pp. 146–8 (it turns out to be a multiplier–accelerator model), there is another stock ratio that relates to production. It is even possible to generalize it a bit so that the target wealth relation and the stock output relation are themselves allowed to have arbitrarily linear distributed lags. It is possible to find the arithmetical result which is given on p. 148 and equation 38 which gives the description of the mean lag. However, the lag relationship, the solved out relationship of income to G/θ, that is to say, to the fiscal stance, is a very complicated one, it has both positive and negative coefficients and a pattern which does not seem to be systematic. This implies that the mean lag itself has no descriptive value, it does not say how closely the left hand time series will follow the right hand time series. Professor Solow said he could produce the simplest possible moving average process of this kind in which the mean lag is zero but the left hand side lagged behind the right hand side; or he could find processes in which the mean lag is negative but nevertheless the left hand side series did not lead the right hand side series. He was therefore dubious about regarding $1/\theta$ as the multiplier that Her Majesty's Government ought to be thinking about from quarter to quarter, or year to year.

Professor Solow also pointed out that if nominal income is growing, either because there is real growth or because the price level is increasing, the relevant steady state condition is not a balanced budget but a deficit, the size of which is such as to keep the stock of public debt in nominal terms growing at the same rate as nominal income. The steady state multiplier for this case may be calculated – it seems to be smaller the faster is the rate of growth and the greater is the target wealth–income ratio.

Finally Professor Solow was not sure whether Professor Godley wished to stick to the last paragraph of his paper for, as with Professor Malinvaud, it had brought Professor Solow up short. He felt that it is simply neither useful nor true to say that there are in the longer run no supply side limitations on real output so that presumably there is no such thing as excess demand in the medium or long run. While it is always possible for a single economy to import labour and capital, it is not really appropriate for Keynesian economists to regard the international market in labour as the kind of smooth frictionless market that they criticise in the descriptions of domestic labour markets by non-Keynesian economists! It is true that in the long run there are fewer exogenous variables than in the short run, one reason being that the long run is defined that way. But to say that there are fewer does not mean that there are none.

The general discussion opened with the comment that this session provided the right opportunity for a discussion of applied Keynesianism, in particular the processes of short-term forecasting, model building and the potential for demand management to control the level of real output. Keynes did not develop this applied science, indeed it is not even clear that he would have been sympathetic to the methods involved, but it was developed in a climate of Keynesianism and the models used are in essence Keynesian.

This science has enabled us to reduce quite significantly the uncertainty associated with a forecast over about a year ahead – a modest achievement of real practical value, both to business and to government. Even a government which has no commitment to demand management wants to know what tax revenue it may expect over the next twelve months. It was considered that monetarist models derived from a study of monetary aggregates had been considerably less successful, and had run into problems of measurement and estimation which were much more damaging than those that remain in the Keynesian framework. The new classical macroeconomics had not provided an operational alternative to the Keynesian methods of short term analysis either. This is a pragmatic judgement and it is not meant to imply that Keynesianism was the only foundation and that forecasting and Keynesianism are necessarily bound up together.

While the knowledge obtained could be used to help control and stabilize levels of real output, in fact it has not been so used recently in this country and, even in the heyday of forecasting and demand management, the objective of policy was as often as not directed to the balance of payments.

The analysis, it had been emphasized, was short term; in the medium term there is not a very long track record and, such as it is, it is very bad. This suggests that a somewhat different method of analysis was needed in order to forecast for periods of say five years ahead. In particular, there is need to think more about the way the supply side is determined, especially about the way in which the forces of supply and demand are reconciled by the private sector in the medium term. This would also require that the process of inflation be modelled as endogenous to the system.

How did Professor Godley's paper fit into this pattern of development? There were said to be two good reasons for including stock variables rather than concentrating solely on flow variables in the explanation of expenditure. First, in their absence there is no integral feedback process on expenditure. For example, if there is no feedback from company sector liquidity to company sector expenditure, there is in effect a sink down which income can disappear and have no subsequent effect on demand at all. What Professor Godley has done – it has been attempted in other models as well – is to include stock variables in a way that removes this problem. The second reason why it is interesting to include stock variables is because they provide the anchor on which the stability of the system can be based, for example, by the effect of a variable price level on a predetermined level of financial stocks. If it were possible to integrate the sort of analysis suggested by Professor Godley's paper with an endogenous model of the price level and to implement this empirically, it might be possible to get empirical answers to some of the questions that were considered in the abstract in the sessions of the day before.

It was next pointed out that Professor Godley's model had a real whiff of monetarism about it in that not only do ratios and stock–flow relationships figure prominently in the monetarist approach, in this case, a quantity theory which works on the national debt rather than on money itself, but also the economy is regarded as operating 'very near' the steady state.[1] (It also would be hard to generate cycles with Professor Godley's approach because there is no theory of durable stocks in the model.) It was added that a system which starts by setting up a national debt to income ratio bears a remarkable similarity to the kind of thinking that has gone on in Whitehall, the thinking that in particular led to the medium term financial strategy. If one of Professor Solow's suggestions is adopted and it is supposed that there is a national debt to income ratio of one half and a steady rate of inflation of 10 per cent, then there will be a budget deficit of 5 per cent of the national income. A lower rate of inflation would be associated with a lower rate of deficit, which has led some to argue that lowering the deficit will lower the rate of inflation – whether in fact it will do so rather than have an impact on output cannot be answered by Professor Godley's model, so that even though it is agreed that stocks and flows must be consistent with one another, the answer to the above question is ultimately an empirical one.

A difference in the two models in Professor Godley's paper was noted. The first model works off an exogenous variable, inventories, with which go credit creation. If it were to contain a capital–output ratio as well as a wealth–income ratio, it would run into a Harrod-type instability problem. The second model solves this problem in an essentially Keynesian manner; the role of the national debt in the system is to make consistent the demand and supply of wealth in total. It was felt that the model badly needed re-emphasizing in a disequilibrium connection.

This suggestion was countered by the following considerations. In the 1960s there were some who were optimistic enough to believe that once there was an adequate econometric model of the economy it would provide all the answers that were needed about the future path of the economy and would allow policies to be designed that would improve the performance of the economy. Professor Godley's model belonged within this approach. What it failed to come to grips with is an important piece of empirical

---

[1] Later in the discussion Professor Solow came to Professor Godley's defence, saying that he should not be labelled a monetarist because it was wrong to concede to monetarists the capacity to divide one number by another.

information, namely, that monetary velocity (however measured) is a random walk with a relatively large variance which occasionally is subject to discrete jumps. The variance itself reflects unanticipated shifts in the demand for money and in the supply of output, shifts which cannot be accommodated by policy. The better course therefore is to concentrate on policy rules which might serve to reduce variability rather than think that it will ever be possible to model how and when the variability will occur. To do so is to miss the point not only of the recent rational expectations argument but also of a paper by Friedman in 1953. There, he pointed out that if there is uncertainty about the future it is impossible to be sure whether the actions that are taken in the present will increase or reduce variability.

The question whether Keynes treated the money supply as endogenous was raised. It was pointed out that in his finance motive article of 1937 in reply to Ohlin, Keynes clearly treated it as endogenous. He further pointed out that the marginal propensity to buy securities out of new saving was not unity so that even if planned saving and planned investment were equal it did not follow that the flow of new issues would equal the flow of funds seeking them, a puzzle which Lord Kahn analysed in his *Manchester School* articles on liquidity preference and the new issues market.

Next, the definition of the financial assets which people desire to hold on the key wealth–income ratio in Professor Godley's model was scrutinized. If they were money or liquid assets there certainly was a whiff of monetarism in his model. The other possibility was a wealth–income target which people wished to build up to gradually over their life times. It was hard to make sense of any definition in between these two extremes. Suppose that all real assets are represented by some form of financial assets and that capital gains and losses are ignored. Then the total wealth of the community equals the total of financial assets. Suppose that there is an autonomous increase in exports and that the simple Keynesian multiplier works instantaneously. Then Professor Godley is looking at the rest of the story, that is to say, what people do as their assets grow as they are saving, how will this affect future saving and, given the fixed ratio between wealth and income, how the budget deficit will so adjust itself as to get the economy to a long-period equilibrium with $Y = G/\theta$.

The discussion then returned to the question of whether or not there are long-run supply constraints. It was argued that exhaustible resources in principle could be such a constraint but that in fact technical progress had offset this effect in the past. Professor Malinvaud's argument that the economy may be sunk in a deep supply depression because of low profitability, against which demand expansion is powerless, was then considered. It was pointed out that the reason for low profitability was low investment expenditure and so low demand overall. Professor Malinvaud, however, attributed low profitability to 'too high' real wages – a long-run supply constraint. But if the Cambridge view of distribution is accepted, real wages are determined in the commodity, not the labour market: wage-earners can only determine money wages, and a rise in demand *will* bring with it a rise in profitability. It was further added that once Keynes's analysis was extended to long-run problems, the analysis of the evolution of potential output and its interrelationship with effective demand were very much to the fore in the writings of Keynesians, for example, Harrod, Reddaway, Joan Robinson, Richard Kahn and Luigi Pasinetti. A further point relating to policy was added. If the government were to act on the basis of Professor Godley's paper and stabilize demand at a high level, would not this undermine the basis on which post-war stabilization policy was erected, that the government would stabilize demand and the unions would keep real wages by and large in line with productivity?

Mr. Cripps replied to the comments as follows:

He said he was replying because he and Professor Godley had been working very much together on the issues that were discussed. What they were doing was Keynesian monetary economics; it was not neoclassical let alone general equilibrium monetary economics. He wished, first, to discuss the stability and the nature of the dynamics in the model and what the mean lag proposition really meant. The formal model in the paper is extremely simple, at a high level of abstraction from reality. One approach which theorists follow is to make models more complicated in order to make them more realistic. Professor Solow is correct to observe that if the present model is made more complicated, it becomes a general dynamic model with an extremely mixed range of possibilities, including the possibilities of explosion and cycles. Mr. Cripps felt that diminishing returns set in very rapidly to the application of these procedures; instead, it is better to see whether, when orders of magnitude from reality are put on the coefficients in the simple model, the model itself gives a sensible diagnosis in practice of actual dynamic behaviour.

There is a confusion about dynamics which stems from the style of presentation in their book and in the paper. It concerns the scope and definition of financial assets as used in the very simple model. In the simple model, the concept does two jobs. First, changes in financial assets close off the difference between expenditure and income in the flow system – the net financial acquisition of the private sector excluding inventory adjustments. Secondly, they record the changes through time in the stocks of assets about which people are supposed to have some kind of behavioural objective. When such a model is applied to real life, these two things must be distinguished and the one concept and one symbol cannot be used with two sets of ideas. These stocks consist of heterogeneous objects, some assets, some liabilities, with the result that in a more refined model the whole concept of what is meant by a mean lag loses definiteness.

Their propositions were not meant to hinge on a constant relation of assets to income. What they were attempting to do was to show how the fiscal system might serve to stabilize the stock system (stabilization of the flow system is a concept which is familiar to Keynesians). The economy is put on an auto pilot – the government can aim the system at whatever G/θ level it wishes and the auto pilot will take care of all the monetary adjustments necessary for it to get there, subject, of course, to cycles, the importance of which needs to be tested.

The final point which Mr. Cripps wished to make concerned the important proposition of inflation neutrality which on the whole had been either ignored or misunderstood. It had been suggested that the inflation process should be made endogenous in a complete model and only then could what happens in the real system be discovered. What Mr. Cripps and Professor Godley are trying to say is that to a reasonably good approximation this approach may be short circuited by thinking of monetary processes operating directly in real terms. Monetary behaviour is a real phenomenon and monetary processes adapt to inflation rather than constrain it. The proposition about the near inflation neutrality of the economy may be false or true but that is an empirical question, certainly it cannot be ruled out on purely theoretical grounds.

5

What would Keynes have thought of rational expectations?

AXEL LEIJONHUFVUD

INTRODUCTION

The Keynes Centenary celebrations would be more festive if the Keynesian tradition were in intellectual good health and vigor for the occasion. Unfortunately, it is not. Unsuccessful policies and confused debates have left Keynesian economics in disarray.

In recent years, the intellectual excitement in macroeconomic theory has centered around the development of the rational expectations approach. Many economists have concluded that rational expectations spells the end of Keynesian economics – and many more seem to fear that this is so, even while they dispute it. What has caused the most commotion, however, is not so much rational expectations *per se* but rather the so-called New Classical Economics. *Rational Expectations* is but one of the characteristic components of NCE. The other two are *Monetarism* and *Market Clearing*.

It does not seem particularly fruitful to speculate on how Keynes might have reacted to theoretical developments taking place thirty years or so after his death.[1] Economists who still regard themselves as 'Keynesians' (in some sense) will, however, have to define their positions *vis-à-vis* these new developments. What should we learn from this recent work? What criticisms of Keynesian economics have to be accepted? What lessons of Keynesian economics must not be abandoned? How can they most persuasively be reasserted?

The relevance of Keynes's contributions to current concerns is best reaffirmed by providing good, clear answers to these questions. Many

---

[1] In the past, I have sometimes been accused of claiming knowledge of 'what Keynes really meant'. The present title was assigned to me by Royal (Economic Society) decree. In trying to write a paper to fit it, I have had occasional bouts of the unworthy suspicion that it was meant to goad me into some sort of spiritualist seance before witnesses. I would like to declare from the outset, therefore, that I have not been in touch with Maynard about this!

retorts to the New Classical Economics have been impatient outbursts, tinged with moral indignation. They have gotten us precisely nowhere. Quite generally, Keynesian economics has adapted badly to opposition. As a consequence, it is losing the battles for the best young talent in economics. In the United States, this has been true for a decade or more. To the younger generation of economists, Keynesian economics – all of it, not just Keynes himself – belongs to the history of economic thought.[2]

MONETARISM IN THREE LESSONS

How did Keynesian economics end up in such a sorry state? Although some of us have not conceded defeat, it is obviously a widely held view that Keynesianism was vanquished by Monetarism. James Tobin has distinguished two Monetarist creeds: Mark I and Mark II.[3] It is useful, I think, to distinguish two stages in the development of his Mark I Monetarism and, correspondingly, to recognize three stages of the long controversy.

In the first stage, through the mid-1960s,[4] the discussion concerned the Monetarist causal interpretation of money–income correlations. The stability of the demand function for a well-specified stock of 'money' and the predominance of supply over money demand in the determination of that money stock were the core tenets of this Stage I Monetarism. In claiming that monetary policy would be an effective regulator of nominal income this Monetarism differed markedly from Keynesian views of that time. In almost every respect the policy doctrine advanced by Friedman and Brunner was diametrically opposed to that of the Radcliffe Report.

In the second stage of the controversy, many Keynesians embraced the Phillips-curve and the Monetarists challenged its stability. Arguments based on the anticipation of inflation became central to the debate for the first time. Although not logically entailed by labor-market anticipation of inflation, the Natural Rate of Unemployment hypothesis was made a Monetarist doctrine. This natural rate doctrine sharpened the crowding-out arguments against fiscal stabilization policies. The Monetarists found use for the anticipated inflation model (AIM) also in accounting for

[2] A recent Lucas & Sargent paper (1979) is entitled 'After Keynesian Macroeconomics'. (It deals, however, to a very large extent with econometric issues outside the scope of my discussion).

[3] Tobin (1981). For the material in this section, see also Laidler (1981, 1982).

[4] Friedman's (1956) 'Restatement' through the years in which Friedman and Schwartz's (1963) *Monetary History* and related works by Cagan, Brunner and Meltzer were absorbed by the profession.

Gibson's paradox, i.e. the (pro-cyclical) pattern of nominal interest rates. Friedman's presidential address (1968) authoritatively summarized this Stage II Monetarism.

In the third stage, Lucas (1972) succeeded in providing a model, carefully built on rational expectations foundations, within which Friedman's (1968) conjectures about the short-run and long-run Phillips curves hold true. A breakthrough in the systematic modelling of informational assumptions, this immensely influential paper married the rational expectations approach to Stage II Monetarism from the outset. Sargent (1973) generalized the policy-ineffectiveness proposition which was then further developed by Sargent & Wallace (1976) and Barro (1976). The 'New Classical Economics' gained currency as the label for this Stage III Monetarism.

The reason for distinguishing between the Stages I and II is that the former is capable of a 'weak' and a 'strong' interpretation of the money–income correlation. In the strong version, exogenous changes in a purely supply-determined money stock interact with a stable money demand function to 'cause' the observed movements in money income. The 'weak' version allows a reciprocal influence from real income movements via real money demand to the money stock. The weak version nonetheless implies that control of the money stock will yield control of money income. Recall the oft-quoted summing up of Friedman and Schwartz's *Monetary History*:[5]

Mutual interaction, but with money rather clearly the senior partner in longer-run movements and in major cyclical movements, and more nearly an equal partner with money-income and prices in shorter-run and milder movements – this is the generalization suggested by our evidence.

Sufficiently diluted, Stage I Monetarism can be made weak enough, obviously, to be stomached by almost all Keynesians, most of whom use a stable money demand function in any case. Stage II Monetarism, however, pretty much excludes this weaker interpretation. In the absence of monetary shocks, employment stays at the Natural Rate level. The permanent income corresponding to the Natural Rate of Unemployment determines the demand for real balances which is, therefore, a constant in the absence of monetary shocks. This leaves us with 'money causes income', *without* the reciprocal influence. It is this strong version, consequently, that is carried over into Stage III New Classical Theory.

Where then did Keynesianism founder? At Stage II, obviously, on the Phillips-curve or, more generally, on the failure to incorporate inflation rate expectations in the Keynesian model. When the American inflation

[5] Friedman and Schwartz (1963), p. 695.

picked up steam, the misbehavior of the Phillips-curve and the inflation premium in nominal interest rates became obvious for all to see. Monetarists, who had predicted these things by reasoning from the neoclassical anticipated inflation model, made enormous headway within the economics profession and without. Keynesians, who had continued to argue the usefulness of the Phillips-curve and to disparage the empirical relevance of the anticipated inflation model, lost face and lost influence.

It was a debacle. A bad enough debacle that the profession proclaimed the long controversy a Monetarist victory and, by and large, turned its interest elsewhere. This collective reaction left a number of things muddled.

First, the Phillips-curve and Gibson's Paradox were both late-comers among the issues of the Monetarist controversy. When the verdict was rendered on the basis of the obvious significance of inflationary expectations, the *original* (Stage I) issues were not thereby settled. Rather they were forgotten – or at least tabled for a number of years. I would agree with Tobin that 'the question whether money causes income or income money or both is still undecided'.[6]

Second, the stable Phillips-curve had not been an integral part of earlier Keynesian theory. It was added on to that theory in the 1960s, not without opposition by some Keynesians.[7] It is not obvious, therefore, that the destruction of this excrescence by unfolding events should be regarded as tantamount to the demolition of the central structure.

Third, although the Natural Rate hypothesis is pedagogically effective as the polar opposite to the stable Phillips trade-off hypothesis, it is not the case that empirical rejection of the latter establishes the former. Suppose that fully anticipated, purely nominal shocks have no employment effects. Other things (such as changes in the 'marginal efficiency of capital') might still have such effects. The ability to anticipate inflation (or 'absence of money illusion'), then, does not by itself imply some sort of strong stability of the economic system around full employment, be it 'Natural' or not.

THE OUT-OF-FOCUS KEYNES

What do the Three Stages of Monetarism have to do with Keynes? How do we bring Keynes into some sort of relation with developments decades after his death?

In all the debates over Keynesian economics in the last twenty years or so, there is one Keynes that has remained curiously out of focus. This is true also of my own writings. I mean Keynes, the monetary reformer. After

---

[6] Tobin (1981), p. 41.

[7] See esp. Phelps (1968). I may also refer to my own comment, *ibid.*

more than fifteen muddled years of inflation, preoccupied as we are with intractable problems of monetary stabilization, it seems natural to give some thought to the Keynes who gave so many years of his life, from Versailles to Bretton Woods, to the cause of a stable and workable international financial order.

The Phillips curve debacle coincided in time with the elimination of the last vestiges of the Bretton Woods system. The heritage of Keynes, the theorist, came to grief when the legacy of Keynes, the monetary reformer, had been squandered. Is this just a curious coincidence? Or should we make more of it?

Keynesian theory failed to incorporate inflation expectations. Before the Great American inflation, the theory was widely accepted as an adequate guide to reality. Once the inflation picked up momentum and became both high and volatile, the Keynesian neglect of nominal expectations became fatal. But the international monetary order that Keynes had striven for should have had responsible international central bank policy by the reserve currency countries and everyone else disciplined by fixed exchange rates. In such a regime, rational agents should not have volatile nominal expectations and a theory in which they do not is appropriate to the regime.

This is a rational expectations argument. The concept of 'monetary regime' figures prominently in the more recent rational expectations literature. It links expectations and institutions. It may be defined as follows: A monetary regime is a system of expectations that governs the behavior of the public and that is sustained by the consistent behavior of the policy-making authorities. Since the responses of an economy to shocks or to policy-actions depend on the public's expectations, we need, in effect, a different short-run macrotheory for each different regime.

The regime approach is a highly useful one – certainly, one of the most useful developments to come out of the rational expectations movement so far. I suggest we use it on Keynes and ask what regimes (if any) his theory would fit and also what his opinions were of various regimes. First, we need to consider his treatment of expectations.

EXPECTATIONS

It used to be one of the proud boasts of Keynesian economics that it incorporated expectations in a significant way. Sir John Hicks in his first review of the *General Theory* gave pride of place among the book's contributions to its treatment of expectations:[8]

---

[8] Sir John Hicks (1936), reprinted as '"The General Theory" a First Impression', in Hicks (1982), p. 86.

If we assume given, not only the tastes and resources ordinarily assumed given in static theory, but also people's anticipations of the future, it is possible to regard demands and supplies as determined by these tastes, resources and anticipations, and prices as determined by demands and supplies. Once the missing element – anticipations – is added, equilibrium analysis can be used, not only in the remote stationary conditions to which many economists have found themselves driven back, but even in the real world, even in the real world in 'disequilibrium'.

This is the general method of [the *General Theory*]; it may be reckoned the first of Mr Keynes's discoveries.

The claim Hicks made for Keynes was that, by bringing in expectations in the right way, he had succeeded in significantly extending the scope of equilibrium analysis. This is precisely the claim now being made for Lucas, Sargent & Co. although for rather different reasons. Keynes extended the use of the Marshallian equilibrium method by treating long-term investment expectations as *exogenous* determinants of his short-run income equilibrium. Lucas extended the use of neo-Walrasian equilibrium analysis by making short-run nominal expectations strictly *endogenous* again while shifting to a stochastic equilibrium concept that allows realizations to diverge from expected values.

By the early thirties, business cycle theorists had come to realize that use of the equilibrium toolbox could be strictly justified only for stationary and perfect foresight processes.[9] This pretty much excluded business cycles – and there was no other toolbox. Keynes's new method successfully *evaded* this dilemma. Lucas's new method attempts to *solve* it.

That, however, is not the whole story. Keynes' innovation concerned the long-term expectations of real magnitudes, while NCE theory has dealt mainly with the short-term expectations of nominal magnitudes. Keynes, on the whole, ignored nominal expectations and the rational expectations pioneers have only recently begun to turn their attention to long-term investment expectations.

Keynes' own treatment of short-term expectations should give pause to anyone tempted to attack the NCE on the grounds that it assumes too much foresight on the part of agents:[10]

it will often be safe to omit express reference to *short-term* expectation in view of the fact that in practice . . . there is a large overlap between the effects on employment of the realized sale-proceeds of recent output and those of the sale-proceeds expected from current input . . .

[9] See, again, J. R. Hicks (1933), reprinted as 'Equilibrium and the Cycle', in his (1982). Compare also Robert E. Lucas, Jr, (1980), reprinted in his (1981), esp. section 5.

[10] See Keynes (1936), pp. 50–1. My colleague, Robert Clower, reads this passage simply as assuming static expectations. Even on that reading, however, the solution states of Keynes' model will be perfect foresight equilibria.

The omission of 'express reference' is achieved, of course, by simply equating expected and realized real income, a procedure subsequently imbedded in the Keynesian cross, in *IS–LM*, and thus in the entire Keynesian literature. This is 'perfect foresight' such as the rational expectations people have not allowed themselves to indulge in! Keynes, I would think, should have appreciated the considerable weakening of this assumption achieved through the use of a stochastic equilibrium concept.

Long-term expectations are another story. In the early stages of the rational expectations debate *the* issue was the Phillips curve and the focus, therefore, was entirely on expectations over the most immediate future only. The ability of agents to infer more-or-less correctly the immediate price-level consequences of current monetary policies were emphasized to the neglect of their inability to infer much of anything about the future nominal values that will emerge from longer sequences of discretionary policy actions.[11] As a consequence, this early rational expectations literature provides very little in the way of theoretical foundation for the opposition to inflationary policies (and discretionary policies in general) that also characterizes it.[12] This temporary neglect does not mean that the rational expectations approach implies negligible social costs of inflation. Nor does it mean that it somehow precludes sensible study of this problem on which Keynes held such strong views.[13] On the contrary, progress beyond the point reached in the *Tract* requires, I think, careful specification of the 'inflationary regime' in question – requires, in other words, a rational expectations approach.

Nonetheless, long-term expectations pose the question of how far the endogenization of expectations can be taken. Elsewhere, I have used a distinction between 'well-behaved' and 'ill-behaved' expectations.[14] Well-behaved expectations bear a stable relationship to the observable state variables of a macroeconomic model and can therefore be treated as fully endogenous. Expectations are 'ill-behaved' if not explainable by the model. If, in addition, they are unobservable (or unmeasurable), ill-

[11] See Leijonhufvud (1981b, 1983a).

[12] That the New Classical Economics does not provide sufficient reasons for its strong aversion to inflationary policies is a complaint often voiced by critics. See, e.g., Tobin, *op. cit.*, or Hahn (1983), pp. 101ff.

[13] Keynes (1971b) 'Preface'. It is true, of course, that Keynes's thought changed and developed from the *Tract* on. It is also true, however, that the world of the *Tract* resembles our current regime of fiduciary standards and flexible exchange rates more than does the world of the *Treatise* or that of the *General Theory*. One must insist, moreover, that we do not have evidence from Keynes's later years that would indicate a change of mind on his part with regard to the consequences of inflation.

[14] Leijonhufvud (1983a).

behaved expectations will spell trouble for our ability to forecast.

In these terms, Keynes's short-term expectations were (excessively) well-behaved but his long-term expectations ill-behaved in that they shifted for reasons not incorporated in the model. The rational expectations approach to this problem will, of course, be to strive for a behavior-description in which long-term investment expectations are completely endogenized.[15] Keynes would presumably have raised philosophical objections to so foolhardy an attempt to harness the 'dark forces of time and ignorance' with the actuarial calculus.

From the standpoint of rational expectations methodology, a refusal to attempt to *endogenize* all expectations is perhaps nothing but obscurantism. The Keynesian trick of explaining income movements by invoking exogenous (and perhaps also unobservable) 'shifts in MEC' appears as nothing more than putting a verbal label on our quantitative ignorance. Clearly, we are better off the more success this ambitious rational expectations programme has. Meanwhile, a label for one's ignorance is a very useful thing – if it helps remind one that one *is* ignorant.

PRICES AND QUANTITIES

During the course of the Monetarist controversy it was often said that the two sides differed in their explanations of changes in nominal income but 'were in the same boat' when it came to explaining the breakdown of nominal income changes into their price and quantity components. But surely the two approaches do not belong in the same boat? Throughout the entire history of modern macroeconomics, I feel, there has been something profoundly unsatisfactory, something thoroughly befuddled, about our handling of the relationships between nominal and real magnitudes.

I have no precise diagnosis of what has been the problem. I do have a hunch about it, namely, that the trouble may stem from a failure to keep straight the differences between monetary (or nominal) and real business cycle hypotheses.

Any business cycle 'story' will have, as two of its elements, first, a shock or disturbance and, second, the failure of some endogenous variable or variables to adjust appropriately to the shock. The disturbances can be nominal or real (or, of course, mixed) and so can the adjustment failures. Thus, we obtain the 'Swedish flag' classification of Figure 1, where the mixed cases are slighted for the purposes of the present discussion.

[15] Early in his career, Lucas was best known for his work on investment. He returns to it, in context of a complete macromodel and from a rational expectations perspective in his (1975). For the growing interest of the rational expectations group in explaining the cyclical behavior of investment, see the 'Introduction' to Lucas (1981) and for recent work, e.g., Kydland and Prescott (1982).

Figure 1 Adjustment 'failures'

Shocks		Nominal	Mixed	Real
	Nominal	N/N $dM \mid \bar{w}$		N/R $dM \mid \tilde{E}(r)$
	Mixed			
	Real	R/N $dMEC \mid \bar{w}$		R/R $dMEC \mid \bar{r}$

A '(purely) nominal disturbance' is one that requires a scaling up or down of all nominal values for the re-equilibration of the system. Thus, nominal shocks are neutral by definition. A 'real shock' is one that requires some reallocation of resources and, correspondingly, changes in real relative prices. Keynes's shifting 'marginal efficiency of capital' is the case we will deal with here (oil-shocks and other newfangled inventions will be · ignored). MEC shocks change perceived intertemporal opportunities and require, therefore, adjustments in intertemporal prices, i.e., in the structure of real rates of interest.

In a nominal/nominal (N/N) theory, the disturbance requires a rescaling of nominal values. A truly exogenous change in a purely supply-determined money stock might approximate such a case. If money wages (for instance) were to be inflexible – for whatever reason – the maladjustment would show up in changes in employment. Friedman's (1968) explanation of deviations from the natural rate of unemployment exemplifies this brand of theory.

In the diagonally opposed R/R case, the MEC shift requires a reallocation of resources between production for present and production for future consumption. (To the extent that intertemporal substitution elasticities in labor-supply vs. leisure choices are of significant magnitude, it may also call for a change in the present 'natural' level of employment.) If the intertemporal price structure proves inflexible, saving and investment cannot be appropriately coordinated and the maladjustment, again, shows up in changes in employment. Keynes's (1936) *General Theory* is, of course, of this variety.

If we could have had a Monetarist controversy of this clear-cut N/N versus R/R variety, modern macroeconomics would be more easily understandable than is now the case. That a failure of nominal values to adjust to a nominal disturbance will mean trouble is not a very complex idea. That a failure of relative prices to adjust to a real disturbance likewise spells trouble is not that much harder to grasp.

The actual discussion has seldom been that straightforward. First, the most widely accepted version of Keynesian economics combines shifts in MEC with rigidity of money wage rates. This R/N story is not at all as transparent as our first two examples. If we start with a real disturbance requiring changes in the allocation of resources and in relative prices, but not in the level of nominal values, why should rigid money wages give us trouble? At best a crucial link is missing from this story. At worst it is confused.

One of the consequences of 'Keynesian' economists shifting their ground in this way was a rather confused altercation with the Monetarists over unemployment theory. In this discussion, the Monetarists – who are obliged to invoke some nominal adjustment failure to explain how the real cycle results from nominal shocks – were steadfast in denying any rigidity of wages, while the Keynesians – who should have no particular use for the assumption – eventually made it the touchstone of Keynesian doctrine.[16] Probably, nothing could have done more to make wage-rigidity seem an essential Keynesian tenet than the objections to it from Karl Brunner and Milton Friedman.

At the same time, of course, Friedman assumed temporary 'stickiness' of wages to explain how nominal shocks would cause temporary deviations of unemployment from its 'natural rate'. In constructing an equilibrium model with the properties conjectured by Friedman, Lucas transformed the temporary maladjustment into an intertemporal one. The canonical version of NCE, therefore, has nominal disturbances causing misperceptions of the real rate of return which give rise, in turn, to intertemporal substitution adjustments in employment.[17]

Thus, the New Classicists have, in effect, shifted the Monetarist position from a N/N one to a N/R one. This moves the muddled conflict over unemployment theory onto the R/N to N/R off-diagonal, which frankly does not help much. It leaves us with Keynesians blaming sticky money wages confronting Monetarists blaming real return misperceptions.

The slow quadrille continues. It may be that most American Keynesians see little difference between the R/N and N/N positions. From *IS-LM*, one learns that both monetary and real shocks can produce changes in nominal income; it appears, then, that the point one must insist on is that changes in nominal income produce changes in real output and employment only if money wages or prices are sticky. Quite a few former Keynesians, moreover, have come to agree that it takes monetary impulses to produce aggregative movements. These people actually occupy the original Monetarist position (at N/N) but still regard themselves as quite non-Monetarist

---

[16] E.g., Okun (1981), Gordon (1981), or Solow (1980).

[17] See Lucas (1975) and Barro (1980).

in their insistence on the inflexibility of wages; they do so with some reason since the leading younger Monetarists have vacated these premises in favor of a position (at N/R) allowing a principled insistence on market-clearing wages.

Meanwhile – are you following me? – doubts have arisen in the Rational Expectations camp concerning the Monetarist causation hypothesis. Indeed, Sims has moved already from a reconsideration (1980) to rejection (1983) of the monetary business cycle explanation. Here I must ask you to stand by for further developments. It is, as yet, too early to tell whether Sims will lead the New Classical Economists to occupy the original Keynes position (at R/R), while the Old Keynesians make themselves at home in Friedman's quarters (at N/N).

This will remind you, I am sure, of that great Cambridge contemporary of Keynes, Sir Dennis Robertson (1954):

highbrow opinion is like a hunted hare; if you stand in the same place, or nearly the same place, it can be relied upon to come round to you in a circle.

Whether Robertson was here expressing a Rational Expectation or merely voicing the autoregressive prejudice of his five lagged decades in the profession, I will not presume to judge. If, in this clockwise dance, highbrow opinion were to come back to 'nearly the same place' as Keynes, it may still not be perceived as a vindication, for by now the term 'Keynesian' is little more than a label for the hindmost.

The long controversy between Keynesians and Monetarists is thus a very complicated story. That acknowledged, I will proceed 'as if' the basic conflict, all along, had been between a Keynesian real disturbance/real maladjustment theory and a Monetarist nominal disturbance/nominal maladjustment theory.

MONETARY REGIMES

There are two basic but contrasting conceptions of how control of nominal values can be achieved which we may call the *quantity principle* and the *convertibility principle*, respectively. Monetary regimes may be distinguished inter alia according to how closely they approximate a system of pure quantity control or one of pure convertibility control.[18]

The quantity principle seeks control of the price level through control of some monetary aggregate usually referred to loosely as the 'quantity of money'. The logically tidiest version of such a system will be on a pure fiat

---

[18] I have discussed the material in this and the following sections more extensively in my (1982a, 1982b).

standard. It requires central banking. The private sector must be prevented from creating perfect substitutes for the government controlled 'money' since otherwise control of the latter might not achieve control of the general price level. Hence the system usually has government monopoly of the note-issue and more or less far-reaching governmental control of the banking system. Basically, the government decides on the quantity of money and the private sector sets the price level.

An extreme version of this regime would arise if the government, in changing the quantity of money, did so only by means of currency reforms that change the nominal value of outstanding contracts and of the real balances held by the public. (The 1958 French replacement of old by new francs is an example.) In this unrealistic case, the 'nominal scalar' case, the government could directly manipulate the nominal scale of all real magnitudes.

The convertibility principle, in contrast, requires the government to set the legal price of some commodity (such as gold), allows banks to produce 'money' redeemable into the commodity, and lets the private non-bank sector decide the quantity of paper money and bank deposits it desires to hold. Suppose, just for a moment, that the government could set the legal nominal price of a basket of commodities, and that redeemability of money into baskets could be made operable. Such a 'basket case' monetary regime would be the diametric opposite to the 'nominal scalar': the government sets the price level and the private sector determines the quantity of money.

We may thus consider a spectrum of institutional possibilities with the commodity standard regimes towards the convertibility control extreme at one end and the fiat regimes toward the quantity control end. Early banking history shows us systems relying altogether on convertibility for monetary control. The present system retains no shred of convertibility, but relies altogether on governmental quantity control. In between, we could array, in rough historical sequence, the managed gold standard, the gold exchange standard, and the Bretton Woods system in its various stages of ascendancy and decline. The historical process has not been a smooth and gradual transition from commodity to fiat standards, of course. War-time lapses into inconvertible paper were repeatedly followed by the reestablishment of regimes in which convertibility had a more or less significant role to play. With some backing and filling, the secular process has nonetheless been one away from convertibility and toward quantity control of fiat money.

Most of the historical experience relevant to the present discussion is not well represented by either of my two extreme cases. Nonetheless it is instructive to note what kind of monetary theories and monetary policy doctrines would fit these extremes. We should also ask what relationship might be established between the previous classification of business cycle theories and the present one of monetary regimes.

Obviously, the quantity control fiat standard is made for Monetarist theory. In Friedman's theory (particularly, Stage II), the central bank sets the quantity of money and the private sector adjusts first nominal income but ultimately only the price level. The monetary authorities can control nominal magnitudes but, in equilibrium, real ones are beyond their grasp. Attempts to control what cannot be controlled produce undesirable results. Pursuit of a low interest target, for instance, would eventually produce an explosive inflation. Monetary policy should be directed at monetary targets and the latter should not be adjusted with an eye to variables, such as employment, that are ultimately beyond nominal control. And so on.

The (unrealistic) case of 'basket convertibility' would be a convenient one for Radcliffe monetary policy doctrine. The price level is set and the public rationally expects its future to be regulated by convertibility. The non-bank public's trading of real IOU's for real deposits with the banking system determines the monetary aggregates. To the extent that the central bank can affect the terms of this exchange, i.e., mainly the real rate of interest, it will have some small degree of influence on real investment, output and the real money stock, but control of the nominal scale of real magnitudes in the economy is essentially beyond its powers. Monetary policy operates within narrow limits to affect real credit conditions and liquidity. The use of interest targets does not carry any imminent danger of nominal instability in this setting where both the price level and price expectations are kept in check by convertibility.

Now, of course, not even the late 19th century gold standard resembled this 'basket convertibility' regime at all closely. It had an anchor for nominal values in the sense that price level fluctuations were constrained to those of the relative value of gold in terms of other commodities. Mean reverting price level expectations helped stabilize prices. Even so, a variable supply of new gold, a small and price-inelastic non-monetary demand and a vanishing non-bank monetary demand meant that the bounds which gold-convertibility put on the price level could be uncomfortably wide. The wider these bounds, the more room the system gave for the 'Credit Cycle', as Keynes called it.[19] Management of the standard, for reasons beyond merely protecting the solvency of the banking system against 'drains', became increasingly desirable.

The last attempt, in the 1920s, to control nominal values through gold convertibility ended in total disaster. Convertibility for the public disappeared and was never seen again. One by one, the features of the

---

[19] Keynes (1971b)

commodity standard were removed, making central bank control increasingly important. With redeemability gone, the public could no longer protect itself against inflationary policies. Until 1971, small open economies were still disciplined to some degree by fixed exchange rates but retained a significant ability to sterilize reserve flows, particularly in periods when capital flows were restricted.[20]

The international system of multiple fiat regimes, snakes, tunnels, dirty floats, and flexible exchange rates is far removed from the old gold standard world. But although the peoples of the Western world have had to become accustomed to the instability of nominal values and even though the correct anticipation of nominal changes is of the utmost importance in such a setting, the present system of multilateral monetary mismanagement does not closely approximate my 'nominal scalar' extreme.

So, our historical experience lies well inside these extremes. But the never-ceasing theoretical debate juxtaposes two traditions of monetary analysis each of which interprets that experience as if it 'essentially' belonged close to one of the extremes. Very often, moreover, the battle between Monetarism and the 'New View' over the interpretation of some regime midway between the extremes is carried out in terms that suggest that the two theories are regarded as mutually exclusive so that one must be True and the other False.[21] My own unprincipled belief is that both theories are about half true and that we can be dangerously misled if we base policy wholly on one to the total exclusion of the other.

REGIMES AND CYCLES

Turning now to business cycle theories, it is clear that those postulating purely nominal shocks are relevant only at the fiat extreme, whereas at the convertibility extreme only real shock hypotheses are admissible. The (strong) Monetarist causal chain from exogenous money shock via nominal inflexibility to real output and employment is familiar. The Keynesian chain from changes in real intertemporal prospects via real interest rate maladjustments to real income and endogenous movements in inside money, even if familiar, is out of fashion. We may sketch both an equilibrium and a 'disequilibrium' version of it.

In the equilibrium version, we start with a rise (exogenous in relation to the model specified) in the future real income perceived as derivable from present factor employment in some sizeable sector of the economy. All

[20] For an assessment of the scope for independent monetary policies, cf., Darby, Lothian *et al.* (1983).

[21] For the strong anti-Monetarist position, see Kaldor (1982).

agents are equally informed about this change in the situation and all evaluate it in the same way. The entire system responds as would Robinson Crusoe therefore. Suppose, for the sake of argument, a high degree of intertemporal elasticity of labor/leisure substitution, so that we obtain a significant supply response to this change in the future return to present labor. This will allow a temporary equilibrium employment expansion in one sector without equal contraction elsewhere. Hence, the natural rate of unemployment is not a constant but depends on the marginal efficiency of capital. The expansion of output is financed by an expansion of bank and non-bank trade credit. As income increases more real money balances are demanded so that the additional saving matching the increased investment ends up being partly intermediated by the banking system. Investment, real interest rates, and employment all rise and the expansion of the banking system (and of non-bank credit) allows this to happen without downward pressure on money prices.

Note that this sketch follows the rational expectations equilibrium groundrules, although it is non-Monetarist. The money stock varies with income for purely endogenous reasons. Employment covaries with money income for reasons that have nothing to do with nominal misperceptions or other maladjustments of wages or prices.

The disequilibrium version is the Wicksell–Keynes story. Here it is *not* the case that all agents get the same information. Individual firms see improvements in the future return to present activity, but no one has an overview of what is happening to the economy-wide marginal efficiency of investment. Since, historically, the average real rate of return has not been a volatile variable, speculation stabilizes the real rate of interest and firms adjust their rates of investment to it. When the real interest rate fails to find its 'natural' level, household saving and business investment are not properly coordinated. In the upswing, (over)-expansion of credit allows investment to exceed planned saving, putting upward pressure on money prices and wages. In recession, the contraction of credit will similarly put downward pressure on prices. The cycle, therefore, would leave a Phillips-curve pattern of observations even in this system where nominal values are anchored by convertibility.

Suppose this is a serviceable description of the kind of cycle that occurs towards the end of our spectrum where convertibility more or less guarantees against the occurrence of purely nominal shocks. What then happens to the cyclical behavior of the economy as the historical trend away from convertibility control takes it towards pure quantity control? What does *not* happen is that the Keynesian R/R cycle fades out to be replaced by a Monetarist N/N cycle. Two things might happen. *Either* the quantity control is handled in such a way that shocks requiring adjustments in the nominal scale of real magnitudes do not occur; *or* it is mismanaged in which case a N/N cycle is superimposed on the R/R one.

Recent history presents us with about two decades of one and two of the other. What seems most interesting about the Bretton Woods regime in retrospect is that a system of expectations basically appropriate to an economy with convertible money was sustained by quantity control and with the central convertibility mechanism removed. A system of price level expectations consistent with the convertibility principle means that people expect prices to revert to the longer term trend if and when they go above or below trend. For such expectations to be maintained when the economy is not in fact on a standard where non-discretionary, objective factors determine the trend, the central bank must, in effect, 'mimic' such a standard. It does so by imposing monetary restraint above trend and applying monetary stimulus below it. The government must also maintain the faith that this pattern of behavior will be continued indefinitely. An (at least implicit) monetary constitution will be of help in this regard. For small open economies, a habit of defending a fixed exchange rate may be the way to accomplish this task – if, that is, the reserve currency country behaves responsibly. This can be a big 'if'. In any case, public confidence in the indefinite maintenance of this pattern of monetary control will require budgetary policies consistent with this objective.[22]

In the United States, monetary stability was maintained in this way until the mid-sixties. With the private sector firmly expecting a quite low and not very variable rate of inflation, the Federal Reserve System could affect the availability and price of 'real' credit to some extent. Monetary policy could play a limited, but constructive role in attempts to stabilize employment. But the continuance of the regime required continued restraint on the part of the authorities.

The one-time Keynesian (or Radcliffe) doctrine of the 'ineffectiveness' of monetary policy would seem to have served, however inadvertently, as a myth protecting the Bretton Woods regime. Like the belief in the stickiness of nominal wages, it is a doctrine fitting a true convertible standard – where the monetary authorities cannot play around with the nominal scalar, rational agents will not expect that adjustments in the nominal scale of contracts will be needed. When the Friedmanite doctrine that the quantity of money is an effective regulator of nominal income gradually gained acceptance, however, it was inevitable that advocates of discretionary policy would put it to use. To economists who explained unemployment by the stickiness of money wages, this Monetarist doctrine suggested that the

---

[22] See the 'Unpleasant Arithmetic' of Sargent and Wallace (1981), and Keynes's advice to Poincaré quoted on p. 199 below.

stock of money might serve as an effective regulator of employment. If so, it was almost a moral imperative that it be used. But vigorous manipulation of the supply of outside nominal money will destroy the system of expectations that makes nominal values relatively inflexible. The Phillips curve will then start to misbehave.

INVOLUNTARY UNEMPLOYMENT

At the outset I noted that the New Classical Economics was made up of Rational Expectations, Monetarism, and Market Clearing. It remains to comment on the last of the three.[23]

The equilibrium approach has caused more uproar among Keynesians than any other aspect of the work of Lucas, Sargent & Co. The reason is that the market clearing assumption is taken to be inconsistent with 'involuntary unemployment', a concept which most Keynesians feel obliged to defend to the bitter end of their creed. Much ink has been spilt and a considerable volume of hot air expanded, therefore, in criticizing or satirizing the rational expectations approach on this score. From the rational expectations side, scorn is heaped on the arbitrary fix-price constraints of 'disequilibrium' theory while the concept of excess demand is declared inoperational and the notion of 'involuntary' behavior spurned as inexplicable in utility-maximizing terms.

In my opinion, however, the issue has hardly been joined, so that not much can be sensibly said about the debate as it relates to Keynes. One reason for this is that few, if any, people on either side care much about what Keynes might have meant by 'involuntary unemployment' and that most proceed to use the term as if whatever associations happen to come to mind are good enough at least for polemical purposes.[24] The term, without a doubt, is one of the most unfortunate new coinages in the history of economics. The problem to which the term refers is not therefore nonsensical. Keynes was concerned with a *systemic* problem that could be defined neither in terms of individual decision situations nor in terms of

---

[23] The following remarks will deal only with 'involuntary unemployment' which is the aspect of the matter that has the most to do with Keynes. For a broader discussion of the equilibrium methodology of the New Classicists, see the last section of my (1983a) and also my (1983b).

[24] Lucas (1978), for example, concludes his discussion of the concept as follows: 'In summary, it does not appear possible, even in principle, to classify individual unemployed people as either voluntarily or involuntarily unemployed depending upon the characteristics of the decision problems they face.' Lucas may have had in mind, perhaps, Barro and Grossman (1971), Benassy (1975), or Malinvaud (1977), etc., but his comment is simply irrelevant to Keynes's concept.

interactions between buyers and sellers in a single market. His 'involuntary' unemployment is the result of *effective demand failures*.[25]

Two distinct effective demand failures are involved in Keynes' persistent involuntary unemployment state. One is the intertemporal (R/R) one discussed above which arises because[26]

a decision not to have dinner to-day . . . does not necessitate a decision to have dinner or to buy a pair of boots a week hence or a year hence or to consume any specified thing at any specified date.

Hence, it does not pay to organize all the markets for specified things at all specified dates. In their absence, it is possible to have an effective excess supply of present goods to which there corresponds a notional excess demand for future goods which is nowhere registered in a market. The other one, predicated on the prior occurrence of the first, occurs between the spot markets for labor and for consumption goods because unemployed people without money cannot bid for consumption goods so that an effective excess supply of labor may have as its Walras' Law counterpart an ineffective excess demand for goods.

Now, this kind of situation does not have fix-price rationing as a prerequisite. Suppose atomistic markets where, every day, sellers of commodities and buyers of labor post prices and wages and buyers of commodities and sellers of labor have to decide on their demand-price and reservation-wage schedules.[27] These prices are set using the best information available. Suppose further that agents find a way to carry out all transactions compatible with these prior valuation decisions. 'Markets clear'. If, however, the system has been perturbed in some way such that not all agents are equally informed about the developing situation, these information asymmetries will make realized transactions deviate from their 'equilibrium' volume (if by 'equilibrium' we mean the transactions

---

[25] One should recall that the Keynesian categories of 'frictional' and 'voluntary' unemployment covered vast territories, and especially a number of possibilities that latter-day Keynesians often like to bring into their quarrel with the rational expectations equilibrium theorists. The *General Theory* (1936, p. 6) briskly lumps into the *voluntary* category, for instance,

'unemployment due to the refusal or inability of a unit of labour, as a result of legislation or social practices or of combination for collective bargaining or of slow response to change or of mere human obstinacy, to accept a reward corresponding to the value of the product attributable to its marginal productivity'.

Note especially that the '*inability* . . .' is 'voluntary'!

[26] See *General Theory*, p. 210.

[27] This is basically the conception from which I began in my (1968b). It will not serve very far before a more structured picture of how trade is organized in the system becomes required. Cf. Robert Clower (1975).

that would be consistent with plans based on some universally shared view of what the true situation is). So the 'market clears' at a 'disequilibrium' volume.

In the first round of a Keynesian recession, demand price schedules for capital goods shift down because expectations about their future rental values have deteriorated and the rate of interest at which expected rentals are discounted has not declined commensurably. The derived demand for labor in those industries consequently declines but suppliers of labor, who have little reason to believe that realizable real wages have declined throughout the entire system, keep their reservation wages up. So the market clears at reduced employment with not much change in the observed wage-level.

Now, this first round outcome may be described in various ways. To say, as I once did to my frequent regret, that 'In the Keynesian macrosystem the Marshallian ranking of price- and quantity-adjustment speeds is reversed'[28] is too mechanical to be helpful. It reads as an open invitation to fix-price rationing modelling of the sort that pays little attention to the determination of prices. In my 1968 story, prices were not 'rigid' but held up temporarily (in atomistic markets) because of speculation based on 'inelastic expectations'. This story does not give both sides of the labor market the same information sets. But it does not otherwise differ significantly from the way in which later rational expectations models deal with variations in employment.[29]

In the New Classical models, however, tomorrow's another day (drawn from the distribution of pretty nice days). Tomorrow you try it again, starting from scratch. Today's decline in employment has no persistent consequences. (A reason for persistence, in fact, has to be invented.)

In Clower's version of the Keynesian story, the temporary curtailment in employment means that tomorrow's consumption demand is constrained by today's realized income. The derived demand for labor in the consumption goods industries is now also affected. By a familiar route, multiplier repercussions bring the system into a state where the inability of

---

[28] Leijonhufvud (1968b), p. 52.

[29] An important class of rational expectations models, exemplified by Barro (1976), have what amounts to Hicksian 'inelastic expectations' as a central feature. Most of the 'action' in realized transactions comes from a term in the supply and demand functions which measures the difference between current and expected future price. When the expected future price fails to reflect a disturbance appropriately, the result is speculative intertemporal substitution effects that affect the price and volume of transactions in the spot markets.

Asymmetries of information between the two sides of the market are against the rules of the game that apply to this class of models, however. They occur only in the market where the central bank conducts its open market operations.

the unemployed to back their notional consumption demands with cash is a major reason for the persistence of unemployment. The unemployment that persists in the system *for this reason* Keynes called 'involuntary'.[30,31]

Now, I will agree that the theory of effective demand failures raises more questions than it answers and, also, that it has made no progress (as far as I know) for several years. But the nature of the problem that it poses should be clear. Individuals interact on the basis of incomplete information. The consequence is a price vector reflecting the incompleteness of information and a pattern of realized transactions which leaves some agents disappointed. Will this set in motion a learning process that leads to a coordinated solution? If price-adjustments were governed by notional excess demands, then neo-Walrasian stability theorems will tell us under which conditions the answer is Yes. Effective demand theory argues, I think persuasively, that there is no reason to suppose that, whatever the trial-and-error process that capitalist economies rely on, the successive trials will in fact be governed by these notional errors. Consequently, *tâtonnement* stability theorems are suspect.

To my knowledge, the New Classical literature contains nothing of any relevance one way or another to these issues. When 'excess demand' is

---

[30] See Clower (1965, 1967), Leijonhufvud (1968b, Chapter II:3), and for second thoughts on how prevalent such effective demand failures may be, Leijonhufvud (1973).

[31] If you will permit one paragraph of self-indulgence, I have this to add. In my 1968 book, my discussion of involuntary unemployment ended on this note:

'One must conclude, I believe, that Keynes's theory, although obscurely expressed and doubtlessly not all that clear even in his own mind, was still in substance that to which Clower has recently given precise statement.'

Although this interpretation was the only one that made sense to me, I was nonetheless conscious of having done a good deal of reading between the lines. A number of colleagues who did not agree that 'one must conclude' anything of the sort poked some fun at the claim. When Volumes XIII and XIV of the *Collected Writings* appeared, I skimmed them solely to see whether my interpolations had been too imaginative. Somewhat to my consternation, I could not find anything that seemed relevant to the problem one way or another! In the Fall of 1974, I visited Cambridge as an Overseas Fellow of Churchill College and took the opportunity of a dinner at King's to ask my host, Lord Kahn, and also Lord Kaldor and Professor Robinson whether the Circus had not discussed Chapter 2 of the *General Theory* and why no background material had come to light. They did not recall any such discussions – which left me somewhat mystified.

Some time ago, Mr C. W. S. Torr brought to my attention that the 'Tilton laundry hamper' had contained the answer. Much of Vol. XXIX is devoted to some discarded introductions to the *General Theory* in which 'the contrast between a Co-operative and an Entrepreneur Economy' is treated as fundamental.

Keynes's 'Co-operative Economy', as it turned out, was one in which labor is bartered for goods, so that the supply of labor is always an effective demand for goods. In his 'Entrepreneur Economy' the Clowerian rule applies: labor buys money and money buys goods but labor does not buy goods. In the entrepreneur economy, therefore, effective demand failures are possible and so, consequently, is 'involuntary unemployment'.

That, I think, should settle the matter. See Keynes (1979), pp. 63–102.

simply dismissed as an inoperational concept, inquiries into its 'notional' or 'effective' nature are somewhat discouraged. The oft-paraphrased point that 'rational agents will act to exhaust perceived gains from trade' may serve very well as a pedagogical note of caution vis-à-vis certain fix-price constructions, but as a contribution to our understanding of the stability of general equilibrium it ranks somewhere below the Law of Jean-Baptiste Say.

This debate, to repeat, has not been joined.

THE 1920S AND THE 1980S

To many people, my assigned subject is worth discussing mostly in so far as it leads up to a stand for or against Mrs Thatcher or President Reagan. It should be developed in adversary terms: Keynes vs. Rational Expectations. Aggregate demand management in a world of sticky wages versus policy ineffectiveness in a world of neutral money. Re-inflation versus continued disinflation.

My own belief, in contrast, is that this way of seeing the issues gets neither Keynes nor the Rational Expectations people right. I do not believe it gets the alternatives currently before us right either.

There was one period, the early twenties, when Keynes had to deal with a monetary regime resembling our own, which is to say, a system of flexible exchange rates, unbalanced budgets, and unanchored fiat currencies. His main reaction to it, evidently, was that it urgently demanded Monetary Reform. The *Tract* was not a book about how best to muddle along from year to year within the existing system. It argued for a change of regime.

The 1920s have recently drawn the renewed interest of balance-of-payments theorists and monetary economists. In a recent paper on the problem of 'Stopping Moderate Inflations', Sargent (1981) compares the methods of Poincaré and Thatcher. He criticizes Mrs Thatcher for carrying through with disinflation without reforming the policy regime and attributes the 1926 Poincaré 'miracle' to a systematic fiscal and monetary regime change.

The diagnosis of the French situation and the precise recipe for the miracle had been given by Keynes more than two years before Poincaré reluctantly acted on these lines. Keynes's diagnosis, item by item, was then exactly the one that Sargent has now rediscovered.[32] For example:

What . . . will determine the value of the franc? First, the quantity, present and prospective, of the francs in circulation . . . (T)he quantity of the currency, depends

---

[32] See the March 1924 'Preface to the French Edition' of Keynes (1971a). Also the 1926 and 1928 commentaries reprinted as 'The French Franc' in Keynes (1972).

mainly on the loan and budgetary policies of the French Treasury.

What course should the French Treasury now take in face of the dangers surrounding them? It is soon said. First, the government must so strengthen its fiscal position that its power to control the volume of the currency is beyond doubt.

Obviously, Keynes had an adequate working knowledge of that 'unpleasant monetarist arithmetic'![33] A more detailed reading of Keynes and Sargent only makes the agreement between the two even more remarkable.

The *Tract on Monetary Reform* is a very monetarist book. Many latter-day Keynesians like to think that Keynes successfully kicked this habit soon afterward and went on to write the *Treatise*, which he in turn discarded as the *General Theory* began to take shape in his mind. But it is also possible to see this progression less as a series of radical changes in Keynes's fundamental theoretical beliefs than as reorientations of his theoretical efforts to meet changing problems.

This characteristic of Keynes's work – that he adapted his theory to changing problems – has often been remarked upon. Practical political economists approve; pure theorists disapprove. Rational expectations economists might recognize in this adaptability of Keynes's something more than an engaging or irritating character quirk. Rational expectations theory tells us that the short-run effects of particular disturbances or policy actions will depend upon the expectations of the public and, therefore, on the regime that the public believes to be in effect. We need a different applied macrotheory for each monetary regime. The lesson is that we all must, like Keynes, adopt our theories to a changing world.

The *Tract* denounced 'instability of the standard of value' in strong, colorful terms. We do not find him retracting these opinions later. Instead, throughout the rest of his life, he strove for an international economic order that would anchor nominal values and provide 'fixed' exchange rates while leaving scope for discretionary domestic policies and, in particular, giving Britain time to adjust.[34] His work in theory, subsequent to the *Tract*, assumed a regime in which the nominal scale of real magnitudes was not being manipulated. The influence of nominal expectations on behavior was correspondingly neglected. His theory did assume, of course, that one would have to face a business cycle even in the absence of nominal shocks. Absence of obstacles to money wage adjustment does not suffice to guarantee rapid convergence on the natural rate of unemployment in this theory, since intertemporal coordination failures ('saving exceeding invest-

---

[33] See Sargent and Wallace (1981).

[34] See Tumlir (1983). I am grateful to Tumlir for insisting in conversation that I should go back and read Keynes on the French franc.

ment') are not corrected by changes in nominal values.[35] The strong version of Monetarism, therefore, cannot hold in this theory.

CONCLUSIONS

Keynesian economics used to be the mainstream. Now, the younger generation of macrotheorists and econometricians regard it just as a backwater, look to Monetarism for navigable channels, and find their real white water thrills in the technically demanding rapids of Rational Expectations. This ageing Keynesian thinks the main channel is still where it used to be. But it obviously has silted up, is full of accumulated debris, and must be thoroughly dredged and cleared, before one can hope that it will see much traffic again.

Mainly, I suggest, the Keynesian tradition has had trouble in keeping the analysis straight on nominal versus real shocks and adjustments. This happened to surface in the squabble over the Phillips curve. But the trouble goes deeper and begins earlier. When I was a student, over twenty years ago, two of the tenets (for example) that were taught to us as 'Keynesian' were (1) that unemployment was due to the rigidity of nominal wages, and (2) that monetary policy could not bring about sizeable changes in nominal income. Both propositions are basically true if we can take a framework of monetary stability as part of the (unstated) *ceteris paribus* conditions. Both are false as matters of 'general theory'. As it happens, you will be all right as long as you firmly believe both of them. Unlearning (2) while still holding on to (1) led to confusion and produced the Phillips curve debacle.

One does not revive Keynesian economics again by insisting that nominal wages are sticky or by denying that governmental money creation causes inflation. The doctrine that unemployment is produced by nominal income changes (without distinction as to their cause) interacting with sticky wages keeps pointing us in the wrong direction, namely, toward using nominal instruments to try to bring about real change.

Keynesians should learn from Monetarism (if need be) that manipulation of the nominal money stock has strong effects on nominal income in discretionary fiat money regimes. From Rational Expectations they should learn that nominal expectations (of price-setting agents, in particular) are endogenous in regimes where the nominal scale is subject to manipulation; also that stabilization policy is better thought of in terms of the design of policy regimes with desirable overall, long run properties rather than in terms of one short-horizon policy choice at a time. But there are also

---

[35] See 'The Wicksell Connection' in Leijonhufvud (1981a), esp. sections IX and X.

fashionable things they should refuse to learn. We do not have sufficient reason to accept the strong version of Monetarism; we have reason to reject the Natural Rate of Unemployment doctrine;[36] and we have no reason to pay much attention to Rational Expectations denials of effective demand failures and the possibility of involuntary unemployment.

We should seek a return to a monetary order that should as far as possible minimize nominal shocks. They do us no good but cause us much harm.[37] A return to monetary stability – *if* we can find a way – requires us to forswear policies that are built on the hope of exploiting temporary money-illusions, or the incomplete indexing of contracts, or other information imperfections. This includes forswearing fiscal deficits financed by borrowing today but by money creation tomorrow.

In a world where the nominal scale were firmly anchored, business fluctuations would presumably still take place (and they would probably leave behind a record of observations looking much like a stable Phillips curve). It is conceivable that these would be socially optimal in some sense or other, but we have no substantive reasons to give much weight to this possibility. The amplitude of these real cycles and the incidence of their social cost can be modified by policy regimes designed to have real effects on real variables: unemployment insurance, functional finance, built-in stabilizers. The lessons of Hansenian Keynesianism would come back into their own.

As in the 1920s, so in the 1980s: the times call for Monetary Reform. That will be easier said than done. Simple money growth-rules, assuming their operational feasibility, are probably too tight as constraints on systems where not only does '(nominal) money cause (nominal) income' but '(real) income also causes (real) money'.[38] We should have no longings for the 'barbarous relic'. And there can be no returning to Bretton Woods. From Keynes, the monetary reformer, we get a useful suggestion on where to start:

First, the government must so strengthen its position that its power to control the volume of the currency is beyond doubt.

but hardly any help beyond that point. As is proper for an economist, I am thus led to a dismal conclusion – namely, we have to start thinking for ourselves.

[36] See my 'Wicksell Connection', *loc. cit.*

[37] See Leijonhufvud (1981b).

[38] For a monetary rule allowing scope for discretion, see the discussion in Leijonhufvud (1982b).

REFERENCES

Barro, Robert J., and Grossman, Hershel I., (1971) 'A General Disequilibrium Model of Income and Employment', *American Economic Review*, March.

Barro, Robert J., (1976) 'Rational Expectations and the Role of Monetary Policy', *Journal of Monetary Economics*, January.

(1980) 'A Capital Market in an Equilibrium Business Cycle Model', *Econometrica*, September.

Benassy, Jean-Paul, (1975) 'Neo-Keynesian Disequilibrium Theory in a Monetary Economy', *Review of Economic Studies*, October.

Clower, Robert W., (1965) 'The Keynesian Counterrevolution: A Theoretical Appraisal', in F. H. Hahn and F. P. R. Brechling, eds., *The Theory of Interest Rates*, London: Macmillan.

(1967) 'A Reconsideration of the Microfoundations of Monetary Theory', *Western Economic Journal*, December.

(1975) 'Reflections on the Keynesian Perplex', *Zeitschrift fur Nationalökonomie*, Heft 1–2.

Darby, Michael, and Lothian, J. R., *et al.* (1983) *The International Transmission of Inflation*, Chicago: Chicago University Press for NBER.

Friedman, Milton, (1956) 'The Quantity Theory of Money: A Restatement', in M. Friedman, ed., *Studies in the Quantity Theory of Money*, Chicago: Univ. of Chicago Press.

(1968) 'The Role of Monetary Policy', *American Economic Review*, March.

Friedman, Milton, and Anna J. Schwartz, (1963) *A Monetary History of the United States, 1867–1960*, Princeton: Princeton Univ. Press for NBER.

Gordon, Robert J., (1981) 'Output Fluctuations and Gradual Price Adjustment', *Journal of Economic Literature*, June.

Hahn, Frank, (1983) *Money and Inflation*, Cambridge, Mass.: MIT Press.

Hicks, John R., (1933) 'Gleichgewicht und Konjunktur', *Zeitschrift fur Nationalökonomie*.

(1936) 'Mr Keynes's Theory of Employment', *Economic Journal*, June.

(1982) *Money, Interest and Wages: Collected Essays on Economic Theory, Volume* II, Oxford: Blackwell.

Kaldor, Nicholas, (1982) *The Scourge of Monetarism*, Oxford: Oxford University Press.

Keynes, J. Maynard, (1936) *The General Theory of Employment, Interest and Money*, London: Macmillan.

(1971a) *Collected Writings IV: A Tract on Monetary Reform*, Cambridge: Macmillan.

(1971b) *Collected Writings V–VI: A Treatise on Money*, Vols. I–II, Cambridge: Macmillan.

(1972) *Collected Writings IX: Essays in Persuasion*, Cambridge: Macmillan.

(1979) *Collected Writings XXIX: The General Theory and After, A Supplement*, Cambridge: Macmillan.

Klein, Benjamin, (1975) 'Our Monetary Standard: The Measurement and Effects of Price Uncertainty, 1880–1973', *Economic Inquiry*, December.

(1978) 'Competing Monies, European Monetary Union and the Dollar', in Michele Fratianni and Theo Peeters, eds., *One Money for Europe*, London: Macmillan.

204   AXEL LEIJONHUFVUD

Kydland, Finn E. and Edward C. Prescott, (1982) 'Time to Build and Aggregate Fluctuations', *Econometrica*.
Laidler, David, (1981) 'Monetarism: An Interpretation and an Assessment', *Economic Journal*, March.
    (1982) 'Did Macroeconomics Need the Rational Expectations Revolution?' paper prepared for a Conference on 'Economic Policies for Canada in the 1980's', Winnipeg, Canada, October.
Leijonhufvud, Axel, (1968a) 'Comment: Is There a Meaningful Trade-Off between Inflation and Unemployment?' *Journal of Political Economy*, July/August.
    (1968b) *On Keynesian Economics and the Economics of Keynes: A Study in Monetary Theory,* New York: Oxford University Press.
    (1973) 'Effective Demand Failures', *Swedish Economic Journal*, March, reprinted in Leijohnhufvud (1981a).
    (1981a) *Information and Coordination: Essays in Macroeconomic Theory*, New York: Oxford University Press.
    (1981b) 'Inflation and Economic Performance', to appear in Gerald P. O'Driscoll, ed., *Money in Crisis: Government, Stagflation, and Monetary Reform*, Cambridge, Mass.: Ballinger Press (forthcoming).
    (1982a) 'Rational Expectations and Monetary Institutions', paper presented at International Economic Association Conference on 'Monetary Theory and Monetary Institutions', Florence, Italy, September.
    (1982b) 'Constitutional Constraints on the Monetary Powers of Government', paper presented at a Heritage Foundation Conference on 'Constitutional Economics: The Emerging Debate', Washington, D.C., November.
    (1983a) 'Keynesianism, Monetarism, and Rational Expectations: Some Reflections and Conjectures', in Roman Frydman and E. S. Phelps, eds., *Individual Forecasting and Aggregate Outcomes: Rational Expectations Examined*, New York: Cambridge University Press.
    (1983b), Review of Robert E. Lucas, Jr, *Studies in Business Cycle Theory*, in *Journal of Economic Literature*, April.
Lucas, Robert E., Jr, (1972) 'Expectations and the Neutrality of Money', *Journal of Economic Theory*, April, reprinted in Lucas (1981).
    (1975) 'An Equilibrium Model of the Business Cycle', *Journal of Political Economy*, December, reprinted in Lucas (1981).
    (1978) 'Unemployment Policy', *American Economic Review*, May, reprinted in Lucas (1981).
    (1980) 'Methods and Problems in Business Cycle Theory', *Journal of Money, Credit, and Banking*, Nov. (Part 2), reprinted in Lucas (1981).
    (1981) *Studies in Business Cycle Theory*, Cambridge, Mass.: MIT Press.
Lucas, Robert E., and Thomas J. Sargent, (1979) 'After Keynesian Macroeconomics', *Federal Reserve Bank of Minneapolis Quarterly Review*, No. 2.
Malinvaud, Edmond, (1977) *The Theory of Unemployment Reconsidered*, Oxford: Blackwells.
Okun, Arthur M., (1981) *Prices and Quantities: A Macroeconomic Analysis*, Washington, D.C.: Brookings.
Phelps, Edmund S., (1968) 'Money Wage Dynamics and Labor Market Equilibrium', *Journal of Political Economy*, August.
Robertson, Sir Dennis, (1954) 'Thoughts on Meeting Some Important Persons', *Quarterly Journal of Economics*, May.
Sargent, Thomas J., (1973) 'Rational Expectations, the Real Rate of Interest, and

the Natural Rate of Unemployment', *Brookings Papers on Economic Activity*, No. 2.

(1981) 'Stopping Moderate Inflations: The Methods of Poincaré and Thatcher', in *Economic Policy in the United Kingdom*, Proceedings of a Conference sponsored by the General Mills Foundation, University of Minnesota.

Sargent, Thomas J. and Neil Wallace, (1976) 'Rational Expectations and the Theory of Economic Policy', *Journal of Monetary Economics*, April.

(1981) 'Some Unpleasant Monetarist Arithmetic', Federal Reserve Bank of Minneapolis *Quarterly Review*, Fall.

Sims, Christopher A., (1980) 'Comparison of Interwar and Postwar Business Cycles: Monetarism Reconsidered', *American Economic Review*, May.

(1983) 'Is There a Monetary Business Cycle?' *American Economic Review*, May.

Solow, Robert M., (1980) 'On Theories of Unemployment', *American Economic Review*, March.

Tobin, James, (1981) 'The Monetarist Counter-Revolution Today – An Appraisal', *Economic Journal*, March.

Tumlir, Jan, (1983) 'J. M. Keynes and the Emergence of the Post-World War II International Economic Order', paper presented at a Conference on 'Tactics of Liberalization', Madrid, Spain, March.

COMMENT

Luigi L. Pasinetti

1. 'What has caused so much commotion among macro-economists in recent years – says Axel Leijonhufvud (A.L.) – is not so much rational expectations *per se* but rather the so-called New Classical Economics', (p. 179), which includes '*Monetarism* and *Market Clearing*' besides rational expectations. But: What would Keynes have thought of rational expectations? A.L. avoids giving a straight answer.

Those who have been close to Keynes have always tended to be very clear about questions like this. To quote Roy Harrod, for example: 'It would be most inappropriate for me to stand up here and tell *you* what Keynes would have thought. Goodness knows he would have thought of something much cleverer than I can think of.' (Roy Harrod, 1974, p. 8).

But A.L. is right in pointing out that the introduction of expectations, in a significant way, into economic theory was one of the innovations of the *General Theory* (G.T.). I would however regard the difference with respect to the new classical economists in a quite different manner. Keynes introduced entrepreneurial expectations into his analysis in order to show how different his conclusions are with respect to the traditional analysis approach of perfect foresight. Lucas, Sargent & Co. are using the rational expectations hypothesis for the opposite purpose: in order to claim results and draw conclusions on economic policy which, in the end, are exactly the same. It seems very unlikely that Keynes would have found this very interesting; for, by its own nature, it is bound to be very limited. In fact, the rational expectations hypothesis has been applied only to short-run expectations and for future events of the 'risk' type, i.e. of that type to which one can reasonably apply a probability density function, and moreover within a very specific theoretical model of economic reality – the Walrasian general equilibrium optimum allocation model. I cannot see why Keynes should have made objections to relying on rational behaviour and thus also on rational expectations, *provided that* these hypotheses are applied to the correct cases and in the correct model.

But there is a more fundamental objection to be raised. If all agents (consumers, entrepreneurs, Government) really knew how our modern market economies actually work, they would surely also know that the Walrasian atomistic competition model is not an accurate representation of reality, and would take this into account.

2. A puzzling aspect of A.L.'s paper is his colourful account of the triumph of the Monetarists and of the debacle of the Keynesians: 'A bad enough debacle' he underlines 'so that the profession proclaimed the long controversy a Monetarist victory' (p. 182). Surely, by 'the [economics] profession' A.L. means the American economics profession, or more precisely the U.S. economics profession. Although it is certainly true that the U.S. economics profession is the most influential one in the world, it would certainly be wrong to take it as representing the whole of the economics profession, even in the Western world. Moreover, by the term 'Keynesians' he surely means the U.S. Keynesians, and not even all the U.S. Keynesians, but rather that particular brand of U.S. Keynesians (no doubt most prestigious and influential) that proposed the 'neoclassical synthesis', which was only one interpretation of Keynes. The (U.K.) Cambridge pupils of Keynes, for example, never thought of it as anything particularly Keynesian. Thirdly, the great debacle to which A.L. refers reduces essentially to the debacle of the Phillips curve. As A.L. himself says, the Phillips curve was *not* proposed by Keynes; it was not even proposed by any specific brand of 'Keynesians'. It emerged on its own, as an apparently successful – at the time – empirical relation between rates of change of prices (and wages) and the recorded rate of unemployment – 'an empirical finding in search of a theory', as Tobin (1972, p. 9) called it. The Keynesians of the neoclassical synthesis picked it up and introduced it into their 'Keynesian' models thinking to have found a solution to the problem of rising prices. It did not work; and that should be the end of it. This does not

imply anything on Keynes's scheme. Even less does it imply correctness of the monetarist theses.

But A.L. points out that the Keynesians of the neoclassical synthesis mistakenly insisted on defending the Phillips curve, lost face and discredited themselves, and Keynes, before the economics profession and the public. If this is so, the U.S. economics profession cannot be particularly proud in drawing illogical conclusions. Inflation was a latent problem in the 1930s, but it became virulent in the 1970s. Had Keynes been with us, 'Goodness knows he would have thought of something much cleverer than' anything we have been able to do. He would presumably *not* have thought of the Phillips curve.

3. The fact remains that the 'Keynesian' scientific community, considered as a whole, is today in serious theoretical difficulties. As it turned out, when – in the 1970s – new problems arose, with respect to those Keynes originally faced, the 'Keynesians' have been unable to go beyond Keynes. And this needs an explanation.

I am going to argue that, fundamentally, the great majority of those who are known today as 'Keynesian' never went beyond Keynes – since the beginning. I want to contend that – although, on matters of practical conclusions, many of Keynes's economic policy recommendations have by and large been followed, and with astounding success (the 1950s and 1960s have been the best periods ever in the economic history of the industrial countries) – on a purely theoretical level, Keynes started a process which was nipped in the bud. His work was not continued.

Let me recall that one of the striking characteristics of the *General Theory* is that it is presented as a novel work of economic theory. Its very opening sentences are clear enough: 'This book is chiefly addressed to my fellow economists . . . its main purpose is to deal with difficult questions of theory, and only in the second place with the application of this theory to practice' (Keynes, 1936, p.v.). From all accounts we have, Keynes was firmly convinced of having reached such a theoretical breakthrough as to be in the very awkward and painful position of rejecting – at 50 – the views that he had 'held with conviction for many years' (Keynes, 1936, p.v.); repudiating not only what he had been taught, but what he himself had been teaching!

The recent publication of *The Collected Writings of J. M. Keynes* reveals quite clearly the extraordinary excitement around Keynes at the time of the birth of the G.T. Keynes and the young economists of the Cambridge Circus are deeply convinced they are living through an exceptional and unique experience. They seem to have acquired the ardour of converts; at last, they 'see the light'. This extraordinary excitement could not be about trivial or minor things. A year before the publication of the G.T., Keynes writes to G. B. Shaw that he 'believe[s] to be writing a book on economic theory which will largely revolutionize . . . the way the world thinks about economic problems' (Harrod, 1951, p. 462). This is a sharp, definite break with the past. It is the whole burden of traditional theory that the Keynes group is prepared to unload.

For this reason, by the way, I would dissent from A.L.'s guess, as expressed in his third paragraph ('The out-of-focus Keynes') and in his final paragraph ('Conclusions'), where he quotes Keynes from the *Tract on Monetary Reform* (Keynes, 1923) and points out similarities of Keynes's statements with those by Sargent today. It seems to me that, very far from giving us any indication on what Keynes (I mean the post-*General-Theory* Keynes) might have said today, any such similarity simply indicates how far we have regressed from the Keynes of the *General Theory*, to find appropriate the perfectly traditional Keynes of the *Tract on Monetary Reform*. But let me return to my main argument.

The relevant thing to notice is that ever since the *General Theory* was published, the great majority of those who then became known as 'Keynesian' have done everything they possibly could to eliminate any revolutionary aspect from the G.T., to expunge from it, bit by bit, what was in contrast with mainstream economics. The process started, it must be said, in England, with Hicks's (1937) famous article, but it was carried out most effectively in the U.S., where the successful Keynesians have been precisely those who have carried out the task of looking for a reconciliation of the Keynesian concepts with traditional theory.

The contrast with Keynes's aims could not be more striking. As against Keynes's advocacy for a break with the past, the response roughly was: Keynes is right, we accept his conclusions, but we must reshape his arguments in such a way as to insert them in our previous theory. I think it is dutiful to mention, as this gathering takes place in Cambridge, England, that the direct pupils of Keynes here have always strongly opposed this trend; they have always determinately insisted on Keynes's irreconcilability with traditional economics; but they have not been listened to.

This being so, the emergence of the New Classical Economics today should not be a surprise after all. If the neoclassical synthesis was an *ex-post* rationalization of the successful practical 'Keynesian' measures, inserted piece meal into an alien basis represented by previous theory, then it should not be surprising that – with a change of the objective situation that renders those practical measures out-dated – one should realize their extraneousness to the basic texture of traditional economics, and that one should logically advocate a return to the 'purity' of pre-Keynes traditional theory.

It may well be that the (supposed) reconciliation with traditional theory (ill-founded as it may have been) was the only way to introduce Keynes in the United States. It may well be that, in the U.S., Keynes would not have been accepted otherwise. Yet, one cannot hope to stave off a return to (theoretically more solid) pre-Keynesian positions on the basis of heterogeneous, *ad hoc*, or contradictory hypotheses. If nothing else, the new classical economists are calling for logical consistency with a theoretical scheme which is at the basis of the great majority of our economics textbooks. The logical deductions of such a theoretical scheme are very clear. Individuals' rational (optimizing) behaviour leads the economic system to optimum positions (in the sense of Pareto), provided that the markets are not interfered with. This is precisely the opposite of Keynes's central message.

To this traditional scheme one cannot object that the behaviour of individuals may be irrational after all. One can, and must, object with the propositions of an alternative, logically consistent, theoretical scheme.

4. The foundations of the traditional model of an optimally functioning atomistic competition market economy were laid down by Léon Walras, more than a century ago. But we had to wait until Arrow and Debreu to grasp clearly the essential elements of its logical structure. It represents a hypothetical economy – as we are told by those who contributed to it – in which the Keynesian problems can never arise (see for example Arrow–Hahn, 1971).

If we are convinced that we live in a world in which typically 'Keynesian' economic problems do periodically arise, let alone the huge problems of less industrialized economic systems, then it is a waste of time, or exercise in self-delusion, to continue to look for guidance at the Walrasian general equilibrium scheme.

Many economic theorists, who had been enthusiastic of Walrasian economics, have recently begun to work with general equilibria of a non-Walrasian type. This is a belated but welcome development.

It is Keynes, however, rather than Walras, that must remain the relevant point of reference, if we want to elaborate a theoretical scheme appropriate to the features of an industrial society. We cannot pretend to find such a scheme ready and clear in the *General Theory*. Arrow and Debreu have themselves come a century after Walras. Keynes did not even have the Arrow and Debreu model before him to criticize. He was brought up in the eclectic tradition of Marshall, the economist of the reconciliation of marginal analysis with the early classical economics. Like all reconciliations of opposites, the Marshallian one worked for a time, until its contradictions began to emerge. And it was precisely Keynes and his group that played the crucial rôle. Their works, considered together, look surprisingly diverse, and even concerned with different problems, at first. But if we look at them carefully and deeply we might begin to see many elements of an alternative theoretical model; in particular we might begin to notice, within their variety, the singularly consistent feature of their common tendency to the elimination of the Walrasian elements from the Marshallian analysis.

Quite simply, this work should be continued.

5. The New Classical Economics that 'has caused so much commotion among macroeconomists in recent years' hasn't really brought anything basically new.

It expresses a conception of economic reality which is quite traditional, and which has always exerted a powerful attraction, especially for the members of the richer classes: Let every individual strive for his/her own selfish interest, within a framework of competitive free markets, and let us accept, without interfering with them, whatever results 'naturally' emerge from the interplay of the impersonal forces of demand and supply. The 'impersonality' of the market forces has been indicated as the objective criterion. And the Walrasian general equilibrium model has provided the theoretical backing.

But the societies that have come into being since the Industrial Revolution are too complex to be looked at with such a naïve scheme. It is indeed Keynes here that brought the real novelty, by starting a search for what is behind the inadequacies of the market forces and for what must be put besides the *laissez-faire* economic policies. The question is not that of throwing them away, but that of using them appropriately; as part of a more general and comprehensive conception of the modern world.

We know quite well that the spontaneous working of the market forces does not produce the best of all situations. It is enough to look around us to see unbelievable oddities. On the world scene, after 200 years of industrialization, there are countries with average per capita GNP's of the order of magnitude of $10,000, and there are other countries with average per capita GNP's of the order of magnitude of barely above $100: a factor of 100 to 1! The great majority of the existing working power is under-utilized or not used at all. In the industrial countries, where the allocative efficiency of the market mechanism ought to show itself at its highest, we observe huge under-utilization of productive capacity and millions of people unemployed (almost all of them belonging to the poorer classes).

It would be absurd to think of the 'market' as a panacea to solve all these problems. Many markets do not exist at all simply because they cannot exist, others can exist only with peculiar characteristics or various forms of 'imperfections'. The traditional scheme often seems to have led too many economic theorists to a kind of obsession with the market mechanism, looked at in itself, idealized, as if nothing else existed, and especially ignoring completely what is behind it or what the market is supposed to be operating on. This is a remarkably peculiar and superficial attitude in a complicated world; an attitude which ultimately leads to a retreat from responsibility.

In industrial societies which are becoming ever more complex and are constantly changing, our needs increase to understand them and investigate them in depth – not only in the way they work, but also in the way they can be made to work. This view relies of course very much on what Man can do; on our abilities to construct and shape the social institutions that fit our aims (including the utilization of market forces when appropriate). It is a view that calls for maturity and responsibility.

We lack, as yet, a complete theoretical scheme to put behind it, or at least we lack a scheme comparable in its essential simplicity to the competitive market economy of the Arrow–Debreu model. But the starting of the remarkable task of building one is among the merits of John Maynard Keynes. This is a task that is not impossible.[1] Keynes called to it his fellow economists from the very beginning of his main work. I would regard this as the still unfulfilled major message of the *General Theory*.

REFERENCES

Arrow, K. J., and Hahn, F. H., 1971, *General Competitive Analysis*, Edinburgh, Olive and Boyd, 1971.
Harrod, R. F., 1951, *The Life of John Maynard Keynes*, London, Macmillan, 1951.
    (1974) 'Keynes' Theory and its Applications' in D. E. Moggridge (ed.), *Keynes: Aspects of the Man and his Work*, London, Macmillan, 1974.
Hicks, J. R., 1937, 'Mr Keynes and the Classics', *Econometrica*, 1937, pp. 147–59.
Keynes, J. M., 1923, *A Tract on Monetary Reform*, London, Macmillan, 1923.
    (1936), *The General Theory of Employment, Interest and Money*, London, Macmillan, 1936.
Leijonhufvud, Axel, (1983), 'What Would Keynes Have Thought of Rational Expectations?', paper presented to this conference.
Pasinetti, Luigi L., (1981), *Structural Change and Economic Growth – A theoretical essay on the dynamics of the wealth of nations*, Cambridge University Press, Cambridge, 1981.
Tobin, J., (1972), 'Inflation and Unemployment', *American Economic Review*, Vol. LXII, 1972, pp. 1–18.

---

[1] I have argued this at length in my recent book (Pasinetti, 1981).

COMMENT

Paul A. Samuelson

It is unrewarding to debate about what the man Keynes would think in 1983 about the doctrines of Lucas, Sargent, and other rational expectationists. Keynes died when he died, and the curve recording the state of his macrodynamic methodologies was not one of those smooth trajectories that lend themselves to confident reliance on Taylor–Maclaurin or other long-distance extrapolations.

It is more rewarding to regard Keynes as an example of a scholar of brilliant good sense. One can then ask, 'How should an informed scholar appraise the new classical school in its rational expectationist version?' This of course is a tall order. Since rational expectations is one of the four important macro paradigms with a sizeable present-day following, the task as described in this paragraph is one that a vast number of articles are constantly being written about. There must be some special reason why, at the centennial celebrations of the birth of John Maynard Keynes, this ongoing research endeavor is especially in season – more in season for example than at a similar festival to honor Joseph Schumpeter's hundredth birthday.

That special reason is not hard to find. Keynes's 1936 *General Theory* had a revolutionary impact precisely because the novel paradigm that it proposed led to analysis and therapies so different from those of pre-1929 classical and neoclassical economics. The new classical economics of rational expectationists is a return with a vengeance to the pre-Keynesian verities.

Utilizing Keynesian methods and insights, I find the modern world poorly described by the depression Keynesian mode. I do not find that the market-clearing neutral-money new classical theory models of the short and intermediate run work well. But if I had to choose between these two extreme archetypes, a ridiculous Hobson's choice, I fear that the one to jettison would have to be the Ur-Keynesian model, which indeed was not one that commanded the main allegiance of Keynes himself.

In short, what Keynes would have thought of the modern classical school is what I think of it: markets do not clear perfectly in the short run and policy interventions can have appreciable real effect for quite a while. But people learn faster these days and the easy Keynesian victories are long behind us.

REVOLUTION AND COUNTERREVOLUTION

Anyone who mastered the *General Theory* in, say, the years 1936–39 was led to believe in quite a different paradigm to explain and understand the world from the models that pre-Keynesians had believed in. When I say pre-Keynesians I mean neoclassical economists in the broad sense of the word neoclassical. I agree with Kaldor that Marshall did not have quite the same view of general equilibrium that Walras did; but their differences fade into insignificance in comparison with the difference between a three-equation macro system of the *General Theory* type and any of the versions of economics that I was taught before 1935.

The 'new classical economics' of Robert Lucas, Tom Sargent, Robert Barro and others is truly a counterrevolution and the same cannot be said of 'monetarism'. If I can believe in Lucas market clearing, then I can no longer believe in the behavior equations and relations of the *General Theory* and this holds both for positivistic description or prediction and for policy diagnosis and therapeutic recommendation. Even Milton Friedman found the new rational expectationism at first unwelcome, since it denied the real evils of systematic mismanagement of money.

I was somewhat saddened to read many of the papers prepared for this conference and to hear much of our discussion. Like the Bourbons so many of us have learned nothing and forgotten nothing. In my observation the way of the world has changed much since the 1930s. Because I regard myself as a serious Keynesian, a post-Keynesian, I have had continually to modify my paradigms and insights. That is not pleasant to do, or easy to do. But it has to be done in the interest of science and I experience no serious qualms of conscience in constantly adapting my Keynesianism to the new cut of the world. To cease to be an old-fashioned Keynesian is not to become a monetarist: I have lost my faith, not my reason.

Having lived through the various stages of unreconstructed Keynesianism, let me describe my view of them.

DEPRESSION KEYNESIANISM

Back in 1938 when the short-term rate of interest in the U.S. was $\frac{3}{8}$ of $\frac{3}{8}$ of 1 per cent, it was sensible to believe in an almost infinitely elastic liquidity preference schedule and to be skeptical about the potency of conventional monetary policy. In the early 1930s when banks were failing, firms were going bankrupt, and mortgages were in delinquency on a macro scale, it was sensible to worry about liquidity traps, vicious cycles of wage cuts and debt deflation, inelastic marginal efficiency schedules. The textbook paradigm of deep-depression Keynesianism (which Maynard himself only occasionally believed in) deserved serious scrutiny then.

The comparative statics of the depression paradigm is about as different from that of Walras's system as one could imagine. Take for example the vital issue of Roosevelt's social security system, which was adopted in 1935. The reasoning of Jevons in the Victorian age, that Britain's coal mines would become exhausted and that she therefore should pay off her public debt, was ludicrous reasoning in the depression version of Keynesian economics. To finance the system in the way it was then decided to do, by essentially pay-as-you-go non-actuarial funding, made more sense: pay-as-you-go would add rather than subtract from the capital stock available to help support workers when they became old; to follow Jevons's orthodox advice might in the Walras–Say paradigm increase the capital stock of future generations, but in the depression whilst the paradox of thrift was valid, following that same advice would most certainly backfire.

NEOCLASSICAL SYNTHESIS

By 1940 simple-minded Keynesianism of the depression paradigm variety had become outmoded hat. It was right that it should be followed by a general model of the *General Theory* in which government policy could hope to use the levers of fiscal and monetary policy to cause the *IS* and *LM* curves of the Keynesian system to shift so as to achieve an equilibrium intersection nearer to full employment and with a mix between capital formation and real consumption that could be shifted toward investment by greater emphasis upon expansionary credit policy and on austere fiscal policy. This post-Depression Keynesian paradigm worked in the Roosevelt–Truman years, and it even continued to work in Europe and Japan into the 1950s and 1960s. If a Lucas had said then that the 1949 devaluation of the principal currencies *vis-à-vis* the dollar would soon be found out and would spend itself completely in price-level changes with few favorable real effects of any duration, he would rightly have been laughed out of court by informed observers of how the world then worked.

Let me stick with my practical example of how to devise a good social security system, bringing the analysis forward in time. It is saying the same thing to say that Milton Friedman was at this time working out the monetarists' paradigm as an alternative to Keynesianism or to say that Friedman was belatedly discovering for himself the elements of Keynesian liquidity theory and demand for money, and was converging toward the post-Keynesian models of Tobin, Solow, Samuelson, and Modigliani. In the systems of all of these scholars, it would have been deemed feasible to accomplish the Jevonian task of adding to public thrift by means of an austere overbalanced fiscal budget, but with the proviso that the fiscal surplus would not be permitted to abort its own thriftiness by causing an insufficiency of effective demand; instead room would be made for 'crowding in', by the Federal Reserve central bank following an easy money policy that could ensure that the ample fraction of resources left over from full-employment consumption demands would be channelled into effective capital formation.

In social security terms, the system could now afford full actuarial funding without fear of the paradox of thrift. And, social security aside, in the miracle economies of the Common Market and Japan, high investment equilibria were maintained throughout much of the 1950s and 1960s. I recognize that neo-Keynesians of the Kaldor–Robinson–Pasinetti–Garegnani school could not countenance this possibility in terms of their preferred fixed-capital. But what killed off the golden epoch of the 1950s and 1960s was not some confirmatory scientific findings pointing in the direction of the doubts of the neo-Keynesian school. Most of the economic world simply stopped paying much attention to their models.

STAGFLATION

What ended the honeymoon of functional finance and, in Leijonhufvud's accurate words, lost to the camp of Keynesianism many of the able economists of younger ages was the dilemma of stagflation. By the end of the 1960s, and with a vengeance after 1973, inflation rates showed a damnable tendency to accelerate at higher and higher (so-called) natural rates of unemployment. The mixed economy was sick; and it was that sickness that opened the way for the virus of the Lucas rational-expectationist new classical economics.

The sickness of the mixed economy, which must be kept distinct from the imperfections of us economists and the decline in our self-esteems and reputations, I must repeat, is in its fundamentals the problem of stagflation. For more than a decade I have been arguing that this stagflation is a basic feature of the humane welfare state that has replaced ruthless capitalism. It changes drastically the behavior equations of the modern macro world, and it itself has to be understood as much in terms of microeconomic incentives and behaviors as in terms of conventional macroeconomics.

As a description of what happens in the real world and as a tool for intermediate-run macro prediction, the Lucas–Sargent–Barro model is a poor tool. Those members of their school who venture an occasional prediction have terrible cricket batting averages. (Barro I recall at a 1974

Federal Reserve academic consultants' meeting had the grossest squared-error of unemployment estimate that I had heard that year; with apologies for picking on him as one daring occasionally to venture a view, I mention a recent Goldman-Sachs report trying to test the Barro view that when Reaganomics promises large structural deficits in the mid-1980s, that will lead us rational bequeathers to step up our private savings now: there have of course been no such stepups discernible in private savings. I have had fun with the Barro–Rush regressions purporting to predict nominal GNP changes from surprises in M: until these regressions were tamed by autocorrelation corrections barely consonant with their spirit, they led to fantastic extrapolations. Sargent's resurrections of 1923 currency stabiliz-ations, I must report, although they have not been useful in leading us to expect Reagan victories over inflation at little real cost, have in my view slightly prepared us for somewhat better anti-inflation success than earlier Tobin and R. J. Gordon regressions had suggested to me. However, thus far the dicta by the rational expectationists on the miracle that can be expected to follow the establishment of credibility have themselves lacked credibility (and, often, have lacked operational meaning).)

SUMMING UP

Having written on Keynes so many times in this centenary year, I fear to repeat myself. Let me say again that the Keynesian system is better than Keynes the man. Even when we are forced into empirical and policy inferences that are quite the reverse of those appropriate for 1936, we modern economists are using the tools that were not part of economics before Keynes wrote. When Friedman writes down a monetarist model or Meltzer writes down one of his versions, readers note that there is a complete isomorphism with models written down by Keynesians like Tobin or Modigliani – and all of them are different, distinctly different at the methodological level, from the Walras–Debreu or Knight–Viner models of my pre-Keynesian schooling.

Yes, the Keynes model needed, and needs, better exact foundations. But as a student I learned by 1937 that it is better to have a model with inexact foundations that gives you a good grip to handle reality than to wait for better foundations or to continue to use a model with good foundations that is not usefully relevant to explain the phenomena that we have to explain.

The fiction that Keynes assumed rigid wages was found to be a useful fiction. That was so even if one could be persuaded by his purported demonstration that wage cutting might induce such perverse dynamic effects as to be incapable of helping the unemployment problem.

Yes, American Keynesians like me believed that imperfections of competition and deviations from strict constant returns to scale are an important part of the Keynesian under-employment equilibrium story. We knew that the Fortune 500 corporations were there to stay and we also knew that Chamberlin–Robinson diagrams didn't explain why the system was so Pareto-nonoptimal in 1933 and so much more nearly Pareto-optimal in 1929 or 1952. Keynes-cum-Chamberlin-and-Means would have been better than Keynes alone, but we pragmatists were grateful for what we had.

In closing I warn us Keynesians against the vice of complacency. Let us not be *un*reconstructed Keynesians. Let us be *reconstructed* Keynesians – reconstructed by the reconstruction of the world itself.

DISCUSSION

The discussion opened on a point of fact, the claims on p. 184 of Professor Leijonhufvud's paper concerning Keynes's assumptions about expectations in the *General Theory*. First, it was argued that Keynes modelled long-term expectations in real terms. It was pointed out that (expected) quasi rents are measured in monetary terms. Secondly, while it is true that *for convenience* Keynes assumed in Chapter 3 that short-run expectations were realized (in Chapter 5 he discussed what would happen if they were not), it is incorrect to imply that he used a perfect foresight model throughout the *General Theory*. It was added that the expectations of firms were missing from modern macroeconomics displaced, first, by labour's expectations of prices and now by expectations about the monetary regime (an inclusion which must be welcomed in its own right). In the framework of Chapter 21 of the *General Theory all* those elements are present. It is too general a framework to cope with at any particular time as it is important to focus attention on the area where expectations are most volatile at any particular time. Nevertheless, in a general framework, all three types of expectations must be included.

Next it was pointed out that there are two forms of rational expectations, the weak form which is true but tautological and the strong form which Lucas used. The latter implied a very particular relationship between the past, the present and the future, the sort of exact relationship that would not even be necessarily true in physics. Keynes argued that there were certain relevant phenomena for which no probability distributions existed. This ruled out the strong form of rational expectations and ensured that money matters in our sorts of economies in both the short run and the long run. He also argued that economies could be analysed by models which assumed stationary expectations and by those that assumed shifting expectations, stressing that it was the models which changed as the purposes for which they were created changed, not the underlying economy itself.

Keynes dealt with uncertainty and expectations in Chapter 12 where he was discussing the stock market. This approach was fundamentally different from that of the rational expectations school but not that different from the qualifications to rational expectations that Lucas, for example, had to make in order to explain business cycles. There are a limited number of people who are well informed, there is a range of people with differing degrees of information, and the first group make money from the second. They do so because uncertainties about the future are so great that it is better use of their scarce time to be thinking how to make money out of mugs than it is to think about whether it is better to sink an oil well. In retrospect the chapter does not read that well because Keynes greatly exaggerated the impact of stock market volatility on the real economy. (If he were writing today he would have applied the same principles to exchange rates.)

It was next argued that rational expectations is an assertion about how people learn to form expectations about events that can be specified in the form of probability distributions, the sort of uncertainty that is related to earthquakes, rainfall, that is to say, uncertain events that are exogenous to the economic system. This excludes endogenous uncertainty, expectations about other people's decisions, especially in oligopolistic settings (for example, Keynes's example of a beauty contest). The point is not that you cannot fool everybody all the time, as Friedman pointed out, but that people may fool themselves. Keynes wished to design policies which would prevent this happening.

As a point in the history of thought, while the Phillips curve may have been a crucial feature of post war Keynesianism in the United States, that was never true of the United Kingdom. Phillips' article was not well received by British Keynesians when it was first published because the basic model was thought to be far too mechanical, that the market determining wages was too complicated to be modelled in this way. It never became an article of faith.

The discussion moved to the proposition that the theory of rational expectations emphasizes the extent to which the effectiveness of public policy may be determined by the reaction to it of public opinion. Keynes, of course, was well aware of this. Thus he referred to the possibility that an expansionary fiscal policy might weaken industrial confidence if its purpose was not properly understood. Later, rational expectations – to use the modern term – came to be regarded as *favourable* to Keynesian policies. For example, the confidence felt in automatic stabilizers would help to ward off fears of cumulative recession. By contrast, monetarists hold that rational expectations will render public action impotent if this action is foreseen. Why is there this difference? The explanation must lie largely in the fact that a rise in monetary expenditure is assumed by monetarists to vent itself wholly – after perhaps a short lag – in raising prices. Expansion will be inflationary and the aim will be to cheat – or impose an 'inflation tax'. If, however, people are aware beforehand of the intentions of the public authorities, they will take protective action, as far as contracts permit, and will thus frustrate the policy. By contrast the usual Keynesian assumption was that output would rise with rising expenditure. It would not then be a case of the authorities fooling the people. Co-operation rather than confrontation was envisaged.

The difference between the two predictions must obviously reflect differences in what is assumed about the degree of slack in the economy when expenditure is increased.

Professor Leijonhufvud had referred to the debacle of Keynesianism. There had also been a debacle of monetarism. For the rise in OECD unemployment to the huge figure of over 30 million was clearly not anticipated by monetarist advisers. Nor is there any convincing monetarist solution. This does not mean that the right course is simply to revert to the earlier policy and increase expenditure until full employment, in some sense, has been reached. As has long been recognized by some economists, expansion on that scale would need to be accompanied by changes of regime, notably in the labour market.

While one of the discussants did not wish to sound too much like an unreconstructed Bourbon and while it had to be conceded that American Keynesians were too slow to introduce price and inflationary expectations in their models and too quick to embrace the Phillips curve as Friedman's missing equation in macro models, there were two points about this history which should be made. First, no United States administration deliberately took a ride up the Phillips curve in order to obtain lower unemployment at the expense of higher inflation. None of them wanted higher inflation and various of them adopted wage-price policies during expansions in order to limit the possible inflationary results of expansionary policies. The mistakes made in 1968 were done against the advice of Keynesian advisers and other economists and for not entirely discreditable political reasons by President Johnson. In the 1970s the Federal Reserve Board were faced with the agonizing dilemma of how much to accommodate external shocks of unprecedented magnitude associated, for example, with OPEC and the Iranian revolution.

Secondly, on a matter of history of thought, mainstream Keynesians did not believe that demand could be expanded indefinitely with a finite inflationary cost. The Phillips curve was meant to describe a less abrupt transition from the realm of non explosive inflation to excess demand inflation than was implied by the abrupt change in the simpliste model in the *General Theory*. Samuelson and Solow were quite explicit in 1960 about the possibilities of choosing a point on the short-run Phillips curve that would shift the curve itself in the longer run in various directions, including the accelerationist's one. Moreover, it has been a long standing Keynesian view that it is very difficult at all times to maintain price stability and full employment simultaneously without also having an incomes policy.

It was pointed out that as far as forecasting was concerned Keynesian models have done very well, much better than rational expectations models. The proof was that the people who build the first type of models were making millions! The basic difference between the Keynesians, on the one hand, and the rational expectations school and the monetarists, on the other, related to the efficiency of discretionary policies. In the long run it may turn out that they have a role to play but it will be necessary to be far less ambitious as to what may reasonably be expected from them.

Disappointment was expressed at the failure to separate two entirely different issues: rational expectations and 'market clearing' or full wage-price flexibility. The former is increasingly, in some form or other, accepted in decent macroeconomic theory. It is only necessary to mention the work by John Taylor on staggered wage contracting as an example. Anyone must make *some* assumption about expectations. Recent refinements of the original rational expectations models prove to be extremely rich and appropriate for such questions as regime changes, short-term and long-term interest rates and their relation to budget deficits or the exchange rate implications of potential changes in monetary and fiscal policy.

Where the real difference of opinion resides is in the assumptions about wage/price flexibility. It is in this area that the New Classical Economics fails to offer a convincing macroeconomic account of what is occurring and where Keynesian economics insists on the right facts but still owes a persuasive explanation.

Professor Leijonhufvud replied to the discussion as follows:

He said he found it difficult to respond. One of the problems with Keynesian economics is that there are more kinds of Keynesians than you could shake a stick at; he knew because he had tried. Professor Pasinetti said that he (Professor Leijonhufvud) had not answered the question, what would Keynes have thought of rational expectations? He tended to think that Keynes would have had no big objection to making short-run nominal expectations endogenous but he would have objected to the very attempt to make long-run real expectations about real profits endogenous. He would have thought it science fiction to have done so (not that Keynes disliked s.f. – he once favourably reviewed a book of H. G. Wells and ended by saying 'it [was] a large and meaty egg laid by a glorious hen').

Professor Leijonhufvud referred to his 1968 book and his critique of the interpretation of Keynes which said that unemployment was due to the downward inflexibility of nominal wages, an argument that *any* pre-Keynesian economist would have used to explain unemployment. He felt that in the 1960s Keynesian economics was getting into trouble because it refused to straighten out some conceptual problems in its structure. The models which he learned in school did show a clear lineage back to Keynes but there was no inevitability that the arguments needed to develop as they did and land us in the mess that we are in today – there were several different futures, as it were, with the *General Theory* as starting point. His 1968 book was an attempt to go back and see what other alternative futures could have been read into Keynes.

In the paper there is a little diagram, which Professor Leijonhufvud calls the Swedish flag diagram, see p. 187, in which stocks and adjustment failures are classified as nominal, mixed and real. Many Keynesians hold on to some nominal wage rigidity, whether from implicit contract theory or elsewhere, because they think it is what makes them characteristically Keynesians. Professor Leijonhufvud thinks that the move over to this mish-mash and away from Keynes's intertemporal equilibrium story makes Keynesian economics an easy prey to monetarism. Many reacted to his paper by saying that he is a monetarist or a rational expectationist, but he is not, he is one of the other kind of Keynesians you can shake a stick at (and an ageing one at that).

6

The demand-side economics of
inflation

TIBOR SCITOVSKY

When I was asked to speak on inflation at this centenary celebration of Keynes, I admit that I was at first puzzled. Inflation was not a problem Keynes gave much thought to, since it was not a problem of his country in his time. What little he wrote about inflation showed good sense and shrewd insight; but we look up to Keynes for much more than just those qualities, however rare and precious they may be. As I started to think about it, however, I realized that the subject does belong to this conference. For one thing, inflation is a major macroeconomic problem; and macroeconomics, as we understand it today, is largely of Keynes's making. For another thing, it was Keynes who reformed our thinking about monetary problems by departing from his contemporaries' exclusive preoccupation with the supply of money and directing their and our attention to the motivation, and the determinants of the motivation, for holding money. A similar reform is badly needed also in our thinking about inflation. There is nowadays an excessively one-sided preoccupation with the supply of money as the restraining force on inflation, as if prices had an innate, automatic tendency always to rise to the level at which the demand for holding money equalled its supply. I shall try in this paper to restore the balance by focusing attention on the factors that motivate price increases and so motivate the demand for additional holdings of money.

Macroeconomics deals with general economic tendencies that permeate many markets and industries, persist over time, and seem very different from isolated economic changes. We have long taken for granted the existence of those economic tendencies, which seem to develop a momentum of their own, spreading from market to market and retaining their force over time – as if the law of the conservation of momentum governed not only the physical world but economics as well. Yet, one must look to economic forces to explain economic phenomena; and if we want to control them, we must fathom the laws of their behavior and find out how, why and when isolated economic changes become general, economy-wide tendencies.

General equilibrium theory provides a part, but only the lesser part of the answer to that question. It shows that the relation of substitutability causes a given economic change to spread laterally to other markets and to be dissipated in the course of its becoming generalized by affecting more and more markets. The other and more important part of the answer we owe to Kahn and Keynes, whose multiplier theory showed when and how changes in income and output were transmitted vertically from market to market and, far from being dissipated in the process, got magnified – or multiplied, to use Keynes's expression.

Everything that we know about inflation suggests that there, too, a multiplier-type vertical transmission process must be at work, which generalizes isolated price increases into a general price increase and gathers enough momentum to keep the process going. In the following, I shall take up that suggestion, look into the mode of operation of the cumulative price increase and try to find the conditions that make it gather momentum and become self-sustaining.

Prices perform important functions in the market economy: they allocate resources and distribute income. Changes in prices, brought about by changing conditions, adapt resource allocation and income distribution to those changing conditions; and most economists believe that market prices perform better than any other system known today at least one of those functions, the allocative function.

Yet, even the price system does not perform well all the time. Its allocative and distributive functions depend on relative, not absolute prices; and there are circumstances in which a change in conditions that calls for reallocation and redistribution leads to a generalized and parallel increase in too many prices, which fails therefore to bring about the required reallocation and redistribution to the extent necessary. Moreover, because such a general rise in all or most prices fails to reallocate resources and redistribute income, it also fails to eliminate the initial cause of the price rise. That is why inflation, once it has started, tends to continue and is hard to stop. To find the causes of inflation, therefore, one must look for the special circumstances that turn specific price changes into general and parallel changes of most prices and thereby keep them from performing their reallocating and redistributive functions.

Let me begin the search for those special circumstances by analyzing a familiar example: an increase in public sector expenditure. If we focus attention on a closed economy in which all resources were underemployed, so that the increased demand could be fully matched by an increase in supply without creating any upward pressure on prices, any obstacle to the rise in output would change it into a rise in prices. I shall concentrate on the obstacles and their consequences, and will begin by assuming perfect competition. That may seem like a strange assumption to make in a study of inflation but I will soon drop it and at that stage it will pinpoint the role that the lack of competition plays in generating inflation. I shall also go into more detail and differentiate the different obstacles to an increase in output. In equilibrium, of course, there would be not one but many and equally important obstacles, because all scarcities would be equalized on the margin. But we seldom are in equilibrium. Most of the time, one factor is more scarce than the others; and which is the most scarce makes a great deal of difference to the outcome.

For lack of time, I shall consider only three cases. Take first the one, especially common in developing countries, in which manufacturing equipment is the limiting factor. This is represented by the individual firms' rising marginal cost curves; and it causes production costs and product prices to rise along with output in response to the rise in demand. That lowers real wages, raises real profit rates and so redistributes income from labor to capital, all of which tends to reallocate resources in an equilibrating fashion. The shift in income distribution lowers the private sector's effective demand out of unchanged real income; the rise in product prices relative to wages renders profitable the increased utilization of existing equipment through overtime work and multiple-shift operation; and the higher rate of profit makes it profitable to invest in additional equipment and provides additional saving out of which to finance such investment.

In this case, therefore, there is a general rise in prices but no rise in wages, because there is no excess demand for labor.[1] Indeed, there may be continued unemployment, though not Keynesian but Marxian unemployment, due to the insufficiency of the tools of production with which to put labor to work. Product prices will continue rising if the public sector is unwilling to accept the reduction of its take (in real terms) due to the rise in prices; but the cumulative process of rising prices will converge to a higher but stable level, because it causes output to rise, the private sector's share in output to fall, and also leads, in the long run, to a rise in productive capacity. This is the kind of slow rise in the general price level to which many distinguished economists, Lord Kaldor among them, have given their blessing – on the ground that it not only accompanies all fast economic growth but promotes it as well.

As the second case, consider a situation in which labor and productive equipment are both underemployed; but the economy is open and the limiting factor is foreign exchange. Assume further that exchange rates are flexible. Then an increase in public-sector demand will cause output and the

---

[1] When the assumption of perfect competition is dropped, the conclusion that wages don't rise may have to be revised. See p. 237 below.

price of foreign exchange to rise, along with the prices of imports and import-dependent domestic products, while wages and the prices of other products remain unchanged.[2] Since that means a change in relative prices, consumers and producers are put under pressure to reduce their consumption and use of imports and import-intensive domestic products. Here again, the prices of imports and import-dependent domestic products will continue to rise if the public sector refuses to accept the reduction in its real take caused by the price increases; but the rising import prices will converge to a stable level, which will be lower, the less dependent the economy on imports and the greater the foreigners' price elasticity of demand for its exports.

I now come to my third case, a closed economy with plenty of underemployed productive equipment but a shortage of labor; and you will see that in this case alone would excess demand lead to persistent inflation in a perfectly competitive economy. It is not easy, however, to find examples of this case, because businessmen are not so foolish as to build manufacturing capacity that cannot be manned. That is why this is an exceptional case, which usually occurs only in time of war. It may be useful to look at the most obvious example: the assignat period during the Great French Revolution of the 1790s. That was the time of the first hyperinflation recorded by history; and it is customarily associated in people's minds with that great French invention, paper assignats. A no less and perhaps even more important part of the explanation, was compulsory military service.

Threatened with foreign invasion, compulsory military service enabled the French to increase the size of the army, in record time, from under 100,000 men to almost 800,000 men. In a country with barely 27 million inhabitants and a labor force which 60 years later was estimated at only 7.2 million (out of a then population of 36 million), that constituted a very large diversion of manpower, because the new recruits were conscripted not from the unemployable rabble of the Paris streets but mainly from among the most productive and active members of the labor force. The decree of the Committee of Public Safety did proclaim that 'young men will go to the front, married men will forge arms and carry food, women will make tents and clothing, and work in hospitals, children will turn old linen into bandages'; in effect, however, only the first part of that comprehensive plan for total war was actually carried out. Contemporary comments and scattered data showing a fall in output suggest that there must have been a

---

[2] That conclusion may also have to be revised when the assumption of perfect competition is dropped. See p. 237 below.

sizeable reduction in the labor force – at least by 10 per cent and possibly by much more.

At the same time, of course, the need to equip, clothe, house, feed and transport so large an army greatly increased the public sector's demand for the diminished output of that diminished labor force. The way that demand was financed is explained by the disarray of the tax system and credit market of the time; but the only thing important to know about it is that it failed to diminish the private sector's effective demand. The result was a simultaneous excess demand for both products and labor, which led to a simultaneous rise of prices and wages, keeping income distribution more or less unchanged. Since that raised the money value of the unchanged output, private income and (in view of the unchanged income distribution) private demand in equal proportions, government, in order to keep maintaining, supplying and equipping its army, was forced to spend ever-increasing sums in order to keep outbidding the private sector, thereby raising prices, wages and presumably profits to ever-higher levels. Note that with no significant change in relative prices and income distribution, the inflationary process generated no equilibrating forces to make the rising prices converge to a stable level.

That, in a nutshell, is the story of the French hyperinflation; and similar reductions of the labor force in the face of increased or undiminished demand for output occurred also in the Hungarian and Chinese hyperinflations of the mid-1940s and, at least for a while, in the German hyperinflation of 1923. In Hungary, following the siege of Budapest, the city's entire adult population was commandeered (and generously paid) for clearing rubble away and building temporary shelters; in China, the civil war took many millions of people out of the labor force; in Germany, the entire labor force of the Ruhr, the country's industrial centre, went on strike, encouraged and financed by the German Government to protest against the French occupation of the area.

In all those examples, the excess demand for products and the excess demand for labor arose simultaneously from the same cause, thereby shortcircuiting the sequence of events people have in mind when they speak of a price–wage spiral and visualise rising prices to drive up wages and rising wages to drive up prices in turn. The simultaneous occurrence of excess demand in both product and labor markets may explain why the rate of inflation accelerated so easily and quickly in all those countries and reached such astronomic heights. Indeed, hyperinflation, defined as a 10-fold or faster annual rise in the general price level, is probably limited to those exceptional circumstances in which a general shortage of labor is the main obstacle to supply's ability to respond to a rise in demand; and note that that was also the only one of our three cases that, on the assumptions so far made, was truly inflationary.

Let me now drop the assumption of perfect competition and consider what happens when some members of some markets have a conscious influence over some prices. Since people use their power over prices to claim a share in income, bringing them into the picture shifts the focus of attention from the allocative function of prices to their distributive function; and, more particularly, from their occasional failure to perform the first function to their much more frequent failure to perform the second.

When owners of the factors of production ask a price for the services they perform or for the primary or intermediate goods they sell, they claim a part of the value of the output to whose production they contribute. For those prices to stick and the price level to remain stable, the sum of the parts to which they lay claim must not exceed the total of which they are the parts. When that condition is not fulfilled, inflation results, which I propose to call excess-claims inflation, by analogy to excess-demand inflation. A notable difference, however, between the two kinds of inflation is that while excess-demand inflation can start only after supply has reached its physical upper limit, excess-claims inflation can occur whatever the degree of utilization or underutilization of the capacity to produce. The reason is that claims to income are claims not to absolute quantities but to proportionate shares or parts of income. Accordingly, when the prices claimed for the inputs add up to more than the value of the output they generate, the excess can be eliminated by reconciling prices, by increasing productivity, but not by increasing activity.[3]

How does the market economy reconcile prices and distribute income? We have a theory of income distribution under perfect competition but know next to nothing about what happens when competition is imperfect. If one could separate the people with power to influence prices from those who, powerless, face prices on a take-it-or-leave-it basis, one would safely suppose the powerful to increase their share in income at the expense of the powerless; but what happens when no such separation is possible? What, for example, would happen in an economy in which all prices were set by the sellers and all buyers would be price takers? That may be an extreme and oversimplified model; but today's reality is a lot closer to it than it is to the model of perfect competition; and it is an inherently unstable and inflationary model – for reasons that become apparent as soon as one starts analyzing it.

Since everyone of us is both a seller in some markets and a buyer in other

---

[3] Except to the limited extent that increased activity leads to a rise in productivity.

markets, such an economy would give everybody a split personality, a kind of economic schizophrenia, by putting them into a position of power in some markets and a position of complete powerlessness in other markets. That is a natural and harmless position for middlemen to be in: most retailers regularly buy their wares at the wholesalers' set prices and resell them to consumers, with a markup added, at their own set price. But when all or most members of the economy are in that position, powerless against exploitation in markets where they do their buying but able to exploit their opposite numbers in the markets where they do their selling, then any change in economic conditions that calls for a reallocation of resources or redistribution of income will, instead, start a chain reaction of price changes, because everybody who finds his income diminished by a price change he cannot resist will try to recoup his loss by changing some other price in some other market in which *he* has the power to change prices and play the role of exploiter. To do so requires no increase in exploitation; indeed, it is reasonable to assume that everybody already exploits his market power to the full. But when prices are raised against anyone, he will find it profitable to raise his prices in turn by adding his unchanged profit-maximizing markup to his now higher costs. Once that process has started, it is self sustaining and can only be ended by the providential presence of suckers, willing to take the reduction of their incomes on the chin, or by a rise in productivity, which allows some people to gain without causing others to lose. Moreover, since the economic model we are considering is one in which the sellers, not the buyers, are the price makers, the cumulative process whereby one price change leads to another will be biased in the inflationary direction.[4]

I dare say that many of the people who have already contracted the condition of economic schizophrenia in today's economy don't think of it as a disease at all, because they don't connect its ill effects to their cause. Yet, the ill effects are inflation – or the miseries inflicted by attempts to combat inflation with restrictive monetary and fiscal policies – and I will try to show that those ill effects result not only in the oversimplified model I postulated but in practical and more realistic approximations to it as well.

Economists instinctively think of competition as the force that keeps prices stable; but that is false. The necessary condition of price stability is market symmetry, i.e. competition among both buyers and sellers. Perfect competition provides that, because it means equally perfect competition on both the buyers' and the sellers' side of the market; but competition does

---

[4] See my 'Asymmetries in Economics' (*Scottish Journal of Political Economy*, Vol. 25, 1978, pp. 227–37) for the argument that prices set by sellers are more flexible in the upward than in the downward direction.

not have to be perfect, it does not even have to exist for prices to be stabilized. All you need is the mutual offsetting of buyers' and sellers' market power as they exert their pressures on prices. The simplest form of that is when a buyer and a seller confront one another in an isolated market and haggle over price until they manage to hit upon a mutually agreeable one. That then becomes a stable price. In any single market transaction, the price agreed upon divides the gain from that transaction between the transacting parties; and that statement can be generalized from a single market to the whole group of factor markets in which a given producer buys his inputs, provided that the price of his product remains unchanged. The price he agrees to pay the suppliers of his inputs determine the shares of the contributors in the income his output generates; and the sum of all the shares necessarily equals the total income generated, because his own share, which he pays himself for his own input, is the residual that remains after he has paid for all the bought inputs.

That somewhat trivial result is true whether factor markets are competitive or monopolistic and whether the buyers or the sellers have the upper hand in those factor markets; but it ceases to be true, and the situation becomes very different, when product prices are free to change and the producer has the power to change them. For in that case, if, after having signed all his factor-market contracts, the producer finds that he has promised away too much and left himself too little, he can raise the price of his product, thereby unilaterally revising in his own favor the income distribution implicitly agreed upon in his factor-market contracts. In short, costs can push up prices when, and only when, producers have power over the prices at which they sell their output.

I advisedly speak of power over prices rather than of monopoly or oligopoly power, because I want to include political power over prices, manifest in farm-price support programmes and minimum-wage legislation, and because I want to extend the argument also to socialist economies. After all, excess-claims inflation is endemic to socialist economies as well when plant managers have the power to set the prices of their products or to influence the level at which the central pricing agency sets them. That power is crucial, because one of the necessary conditions of excess-claims inflation is the power over prices of the sellers of products, not the power over wages of the sellers of labor.

To raise prices, however, is a very different and much rarer thing than merely to have the power to raise them, because it is not always in the producer's best interest to exercise his power over product prices. Having agreed to or initiated an increase in the price of an input, he can reduce the resulting loss of his profit by raising product prices correspondingly; but that will not eliminate the loss completely if the higher prices of his products discourage their sales. Accordingly, the producer usually regards raising product prices in response to rising costs as a second-best policy, to be resorted to only if no better policy is available. His first-best policy is to resist cost increases and keep costs as well as prices unchanged – provided that that is possible and not more costly than the parallel increase in both costs and output prices.

Whether the producer can resist and avoid the rise in his input prices depends on whether he possesses superior bargaining strength in factor markets to match his superior bargaining strength in the markets where he sells his products. In my model of price-maker sellers and price-taker buyers, that, obviously, is *not* the case, since a price taker's market position is always weaker than the price maker's. Accordingly, under the conditions postulated in my model, the producer's second-best policy of raising product prices in response to rising input prices becomes his first-best policy. That explains one half of the cost–wage spiral that characterizes excess-claims inflation: the half that consists in costs pushing up prices. But the same model also explains the other half of the cost–wage spiral, which consists in product prices pushing up costs. For, when the owners of the factors of production are price makers in selling their services, then they can and will raise the prices of their services in response to a rise in the cost of living which they are powerless to resist.

You will have noticed the important role asymmetrical market relations play in destabilizing the price system. My theoretical model postulates a particularly simple form of asymmetry; but that, while sufficient, is not a necessary condition for excess-claims inflation to arise. Our next task therefore is to leave my model and look instead at the real world to see how, why, and since when its asymmetries approximate the asymmetry postulated in my model sufficiently to generate inflation. After all, quite a few economies have been remarkably stable until not so many years ago: what has happened in recent times to undermine their stability? It will be easiest to answer that question by tracing the gradual change in our economic relations from the atomistic competition in those early markets and periodic fairs, which posed for the economist's idealized picture of perfect competition, all the way to today's bitter conflicts between large oligopolies, organized labor, international cartels, and others of their ilk. The beauty and stability of the early market relations lay in the perfect symmetry of buyers' and sellers' market positions, which resulted from bilaterally competitive bargaining, and which today is only preserved in the textbook model of perfect competition. In the real world, the symmetry and the stability slowly came to an end with the growing size of economic agents.

The first departure from bilaterally competitive bargaining came with the emergence of the wholesale trader as the dominant figure of merchant capitalism. The sheer size of his wealth and scale of operations enabled him to impose his terms on both the small retailers to whom he sold and the small manufacturers with whom he placed his orders. His superior bargaining position in both the market where he bought and in the market where he sold accounted for his large profits and fast growth to great size and wealth; but it did not diminish the stability of the general price level, because the asymmetries between buyers' and sellers' bargaining strengths in the two markets were themselves symmetrical and so mutually offsetting. The upward pressure the wholesaler exerted on the price paid by retailers and consumers was counterbalanced by the downward pressure he put on the price received by the small manufacturers and with it also on their workers' wages and suppliers' earnings. For, remarkably enough, the downward pressure of buyers' market power will counterbalance the effect on the general price level of the upward pressure of sellers' market power, not only when they are pitted against each other in a direct confrontation in the same market, but also when each of them presses against a different price in a different market, and even when the opposing pressures are exerted by the same actor or actors.

The last vestiges of merchant capitalism can still be found in Japan, whose large general trading companies retain to this day their dominance over the part of the country's export trade that originates in small manufacturing firms; and they also seem to have maintained their downward pressure on costs and wages in those small firms – to judge by the failure, during the 1950s and '60s, of costs and wages in those firms to rise in step with the inflationary rise in the level of both consumer prices and wages in large firms and the service industries. That fact has been cited among the reasons why Japan's export prices and export performance were unaffected by her domestic inflation during that period.

In the West, wholesale merchants had yielded their dominant position to manufacturers already by the end of the 19th century. The development of precision machine tools for machining interchangeable parts and the invention of the assembly line on which to assemble them created great economies of scale which not only called for firms large enough to engage in mass production but also yielded the large profits that enabled manufacturing enterprises to grow to great size and market power. As a result, manufacturers gradually displaced wholesalers as the dominant members of the markets in which they sold their products and acquired the ability and habit of setting their prices on a take-it-or-leave-it basis.

At the same time, of course, their increasing size rendered manufacturers equally powerful in the markets in which they bought their inputs and so became wage- or price-makers also in those markets for many years to come. Accordingly, the period of wholesalers' domination was followed by an equally stable period of manufacturers' domination, because that too created a situation of symmetrical asymmetries, in which the impact on the general price level of producers' downward pressure on wages and input prices counterbalanced the impact of their upward pressure on product prices.

Needless to say, there were exceptions to that rule of the manufacturers' power over input prices; but those, at first, were too few and unimportant to endanger the stability of the system. As time went on, however, more and more exceptions were added, until the exceptions became the rule and turned the once symmetrical and stable situation into an asymmetrical, unstable, and inflationary one.

An obvious exception to the rule could be found in the markets for intermediate goods, where producers faced producers and buyers and sellers could not both dominate the same market at the same time. But power relations in those markets and the way they operate are an internal matter of the manufacturing sector and do not diminish the stability of the system, because they do not affect its basic symmetry, which consists in manufacturers as a group dominating both the markets in which they sell to, and those in which they buy from, people outside their group.

A similar and equally harmless exception was provided by the markets in which large and powerful manufacturers sold to large and powerful wholesalers. Here again, what happens in such markets is an internal matter of the business community and does not alter the balance of market power between businessmen and consumers on the one side and business-men and the sellers of primary productive factors on the other side. Exactly the same applies to yet another exception of more recent vintage, the formation of nationwide retail chains and their acquisition of countervailing power in their dealings with manufacturers. Their countervailing power redistributes profits within the business community but does not diminish retailers' power over prices in consumer markets.

More significant exceptions are the markets for primary products, like wool, cotton, corn, wheat, etc., in which the standardization of the product assures bilaterally perfect competition and deprives even the largest buyers of any conscious influence on price. Note that the buyers in such markets are just as powerless to resist a price increase as they are when the price is unilaterally raised by price-maker sellers. That shows that price-maker sellers in input markets are a sufficient but not a necessary condition for creating the costs-pushing-up-prices half of the inflationary spiral.[5] Perfect competition in input markets does just as well. Perfect competitive markets, however, were too few and transacted too small a part of the trade in inputs to endanger stability.

---

[5] The other half of the spiral hinges on product prices entering the costs of inputs.

All the other exceptions to the rule of producers' domination in input markets came very much later, mostly as the result of defensive action taken by various groups of people who felt exploited by the large manufacturers' large profits. The most important of those groups was labor, whose organization into unions managed, in some countries, to substitute collective bargaining for the unilateral setting of wages by employers and to exert a fair amount of pressure in the course of such bargaining.

A second group or set of groups were producers of mineral resources, who formed international cartels in their attempts to reverse the balance of market power and assume the price-maker's role in the markets where they sold. The most recent and spectacularly successful of those attempts was the concerted action of oil producers in 1973. The world-wide rise in price levels that immediately followed was a striking illustration of how costs can push up prices; whereas the second oil crisis of 1978 showed how prices pushed up (oil) costs.

Farmers constitute a third group of sellers of inputs; and they improved the terms of trade between their produce and manufactured goods, in some cases by co-operative marketing, in others by successfully pressing for the enactment of farm-price support legislation. The latter is a form of price setting on the farmers' behalf, the more effective in promoting the inflationary spiral (both the cost–price and the price–cost halves of it), the more it stabilizes the farmers' share in income.

In all those instances, the concerted action of the suppliers of a given input either reversed the balance of market power in their own favor or at least substituted bargaining for prices set by the other side and so presumably brought the two sides' bargaining strength closer to equality. Since every reversal adds to the number of input markets dominated by sellers, each one brings the economy a step closer to my theoretical model of price-maker sellers and price-taker buyers, which we know to be inflationary.

But what are the consequences for price stability of a mere reduction in the disparity between the buyers' and the sellers' bargaining strength? In practical terms, that is the really important question one must answer, because complete reversals in the balance of market power, such as the one that created the 1973 oil crisis, are rare occurrences; and a few of them have taken place in the markets for the most important input: labor. Collective bargaining as the main means of wage determination is confined to a handful of Western European countries; and labor does not, by any means, have the upper hand in all such bargaining situations. In the United States, collective bargaining determines the wages of only 29.8% of all wage and salary earners,[6] the remaining 70% are paid according to wage scales unilaterally set by employers. In Japan, about 35% of the labor force belongs to unions; and they are probably the only ones whose earnings are determined by collective bargaining, given the importance in Japan of the closed shop. In most other countries, including the newly industrializing countries, all or almost all wages and salaries are still set by employers, except in small firms with few employees, where personal bargaining is probably the rule. In the newly industrializing countries that is not an unimportant exception. In Taiwan, for example, 10.1% of the labor force in manufacturing works in enterprises employing less than 10 people; and the percentage would be much higher if all sectors, including retail trade, were included. I also suspect that Japan in this respect is not very different from Taiwan.

What can one make of that variety of ways in which wages are determined? What, to begin with, is the impact of collective bargaining on price stability? It is generally believed to be destabilizing. I go along with that – not only when labor has the upper hand at the negotiating table but even when the opposing parties are evenly matched. After all, I have just argued (see p. 233 above) that perfect competition in input markets is inflationary, because it destroys the symmetry in market relations between input and output markets; and perfect competition is merely a limiting case of bilaterally competitive bargaining between buyers and sellers of approximately equal bargaining strength.

We now come to the puzzling behavior of wage rates unilaterally set by employers. U.S. experience shows that they tend to rise with the cost of living or faster than the cost of living whether or not there is unemployment in the firm's sector and even when there is general unemployment in the economy. Indeed, wages unilaterally set by employers don't seem to behave very differently from wages negotiated by unions, from which one must conclude that the market position of unionized workers is not much better than that of the workers who have no union to represent them.

The implication, however, is not that unions are unable to exert strong bargaining pressure, but that individual workers themselves have also acquired a strong bargaining power of their own, which they exert even when they have no union to represent them. That, at any rate, seems to be

[6] That percentage is considerably higher than the percentage of union members, because it includes workers who, though not union members, are covered by wage contracts negotiated by unions. It is based on surveys made between 1968 and 1972; today's percentage is probably somewhat lower. See Richard B. Freeman and James L. Medoff, 'New Estimates of Private Sector Unionism in the United States', *Industrial and Labor Relations Review*, Vol. 32 (1979) pp. 143–74.

the most plausible reason for the observed practice of employers to initiate wage increases on their own, thereby to keep their workers' earnings abreast of the cost of living and of other workers' earnings.[7]

What is the basis of the individual worker's growing bargaining strength? Often mentioned is the supposedly ever-present threat of forming and joining a union; but a more important basis, I believe, is technical progress, which is gradually but profoundly changing the character of work. What used to be considered the substance of factory work: the need to exert brute force and endure fatigue, monotony, danger, filth, noise and generally unpleasant working conditions, is slowly receding into the past as mechanical power is displacing muscular exertion, repetitive operations are increasingly performed by machinery, and hygiene and safety regulations are better enforced. At the same time, however, the new technology makes many new demands on the worker, requiring him to be vigilant, careful, always on the alert, ready at a moment's notice to avert or deal with unexpected mechanical breakdowns or mishaps, and able to exercise judgment and use his sense of responsibility. Needless to add, today's workers are fully able to meet the many new demands on their various skills and abilities, thanks to better training, better education, and their greater sophistication and self confidence.

The fact, however, that modern technology and modern work utilize such a great variety of the worker's faculties also means that the inevitable differences between different people's talents and abilities come to the fore and become apparent, because they greatly affect the quality and quantity of the work performed and output produced. Within limits, the employer must accept and accommodate those inevitable human differences and the resulting differences between different workers' performances; and in the process *he cannot help accepting and accommodating similar differences* also *in the same person's performance at different times*. The employer's forcible acceptance of such variability in the individual worker's work performance provides the latter with a secret but powerful bargaining weapon.

Work contracts specify wages, hours, working conditions, vacations, sick leave, etc., but cannot, for the reasons just mentioned, specify the quality and quantity of the work to be performed. Accordingly, even when the employer is unencumbered by unions and free to draw up the work contract as he sees fit, he still leaves, and cannot help leaving to his workers a large measure of influence over the profitability and success of his enterprise. They don't even have to make a conscious decision how well or

---

[7] See, however, my 'Market Power and Inflation', (*Economica*, Vol. 45, 1978) pp. 221–33 for an alternative explanation, in terms of the fairness of employers.

how badly to fulfil their side of the work contract, because their morale, feelings towards the firm, and the ambition and enthusiasm they bring to their work depend very much on how well they are paid and treated and make a great deal of difference to their performance and productivity. The greater the influence of workers' morale on productivity, and the greater the producer's awareness of that influence, the more his ability unilaterally to set wages loses its advantage and becomes little more than an empty formality.[8]

My argument implies that modern technology and the resulting change in the character of work have had much the same impact on the balance of market power in labor relations as the collective action of workers through their unions. Moreover, as a moment's reflection shows, those two influences on the balance of market power are not additive but overlapping, which is why I argued earlier (see p. 235 above) that the similar behavior of wages in unionized and non-unionized industries is no indication of the weakness of union power. All it shows is that the individual worker in the new industries has plenty of bargaining strength and is in very little need of a union to represent him and make his bargaining power more explicit. The fast, inflationary increase in money wages in such newly industrializing countries as South Korea, where industry is highly automated and collective bargaining unknown, would be hard to explain without the argument just outlined.

To sum up the argument, the producer's power over the prices at which he buys his inputs has been weakened in most markets over the years – by the sellers' collective action, by legislation, and by the new technology. From the point of view of distributive justice, the change, on balance, was probably to the better; from the point of view of the stability of the pricing system, it was almost certainly to the worse, because it brought the pattern of market relationships in the economy's different markets very much closer to my theoretical model of an unstable system of markets.

The significance of an unstable system of markets is that it tends to amplify into an inflationary process any major price increase brought about by random shocks. Among such random shocks are not only wars, bad harvests and similar disasters; but also the kind of initially non-inflationary price increases discussed at the beginning of this paper. For example, an increase in effective demand during a depression would raise the level of activity and employment in a stable system; and any worsening of the balance of payments and rise in import prices would be regarded as a

---

[8] The argument of the last two paragraphs owes much to the work of the late Arthur Okun on implicit contracts and what he called the invisible handshake.

small price to pay for an increase in real output and income. In an unstable market system, however, the rise in import prices may well turn into an inflationary wage–price spiral and stop the rise in real output in its tracks.

The above is a quick sketch of a very incomplete theory of inflation, with many important parts missing. After all, I haven't even mentioned expectations, one of the main elements in the cumulative inflationary process, never discussed the growth of productivity and its anti-inflationary impact, said nothing about money, on the supply side of the subject, nor about finance, which has much to do with the initial impetus. The points I did cover are the neglected ones in present-day discussions; yet they constitute an important part of the background one has to understand and bear in mind in order to develop a satisfactory cure for inflation, less painful and less costly than the restrictive monetary policies that bedevil our economy today.

COMMENT

A. J. Brown

Professor Scitovsky has put forward an elegant theory of inflation arising from excessive claims on productive resources, in which he aims 'to restore the balance by focusing on the factors that motivate price-increases, and so motivate demand for additional holdings of money'. First, he deals with the case of perfect competition in which someone (he chooses the public sector) initiates extra expenditure. What happens will depend, as he shows, on where bottlenecks are encountered. If it is in capital equipment, with labour still in elastic supply, money wages are little affected, but prices and profits rise, so investment is encouraged and the bottleneck eliminated. Even if the addition to public expenditure is increased to match the rise in prices, the inflation will be limited, because total real output is raised and the real wage-rate is squeezed to make room for the public authorities' additional real requirements. Something corresponding to this happens if foreign exchange constitutes the bottleneck. If, however, it is labour that is scarce, the prices of both goods and labour rise, so household real incomes are not squeezed, and since it is assumed that the supply of labour is inflexible, an attempt by the public sector to insist on the real extra acquisition of goods and services at which it aims will result in an indefinite, divergent, inflation. Professor Scitovsky's point that true hyperinflation has apparently happened only where something went drastically wrong on the supply side is a striking one. It is noteworthy that big inflations of, say, the Latin American and Israeli kinds do not develop a truly explosive character.

The assumption of perfect competition is then dropped, and Professor Scitovsky deals with 'excess claims' inflation in situations where some agents in the economy have power to manipulate prices. Indefinite inflation results if: (1) the agents with this power are predominantly in a position to exercise it as sellers rather than as buyers, (2) each one, by raising his price, can gain for the time being at the expense of others, who are in a position to retaliate, and (3) money supply is sufficiently elastic to allow this to go on – a point that Professor Scitovsky has deliberately left outside his terms of reference for this paper.

This is, of course, a generalization of the process most familiar as the 'price–wage spiral',[1] but it comprehends also the so-called 'wage–wage spiral' (more properly a 'wage–price–wage spiral') and many other variations. It is pointed out that processes of this kind can operate even when the economy is far below full employment, because price-rises, unlike injections of purchasing-power, impinge on proportional shares of the product rather than absolute uptakes of it. Of course, with limited absolute objectives, a convergent process may occur – wage-earners and profit-receivers may get the increase they want in their real incomes by squeezing rentiers, for instance – but given the power to make further temporary gains by unilateral price-increases, there is no obvious reason why the agents in question should stop. They might make a peace treaty if they found the inflationary process sufficiently upsetting, but if human nature lent itself readily to such developments, we should have had universal disarmament long ago.

The application of this doctrine to the stages of development of modern economies makes interesting reading. To come to the present, in the big industrial economies, however, Professor Scitovsky's picture is as follows. Manufacturers mostly dominate the markets in which they sell. This would not create a net inflationary bias if they equally dominated those in which they bought their inputs, but they have largely ceased to do so. Some primary inputs have near-perfect markets, not dominated by either side; some are dominated by sellers' cartels (e.g. OPEC), some buttressed by legislation (agricultural price-support schemes), and so on. But the biggest input, labour, raises more questions. It is true that, as is pointed out, the overall predominance of sellers is still preserved even if, in the labour market, neither side has the advantage in price-setting power, but a prima facie paradox is seen in the fact that wages set more or less unilaterally by

---

[1] See A. J. Brown, *The Great Inflation 1939–1951*, Oxford, 1955. Chapters 4 and 5.

employers do not behave very differently from those set by bargaining with powerful trade unions.

But how widely does the fact hold? It is true that, in relation to the scale of nominal wage-inflation in recent decades, the rates of divergence between different (and probably between differently unionized) groups within a given economy are small. Sometimes they can be plausibly attributed to relative changes in product-market situation (losses of railway footplate workers, gains of coal-miners after 1973), or to assertion of union bargaining-strength (coal-miners in 1972); sometimes to legislative support (women workers in the U.K. generally in the 'seventies).[2] But durable differences in union bargaining-power seem to manifest themselves mostly in fairly constant proportional differences in *level* of wages, such as the advantages enjoyed by newspaper printers in the U.K. Occupations with lower bargaining-power fall behind only up to a point; thereafter they are pulled along partly by employers' fears of recruitment difficulties, partly by recognition of customary 'normal' relationships with other occupations, which should not be changed too drastically. Professor Scitovsky's doctrine that employees' goodwill has to be retained if quality of work is to be kept up seems to fit in here – goodwill depends on a belief that the relative pay position is not too unfavourable by customary standards. But I am inclined to think he underestimates the importance of the organized sections of labour as 'wage-leaders' in the United States and other countries where collective bargaining characterises only a minority of industry, though a substantial one.

Nevertheless, it seems likely that the width of collective bargaining as a mode of pay-determination does have something to do with the liability to 'wage-push' inflation (which may be crudely diagnosed by the coincidence of wage-acceleration with rise in labour's share of the product). The U.K., with three-quarters of employee incomes directly dependent upon collective bargaining of some kind, and with employers weakly organized, is a fairly extreme case. But the mode of organization of the bargaining is important too. The systems which in some appropriate sense are more centralized – Germany, Austria, Scandinavia – have avoided inflation better than the widely-unionized, but looser British structure.[3]

With only minor qualifications, therefore, I should agree that Professor Scitovsky's contribution is highly relevant to current problems of inflation. But where do the economics of Keynes come in? It is true that in most of his

---

[2] See C. T. Saunders, 'Changes in Relative Pay in the 1970s' in Blackaby (ed.) *The Future of Pay Bargaining*, London, Heinemann, 1980.

[3] See A. J. H. Dean, 'Roles of Governments and Institutions in the OECD Countries', in Blackaby, *op. cit.*

work what Keynes had to say about inflation was incidental to his preoccupation with deflation. Nevertheless, his active lifetime included two of the great inflationary periods of modern history, and in the light of what has happened since his death it is useful to trace the relation of his enormously influential writings to what most people would now regard as our main economic problem.

I can do so here only sketchily, by taking four key themes or passages. The first is in the *Treatise*, where he makes the distinction between income- and profit-inflation.[4] This is, of course, tied up with a system of definitions subsequently modified. The former, income inflation, is defined as a rise in the rate of efficiency earnings (with which some concept of normal or equilibrium profits is rather awkwardly included). The latter – profit inflation – accordingly refers to abnormal profits, positive or negative. When one sees these concepts in action in the historical illustrations of Chapter 30,[5] they show a good deal of analytical power. The war period, 1914–18, and the post-war boom, were profit inflations primarily, but the boom, especially, carried an income inflation with it, which continued in the later part of 1920, when profit inflation was dying away. Keynes does not elaborate this instance of possible wage-push inflation, and his examples are otherwise rather short of income-inflation episodes. He passes on to the more immediately interesting profit-deflation of 1921–24, drawing the moral that it was a mistake to use it to reverse an income-inflation, rather than stabilizing at the late-1920 level of prices. There is little clue to what he really thought about wage-determination, but a degree of independence between happenings in the product and labour markets is accepted.

My next stop is the *General Theory*. There, we have a definition of 'true' inflation.[6] It is that in which the whole effect of additional effective demand is in raising the cost-unit; it happens after full employment has been reached, the value of the marginal product of factors having sunk to equality with their supply price. Price may rise before then as effective demand increases, because of falling marginal efficiency of factors and their rising supply-price, but output rises as well. There is, however, two pages earlier, an admission that the wage-unit is likely to increase irregularly as full employment approaches. This is the nearest we come to an anticipation of 'stagflation'.

The invention of the aggregate supply and demand curves is of central

---

[4] J. M. Keynes, *Collected Writings*, Vol. v, p. 140.

[5] *Ibid.*, Vol. vi.

[6] *Ibid.*, Vol. vii, p. 303.

importance for the *General Theory*, but their immediate usefulness for the analysis of inflation is reduced by the decision to measure expenditure in wage-units. The main discussion of the effect of change in the wage-unit in Chapter 19 is concerned with its *decrease* in money terms, and because there is no effect on the aggregate (wage-unit) supply curve, this drops out of the picture, leaving the stage to the aggregate demand curve and its components. It was many years before, at the hands of Patinkin, de Jong, Weintraub and others,[7] aggregate supply was reinserted into discussion of Keynesian theory in a form which allowed supply shifts to have equality of treatment with demand shifts, and the macroeconomics of inflation to be made symmetrical and even then the message did not penetrate as far as it might have done.

Meanwhile, Keynes had tackled the problem of inflation directly and practically in *How to Pay for the War*. That famous discussion is, primarily, in terms of the ex ante inflationary gap in a situation of full employment,[8] and up to a point it is very readily translated into the sort of diagram, with a consumption function and a 45° income line, that did service in teaching the post-war student generations about income equilibrium and the multiplier. We start at full employment, so that increases can be made in nominal income only, but at first we assume complete money-illusion, so that does not affect the analysis. Someone (usually the Government) initiates additional expenditure; increases in factor-incomes and expenditure then take us up a staircase of diminishing steps to the new equilibrium point where the schedule of consumption-plus-government-expenditure cuts the 45° line from above. The next stage is to suppose that the government is free from money illusion and insists on its (real) pound of flesh. This gives the schedule of consumption-plus-government-expenditure a steeper slope, and enlarges the multiplier. Finally, consumers lose their money illusion and can insist on constant real wages. Both the consumption function and the consumption-plus-government-expenditure function then become (from the point of full employment onwards) rays traceable back to the origin, and the steps of the multiplier process expand indefinitely. This is virtually Professor Scitovsky's 'third case' under perfect competition, where labour is the bottleneck, and its scarcity automatically raises money wages. Keynes goes on to modify it by reference to lags in wage-adjustment and to the effects of taxation, especially the heavy taxation of profits which are increased as a share of factor-income by the wage-adjustment lag.

---

[7] See, for instance, D. Patinkin, 'Involuntary Unemployment and the Keynesian Supply Function', *Economic Journal*, September 1949, F. J. de Jong, 'Supply Functions in Keynesian Economics', *ibid.*, March 1954 (and subsequent discussion), and S. Weintraub, 'The Micro-Foundations of Aggregate Demand and Supply', *ibid.*, September, 1957.

[8] J. M. Keynes, *Collected Writings*, Vol. IX, especially pp. 413–22.

The fact that this kind of multiplier analysis has become very familiar should not blind us to the fact that it was once novel. Keynes's comment on his own analysis in *How to Pay for the War* concludes with the wholly convincing statement: 'During the last war I was at the Treasury. But I never at that time heard our financial problem discussed along these lines.' The ex ante inflationary gap calculation with which it starts was, quite explicitly, the basis of British macroeconomic planning, other than manpower planning, from 1941 onwards.

In all this, of course, the main weakness was the absence of any clear theory of money wage formation. Keynes remarks merely that, with a labour shortage, employers will put up less resistance to wage-increases than they would otherwise, and that with a high excess profits tax in operation, 'it will not cost them much to share their profiteering with their employees'. In the British post-war Economic Surveys, which give some account of the macroeconomic planning process for the coming year, the explicit or implicit treatment of the price of labour varies, and, from 1952 onwards, income figures for the coming years are eschewed. It was only in wartime that one could start by assuming that, if there were no ex ante inflationary gap, the price of labour would not rise.

My last reference to Keynes's views is to a single sentence in a letter of 5 June 1945 to S. G. Macfarlane: 'One is also, simply because one knows no solution, inclined to turn a blind eye to the wages problem in a full employment economy.'[9] Although Michal Kalecki turned a rather perceptive eye in that direction, and Lionel Robbins gave a sharp answer to Beveridge's argument for a perpetual labour-shortage,[10] it must be admitted that Keynes was there writing for almost the whole generation of economists and policy-makers who had absorbed the message of the *General Theory*.

That, of course, is why one welcomes Professor Scitovsky's paper as a contribution to discussion on the relevance of Keynes's economics today. In the decade or two after Keynes's death it came to be widely accepted, following Hicks's interpretation, that we are all 'on a labour standard', and we began to believe that the Phillips Curve gave us a key to changes in the money value of labour. It has become apparent that things are more complicated than that. The Phillips Curve proved to be a plaything of expectations and other influences very imperfectly captured, as yet, by econometric wage-equations. The world prices of primary commodities have made rude incursions onto the scene. Formation of prices of manufactures is far from being as well understood as we should like. More

[9] *Ibid.*, Vol. XXVII, p. 385.

[10] L. Robbins, *The Economist in the Twentieth Century*, London, 1954, Chapter II.

deliberate attempts to control the price-level by monetary and fiscal profit-deflation (to use the language of the *Treatise*) have confirmed Keynes's gloomiest accounts of the effects of that process on employment and growth, though great differences have been revealed between the abilities of different national economies to make adjustments that mitigate the pain. At several points in this complex picture, I think the Scitovsky doctrine of asymmetrical market power can assist understanding.

COMMENT

J. Flemming

I am a follower of Scitovsky in three respects: in my undergraduate studies his *Welfare and Competition* held a place in micro-economics close to that of the *General Theory* in macro-economics and I have never regretted the close study of either.

As Scitovsky did his task, I found mine – that of discussing his paper – puzzling; and like him in his puzzlement I shall fall back on a presentation of some of my own work.

The first puzzle is in his claim (p. 223) that 'inflation was not a problem that Keynes gave much thought to'. This is an extraordinary proposition to make of an economist who lived through the inflation of the First World War (from which Britain was by no means immune), was a close observer of the German hyper-inflation, and devoted substantial effort to devising (with considerable success) non-inflationary financing methods for the Second World War.

It is true that the *General Theory* does not provide much evidence of such a concern, and this is a subject to which I shall return, but in his written works as a whole the concern with inflation (and the price level) is a major theme – not obviously dominated by unemployment. There is extensive discussion in both the *Tract on Monetary Reform* and in the central sections of the *Treatise on Money* not to mention *How to Pay for the War*.

My second problem is that I found even less that is relevant to inflation in Scitovsky's paper than in the *General Theory*. A contribution to the discussion of inflation which makes no mention, until the omission is noted in the final paragraph, of either expectations or money, is necessarily very limited and particularly difficult to relate to Keynes who devoted so much attention to both. I am also puzzled by the 'demand side' reference of his title. It is true he does, at one point, consider an increase in Government effective demand but the consequences of this, which is in any case incompletely specified since we are told nothing of its financing, depends entirely on the supply responses subsequently analysed. The greater part of Scitovsky's contribution relates to suppliers' price setting behaviour.

The early part of the argument depends crucially on the unstated assumption that any 'underemployed' factor will be in infinitely elastic supply at given *money* prices (wages, rentals). I can think of no reason why this should, in general, be true. We do not know much about the reasons markets do not clear – but only money-illusion would seem likely to produce Scitovsky's results here.

In the major part of his paper Scitovsky extends to the domestic economy something very like the 'Scandinavian open economy macro-model'. Firms, like Scandinavian countries, are price takers in markets in which they buy (presumably even the labour market) and price setters in the markets in which they sell. This is alleged to produce an inflationary bias relative to a more symmetrical structure. In his *SJPE* article Scitovsky has presented a convincing informational basis for an asymmetry of responses to (perceived, relative) price rises and falls.

Where I have difficulty is in following the inflationary consequences of such asymmetries. Should not the behavioural response relate to movements in nominal price relative to an expected trend?

Why is the effect of such asymmetry classified as inflationary rather than as raising something like Friedman's natural rate of unemployment or lowering Paish's (natural) rate of capacity utilization?

It is not just a matter of choice. If the behavioural response is to price changes relative to expectations, and if the expectations are even weakly rational, the long run effect of changing bargaining structures will *only* be on the natural rates of resource and capacity utilization.

Thus it seems to me that Scitovsky, like the Keynes of the *General Theory*, has addressed the problem of unemployment – albeit structural rather than cyclical – despite the greater relevance of inflation in the 1980s than in the 1930s. An objective function, quadratic and symmetrical in the level of inflation and unemployment, would have assigned negative weight to inflation as prices fell in the early 30s while it would have had much the greater weight, on average, over the last decade. Susan Howson[1] has recorded Keynes's own endorsement in 1920 and 1942 of 'severe doses of dear money' to nip incipient inflationary expectations in the bud at times even of quite high unemployment.

Thus turning back to Keynes I want briefly to address three questions: why is there so little about inflation and the determination of wages in the *General Theory*? How does the undeveloped implicit theory of inflation

---

[1] S. Howson '"A Dear Money Man"; Keynes on Monetary Policy 1920', *EJ*, June 1973.

there (largely in Ch. 21) relate to modern teachings and how does Keynes's prescription for war finance stand up?

I believe that the argument of the *General Theory* is better described as considering the implications of a *parametric* money wage than as being based on a behavioural postulate that labour was in fact perfectly elastically supplied at the going money wage. The advantage of this approach – which is explicit in the work of Barro–Grossman, Malinvaud and others – is that it enables one to conduct arguments about whether, and in what sense, unemployment is due to money wages being 'too high' – or 'too sticky' – without having to discuss the reality of labour market institutions (which would in any case have to change if wages were to be different from what they are).

This method is quite adequate to support the arguments of Chapter 19 that if unemployment is of the kind now called 'Keynesian' anything achievable, in comparative statics, by a lower money wage could be achieved by a larger money supply and that the latter would be both less socially disruptive and would also be less subject to transitional expectational difficulties. As I have argued elsewhere,[2] Keynes's proposition that greater wage flexibility will, for expectational reasons, involve greater volatility of employment, has much to be said for it (even if expectations are rational), especially if the monetary authorities tend to stabilize interest rates – as he generally assumed.

To answer my second question one needs to look at Chapter 21 together with the earlier works on monetary theory and reform. My general impression, based on comparison with the modern literature rather than with Keynes's own reading, is of an electicism I am tempted to call 'monetarist'. Money certainly matters, although velocity is not stable (not only because of interest rate effects but also because of aggregation effects – which may be systematic in certain types of cycle – and also because of innovation). Wages and the price level will tend to be both higher *and* to rise more rapidly at higher *levels* of utilization. Expectations are important. Inflation may occasionally have its policy uses.

Finally, I think that there may be some topical relevance in Keynes's prescription for war-time finance. This relates both to the role of the PSBR and its financing in monetary policy and to fiscal stance generally. The appropriate stance of fiscal policy, as measured by movement of the ratio of national debt to national income, is very sensitive to the appropriate trend movement in that ratio at any time. If Keynes was right that major wars should – at least in part – be debt financed, and if they are likely to recur,

---

[2] 'Wage flexibility and employment stability', mimeo. Published in Spanish in *Información Comercial Española*, 1983.

and if taxes to service debt are such that their deadweight burden rises more than proportionately with revenue, then the trend of the debt/income ratio should be downwards in peace time. How far and how fast it should fall are subjects for more detailed analysis.

I have recently tried to formulate this problem fairly precisely. One issue is the specifications of the distorting tax. I considered two, an income tax and an expenditure tax. The first, by taxing interest, affects intertemporal choice in a way which complicates the problem too much for me. An expenditure tax could be implemented, as is well known, by a tax on either consumption or wages – in a steady state these are equivalent. Their differences in the short run are, however, extreme – it would clearly be perverse to have a temporarily high tax on labour supply in time of war.

In this way one is reduced to a consumption tax. If wars start and finish stochastically (in particular if their occurrence is Poissonian) the tax rate should drift down in peace-time and up in war. More importantly it should jump up on the outbreak of a war and jump down at its end. The effect of the reduction at the end of a war is to raise the purchasing power of savings workers may have made out of wartime earnings – and which are represented by their holdings of the enlarged national debt (and diminished capital stock). This revaluation is very similar to the release of Keynes's post war credits; moreover a consumption tax would be effective even if there were a very good capital market which would undermine post war credits.

All this leads me to conclude that Keynes's discussion of inflation – I have not mentioned his famous essay imputing to Lenin remarks about the subversive efficacy of debauching the currency – is not out-dated; that he did not regard the price level either as arbitrary or inconsequential; and that his war-time remedies might be well worth extending and generalizing to derive prescriptions for public finance in a peace-time economy.

DISCUSSION

Professor Scitovsky opened the discussion in response to the request of the Chairman (Professor Neild) that there be a discussion of what policies should be adopted in the present situation together with a theoretical justification for them. Because the present policies of containing inflation were far too costly in terms of unemployment, bankruptcies, loss of output and loss of growth, an altogether different and more fundamental remedy involving drastic institutional changes was needed. The object of his paper was to facilitate such an approach by analysing the behaviour of people who set prices, who influence prices and the motivation of their behaviour. As he had not got very far in this, his policy suggestions would be very tentative.

If he were correct to believe that the current inflationary process was due to the failure of imperfectly competitive markets to reconcile conflicting claims to income, and to the gradual shift of market power from the buyer's side to the seller's side in one sector after another, certain simple conclusions followed. (It should be noted, though, that it was not only in the labour market, the conflict between labour and capital, that such shifts had occurred, there was also the oil market and there was the end of Bretton Woods as well.) Professor Scitovsky mentioned Professor Meade's proposals and Abba Lerner's idea of keeping the annual increase in value added down to the annual increase in productivity through rationing (this was not unlike the rationing scheme suggested by Kalecki during the Second World War). Professor Scitovsky himself was attracted to another institutional reconciliation, the adoption with slight amendments of the Japanese system of wage payments. In Japan, wages are paid monthly but Japanese wage-earners also receive twice a year bonuses which vary with the size of the profits of the firms concerned. The bonuses are substantial, on average one third of the total annual wage. Professor Scitovsky believed that this scheme had contributed to the very high rate of personal saving in Japan and to the fairly high degree of downward wage flexibility in their system. If it were possible to limit wage bargaining and setting to the determination of bonuses as a percentage of profits before bonus payments and at the same time to keep the monthly wage fixed at a kind of basic wage (which itself could increase with the overall increase of productivity), there would still be a fair amount of leeway for ordinary labour market determination of wages. At the same time, conflicting claims would be much reduced and inflationary pressures in an under-employed economy with them.

Professor Brown began his discussion with a history of the inflationary experience since Keynes died in 1946. The period following the Korean War up to the late 1960s in retrospect looks like a Golden Age. There was very little inflation in the United States or Germany; the United Kingdom slipped a bit, drifted. The slope of the Phillips curve is the operative thing and, in these terms, the United States and Germany had a fairly well behaved Phillips curves with no price expectations term in them. The United Kingdom had a Phillips curve over the trade cycle but not between cycles. In the late 1960s things began to slip more and then came the great commodity price explosion and varying degrees of what could be called fair wage resistance, so that there was an explosion of wages as well. The

Phillips curves all went up to Heaven (except in Germany), then came down again, and since then there have been ups and downs, latterly mostly downs in which unemployment has led prices by a good many lengths. This has made the Keynesian music a good deal more muted than it was.

The clock cannot be turned back because two things have changed. First, primary commodity markets were in the contractionary supply phase of a cobweb (on which was superimposed the oil shock) just when there was an industrial demand expansion which, although big, did not really take the economic systems above the trend line of previous levels of industrial demand. Secondly, there was the explosion of the Phillips curve so that the split between prices and quantities in response to a change in nominal demand changed radically. It used to be one third prices and two thirds quantities up to what Keynes would have recognized as full employment. Now (from the late 1960s) the elasticities of prices in terms of quantities were above 2. Knowledge of this partition is vital for demand management; policy makers needed to be able to rely on it.

Three things are needed now: first, demand management, for exactly the same reason as it was needed in the 1930s and in the 1950s and 1960s. Secondly, an incomes policy is needed because of the perverse behaviour of wages and prices even when there is a lot of excess capacity. Thirdly, there needs to be attention to the supply situation in primary commodities and, in particular, to buffer stock schemes. It will not have escaped the notice of the participants that Keynes gave great attention to two out of three of these, so that, though he is dead, he will not lie down.

Mr. Flemming commented that Professor Scitovsky had called for institutional changes in labour and product markets as a solution to the problem of stafglation. Such reforms might well contribute to long-run health by introducing greater competitiveness and greater flexibility. However, Mr Flemming had difficulty in accepting that persistent inflation is a response to excess claims as he did not see how non-accelerating inflation could reconcile such claims. The benefits of such recommendations must lie either in terms of short-term resource allocations which served to eliminate monopoly profits or, more importantly, in lowering the natural rate of unemployment.

Mr. Fleming would not give such high priority to these sorts of measures now, for a lot of work needs to be done to develop them and the process of change involved might accentuate our acute current problems. The latter could be ameliorated by a better use of more conventional instruments. He had warned several years ago about the dangers of a government committing itself to de-escalating monetary growth as a response to inflation because of the extreme uncertainty of the response of the financial system and labour markets to such a policy. The policy itself requires a degree of precommitment on the part of the authorities and this makes it very difficult for them to respond to the actual unfolding of events. A more superficially cold-hearted approach would be to announce the use of fiscal and monetary policies to keep money demand on some appropriate path and to allow unemployment to rise at a rate of 200,000 per annum if inflation did not respond in an appropriate way. Such an approach would have taken 20 years from when it was suggested to get United Kingdom unemployment to its present level!

Mr. Flemming also suggested that the exchange rate would be a more appropriate intermediate target than monetary aggregates, the behaviour of which had been so puzzling. The basic problem facing the United Kingdom at the moment is how to reduce unemployment without pushing inflation significantly above 5 per cent. He felt there was room for a permanent adjustment of fiscal instruments which would enlarge the deficit now while still leaving it over the cycle at a tolerable level in relation to the trend growth of G.D.P. He would also allow for a devaluation, in order to increase competitiveness, and would offset any effects on the domestic price level by a cut in value added tax. He agreed that cuts in income tax would be more palatable to the present government and that the C.E.P.G. models suggested that they would have a desirable effect on nominal wage demands; however, he was less confident that this was so and so preferred cuts in indirect taxes. He pointed out that such policies involved risks because there were influential operators and opinion makers in financial markets who would not accept the fiscal arguments and could frustrate the policies by actions on the foreign exchange markets. In a situation where public actions are constrained by what private agents believe, and it is concluded that the private agents are wrong, there is no alternative to an intellectual argument to persuade them that they are wrong.

[In the discussion itself reference was made to the paper on an alternative economic strategy in the March 1982 issue of the *Cambridge Journal of Economics* by Professors Hopkin, Miller and Reddaway. Their recommendations coincided with those of Mr. Flemming with one important distinction, that at a time of three million unemployed the three authors argued that there was not much need to worry about the effect of increasing the demand for labour on wage settlements. However, if the proposals were persevered with for a number of years, a better system of pay determination would be needed and this would be provided by a fall in the exchange rate, a reduction in VAT and abolition of the national insurance charge. As Keynes argued in the *Means to Prosperity* it *is* possible to adopt measures whereby everybody becomes better off. The argument that, if the policies were adopted, employers would not stand out against wage increases with the same vehemence was frankly 'rubbish'. In wage negotiations, suppose that on supply and demand grounds employers thought that there ought to be a cut in money wages, of, say, 10 per cent rather than the 5 per cent rise that emerges. If the position is improved so that they think there should be a 5 per cent cut, there does not seem to be any reason why the actual increase should not still be 5 per cent.]

Discussion of Professor Scitovsky's paper:

The discussion opened with an appeal for Mr Flemming to reconsider a little more kindly Professor Scitovsky's basic point that the inflationary process was, over the long haul, primarily an attempt to reconcile irreconcilable claims on income (to which were added from time to time, oil shocks and other imported cost elements). This was followed by an appeal to re-examine Keynes's views on the level of unemployment that practically was associated with full employment, and on money-wage setting. As to the first, the figure of 5 per cent was what Keynes had in mind in 1945. As to the second, his was a theory of relative wages so that if wages were increased at one point in the system, the increase was likely to spread right across the board. Therefore he was very conscious of bottlenecks when analysing what would happen to the general level of wages. For example, in 1937 he was worried that re-armament could bring inflation just because he saw bottlenecks occurring. He did not give much attention to how full employment and wages would interact with one another. Joan Robinson did and there is also an enormous literature from between 1945 and 1950 about their likely interaction, most of it unpublished and in government files.

In the post war period unemployment has increased from about 800,000 to about 4 million – very large movements. When this is analyzed in terms of the natural rate, rarely do people investigate the way in which the labour market is functioning or explain in terms that can be understood why the natural rate should have so changed. The discussant was willing to grant that the natural rate had risen over the last 30 years, perhaps to between 300,000 and 600,000. A criticism was made of the use of the Phillips curve for policy purposes, in that the behaviour of wages over the trade cycle is no more significant than the behaviour of the price of pig iron. Of course, the answer to the question, if 4 million unemployed are created will this have an effect on wages, must be that it will. But the question should not be put in those terms, rather it should be: what happens to wages when much smaller changes in unemployment take place? The Phillips curve is of no help whatever in arriving at the answer. There is no such thing as a theory of nominal wages. In United Kingdom models, wage behaviour is introduced by judgement after the event, as it were. It is extremely difficult to forecast the relationship between changes in demand and changes in money wages over the ranges of variation that are experienced in practice. It was added that a theory of nominal wages is nevertheless needed, particularly in relation to the question of inflation and so the rather imprecise and experimental directions that Professor Scitovsky had opened up were well worth exploring. It is true that they and their policy implications were largely matters of the long run, but it was emphasized that in the long run too lots of people would be alive.

It was thought that the most interesting part of Professor Scitovsky's paper was that he believed that the United States and the United Kingdom had similar problems despite very different trade union organization, because of the modern situation of employer and employee relationships, which implied that wage increases bore little relationship to the unemployment situation in individual industries and in the economy as a whole. Keynesianism had fallen into disrepute because it had not provided a solution to wage cost inflation. While monetary and fiscal policies are necessary there are additional policies which should be explored. It would be helpful to start with countries such as Japan and Austria which faced worse situations than the United Kingdom but which yet managed to avoid the twin evils of inflation and unemployment. The institutions of their labour markets and their political institutions were undoubtedly relevant factors; while it may not be possible to imitate them, it should be possible to draw lessons from them.

The discussion then turned to the role of trade unions in the inflationary process, a discussion that was prefaced by the judgment that inflation was the most serious macro-economic problem. (This provoked a later response of shock, and the comment that the main thing to do was to design institutions which allow inflation to be lived with, as the costs of inflation were relatively trivial.) Trade unions leaders are in business to get rises in money wages and if they do not succeed in doing so the present leaders will be replaced by those who will. It follows that incomes policies which rely on voluntary restraint go against the grain of this institution. It was also pointed out that companies were subject to legislation against monopoly. Yet trade unions had greater monopolistic power than companies. For unions can cause greater social disruption by, for example, stopping the supply of a commodity or a service for weeks or months, which no company would ever dare to do. The powers that trade unions are allowed have built-in inflation in several countries and it is important to think carefully about the implications of their monopoly position.

The distinction was made between the international distribution of income and domestic distributions. Buffer stock schemes were directed to an international division which would neither drive too many producers out of industries nor lead to an unsupportable build-up of stocks. The reason why Keynes was not prepared to leave it to private speculators to do this was that their horizons were too short; what was needed was an intelligent meritocracy which could make decisions with a longer run horizon in view. Such an approach is more difficult now with the advent of multi-national corporations. At the domestic level the purpose of TIP (tax incomes policy) schemes was to iron out incompatibilities while leaving it to the private sector to decide price movements. Keynesianism was destroyed by its own success for it taught people that they did not have to be unemployed in order to be kept in their place – yet democracy and Keynesianism are incompatible unless there are some rules about income distribution.

The discussion next turned to the impact of tax changes, for example, in value added tax, on aggregate supply in Keynes's model. It was pointed out that while a rise in such taxes may tend to reduce aggregate demand, it simultaneously had a similar effect on aggregate supply so that the outcome could well be a rise in unemployment and the price level. The supply aspects of demand management should not be neglected.

Attention was drawn to a population change which was relevant to the changing attitudes and expectations of people on both sides of the wage bargain. It related to people's expectations about price changes as a result of the environment in which they have lived. Twenty years ago, a much larger proportion of people would have lived through periods of price stability or even declining prices than have done so now, when inflation is the norm and price stability is a deviation from trend. This ought to have some influence on the settled point around which wages and other compensations are bargained.

A defence of the Phillips curve as a very useful way of organizing thought about macroeconomic policy was advanced by a participant who learnt macro-economics from Phillips. As a stable trade off relationship it was dead and buried but with price expectations and incomes policies or institutional changes in the labour market included, it was still very much alive. Three hypotheses are embedded in the Phillips curve. First, wage rates are pre-determined at a point in time, they are not determined by a market clearing mechanism, and they change at a relatively gradual rate over time as compared to changes in other variables. Secondly, causation runs from the level of unemployment to the rate of change of nominal wages. Thirdly, wage changes lead causally to price changes. The Phillips curve, so interpreted, leads immediately to the implication that in the short run changes in fiscal and monetary policy will lead to changes in real demand and output which may have to be paid for in terms of increased inflation in the long run.

It was pointed out that there is a need always to distinguish between discrete changes in the price level and rates of change of the price level itself, a distinction which it would have been useful to have made explicit in interpreting Professor Scitovsky's paper. A dichotomy in the Cambridge, England, diagnosis was advanced in that increases in money have virtually nothing to do with inflation while decreases have everything to do with disinflation and unemployment. Together, they led to the policy proposition, 'expand forever and do not worry', which may explain why younger economists do not find this paradigm very interesting.

Professor Scitovsky replied to the comments as follows:

In answering Mr Flemming on non-accelerating inflation, Professor Scitovsky said that inflation is a symptom of incompatible claims being reconciled; if they are not reconciled inflation is quite likely to accelerate. He was glad that the possible irrelevance of trade unions to the inflationary experience of different countries had been mentioned. He was also glad that Austria was mentioned. Austria was a small country; a very special case, where the governor of the central bank, the secretary of the general committee of the trade unions and the head of the federation of Austrian industries had all been in the same concentration camp. They have met once a week for dinner ever since and are able amicably to agree on policy! Finally he had not stressed expectations in his paper because they have received a lot of attention and he wanted to emphasize points which had been receiving much less attention.

Impressions of Maynard Keynes

SIR AUSTIN ROBINSON

Mr. Provost, Mr. Vice-Chancellor, My Lords, Ladies and Gentlemen:

We are met here tonight to do honour to the memory of John Maynard Keynes – son of Cambridge; through all his adult life member of this College; citizen of Britain and of the world.

Son of Cambridge he was in much more than an ordinary sense. Born in Cambridge, his father himself a distinguished philosopher and economist who was later to become Registrary of the University; his mother one of the early students of Newnham, a woman of outstanding ability who was later to become Mayor of Cambridge, Keynes throughout his life had a Cambridge home. In 1943 the City did him the honour of making him High Steward of the Borough of Cambridge.

I shall not attempt to do more than remind others from outside Cambridge of what Maynard Keynes contributed to King's during his forty-four years of membership and his thirty-seven years as a fellow. King's, its welfare, its finances, its buildings, its scholarship, were always at the centre of his pre-occupations. And first as Bursar and later through his bequests he helped to give the College the resources to match its greatness.

Nor shall I attempt (I am not qualified to do it) to describe his contribution to the arts – his share in the creation of the Arts Council, his work for the theatre, for the ballet, for the encouragement of modern painting and in countless other ways. But this cannot be forgotten in any complete picture of Maynard Keynes as he was as a whole and with all his many facets.

My main task tonight is to remind you of his claims to greatness as an economist. Why do I claim greatness for him?

The answer must be that at long intervals there is some outstanding contributor to economics whose work marks a turning point in the subject. He asks a new question and seeks to answer it. After him economics is never

255

the same as it was before. He may not answer the question for all time. But economics is different because of him.

If I confine myself to British economists, I would claim that Adam Smith, Robert Malthus, David Ricardo, Alfred Marshall were turning points in that sense. And without hesitation I would say that Keynes represented another such turning point. The economics of today is not the economics on which I was brought up in 1920.

What right have I to claim special greatness for Keynes?

I think my answer must be this. Economists divide into two very different kinds. The first kind are anxious to put the world right; their interest in economics is as a tool for putting the world right. The second kind are anxious themselves to be right in a minority of one; they are content that any contribution they may make to putting the world right shall be indirect, shall be a contribution through others.

There is no question to which group Maynard Keynes belonged. He was (I wish there was a better name) a do-gooder – a man of action, whose thinking was always a first step towards action. But unlike most of us who are do-gooders, his thinking was never woolly, never slip-shod, never lazily orthodox.

I claim for Keynes a predominance in the economic revolution of the 1930s even despite the powerful claims of the great Scandinavians and the brilliant Poles because, having contributed very largely to it, it was he who broadcast it; it was he who gave it effect. And it is he who nearly fifty years later is still discussed and quoted daily not only in the journals but also in the popular press.

But listening to the discussion at the conference as one who knew him in his lifetime not only as the author of the *General Theory* but as a working economist tackling one problem after another, I cannot help feeling that many of those of the present generation who know him only as the author of a single book are getting him wrong; are failing to understand the sort of person he was and the sort of economist he was.

He was, as I have said, essentially an applied economist, a man of action, seeking the best possible solution of a practical applied economic problem. I have felt that he was being appraised by a group largely composed of theoretical academic economists as if he were a theoretical academic economist.

But that is not Keynes, or not the complete Keynes. I can remember no occasion on which he tackled a theoretical problem which did not have an immediate practical application. He was always concerned with a practical problem.

Faced by such a problem, he tackled it ordinarily in three stages.

First, he analysed the problem in all its aspects more searchingly, more radically than any of the rest of us.

Second, he set out to discover what factors in the situation had created the problem and what factors needed to be changed if a satisfactory solution was to be achieved. Sometimes these factors were institutional; sometimes they were a matter of how a particular institution was being operated in practice; sometimes they were a matter of political policy; sometimes they were a matter of public opinion.

Third, and most important, he went ahead to change some institutional setting, to change the traditions of operating some sacrosanct institution, to change the political policies, to change public opinion, or where necessary to secure the creation of some new institution. He never accepted the inevitability of some obstacle, the sanctity of some institution with long traditions, the impregnability of powerful political figures, the impossibility of changing some dominant public opinion. He was an eternal optimist in the sense that he was never defeatist and never gave up fighting for something that he regarded as necessary.

One can see this three-fold process at work as he tackles the problems of a defeated enemy being made to pay reparations. One can see it as he tackles the problems of the desire of the Bank of England and the Treasury to restore the pre-war parity of exchange. One can see it as he tackles the Treasury view of the inevitability of unemployment. One can see it as he tackles the problems of how to pay for the war.

The book by which he is now almost exclusively known – the so-called *General Theory* – is not to be thought of as designed to be primarily the academic text-book that it has become. It is in effect the thinking-through process regarding employment and unemployment, attempting to clarify the policy and institutional changes regarding such things as investment control, interest rates and monetary policy that were necessary.

I do not think he ever intended it to be a bible for all time or to solve all the possible long-term problems for all time. And since he was always aware of the uncertainty of economic processes channelled through human agencies, I do not believe that he was seeking greater precision than imprecise instruments might justify.

The failure of economic policy during the past few years, I would argue, is not a failure of Keynesian economics but a failure of our generation to analyse clearly the essential preconditions of reconciling a high level of employment with avoidance of inflation, to identify the institutional changes necessary to achieve this, and then to establish first a consensus and then action regarding the making of the institutional changes. We have lacked the leadership and the determination that Keynes could have given us. The uniqueness of Keynes lay in the fact that he was three persons in one. He was a very great applied economist with extreme sensitivity as to how institutions and markets worked. He was a very great, and extremely original and innovative theoretical economist. He was an economist statesman with remarkable gifts of leadership and persuasion. His special greatness lay in the combination of the three.

Where Keynes was, I am convinced, head and shoulders above all but a very few of the economists of our generation was in the much wider range of his knowledge and perceptions. Like most of his generation and my own he had been trained as a general economist, with the whole field of economics as his concern; and he remained through life a general economist, seeing any problem not in isolation but as one element in the whole system and needing to be integrated into the rest of the system.

He never, I think, was guilty of that all too common fault of over-specialized economists of today – failing to see how a proposed solution of a limited problem will react on other elements in the economy.

Equally important, whenever he tackled a practical problem he made himself familiar with the institutions that were involved. He was interested in markets, in how they worked, in the expectations of those operating in them. He was always aware that economic changes are channelled through human agencies in a world of uncertainty, with moods of confidence and lack of confidence, of optimism and pessimism. In many cases he understood these markets because he had operated in them. He had little use, as had Marshall before him, for a mechanistic mathematical economics which could only operate in a predictable world without uncertainty.

But having got his own thinking straight Keynes was anxious to go further and establish, if it were possible, a consensus of thinking among responsible economists. He used to this end his editorship of the *Economic Journal*. To a remarkable extent he dictated the content of economic discussion at any time; he focused it on the issues that seemed to him at the moment to be important and tried to hammer out agreements. We all know the familiar gibe about economists and opinions. But in the 1930s, despite the contemporary advances in economics, there was more nearly a consensus among leading economists than there is today when, with the present multitude of economists engaged in imperfect competition through product differentiation, there is so little agreement even about fundamentals.

For Keynes some measure of academic consensus was a necessary first step towards action. And action required persuasion. And since he wanted action, he wrote not in the esoteric languages of economic jargon or of mathematics for a few colleagues but in the language of those whose comprehension and support were necessary to the achievement of action –

the politicians, the bankers, the civil servants, the financial journalists, the reading public.

And it was because he was one of the great writers of a lucid, pungent English, one of the great creators of the memorable phrase that once read one can never forget, that he was so very much more than just a very original and very radical thinker.

As a creative applied economist he began work with a blank sheet of paper and with his own educated equipment of economics. He did not, as so many attempt to do, spend a long period thumbing through all previous writings on a similar subject. At that time they were in any case not so voluminous as they are today. He became interested in his predecessors only when he had completed his own thinking.

The other thing that must be remembered is that Keynes thought and wrote before the beginnings of private property in ideas, before the enclosure movement that requires any young and ambitious economist to find some rather obvious idea which has not yet been appropriated, label it by his name and extract a toll of bibliographical reference from any unwary trespasser. Keynes was remarkably unconscious of the sources of ideas. We who worked around him were, in our innocence, more interested in truth than in ownership. It was enough for us if, after we had argued with him, the next time we came back to the subject, he retailed to us our own earlier arguments.

We, on the other hand, who were his young colleagues never quite knew which of our ideas were our own and which we had derived from him. He was immensely inspiring, immensely fertile. We often picked up a hint from him and then developed and embroidered it. The present attempts to identify who contributed what to the *General Theory* betray, to my mind, a singular inability to understand the collective thinking of a tightly-knit group led by a dominant creative personality.

His initial thinking was often in some measure intuitive. He saw how some process operated before he could demonstrate it logically. He was, I think, introspective regarding his own thought-processes when he wrote of Alfred Marshall's belief 'that those individuals who are endowed with a special genius for the subject and have a powerful economic intuition will often be more right in their conclusions and implicit presumptions than in their explanations and explicit statements'.

He believed in the progress of economics. He believed in the collaboration of many minds. He would never have assumed that he was writing a book which said the final word. He would have welcomed criticisms and advances. But that does not mean that he would have accepted them uncritically.

Down to the 1930s, Keynes was an orthodox Marshallian, embroidering but never departing from the teachings of his master. It was when he began, in company with Dennis Robertson, to work on price theory that he began to break out and develop the ways of thinking that we now associate with his name. But even then breaking with Marshall was a painful and traumatic experience both for him and for others.

This is no occasion on which to analyse Keynes's great contribution to economics in the form which in these days is principally identified with his name. But let one who has the advantage of having first learned his economics in the 1920s just say this. Our economics was exclusively micro-economics; almost exclusively long-term with Marshall's short-term quasi-rents thrown in. There was complete schizophrenia between value theory and monetary theory; I listened to value theory one hour and bicycled across Cambridge to listen to a wholly unrelated monetary theory the next hour. I moved on to lectures on public finance that were equally unrelated to the other two. There was no macro-economics. There was no employment theory. There was no growth theory. There was no real economic dynamics. We lived in a world that fluctuated, which we believed to be uncontrollable but somehow self-righting.

The change today is not, of course, wholly the work of Keynes. It would be ridiculous to suggest it. But much of it has flowed from the work of those that have learned from him and from the application of methods of thinking that he initiated. If Keynes had never done anything else but write the *General Theory* we should be celebrating his centenary today.

But it is in his second capacity as the man of action that I want at least equally to be claiming greatness for him. He came first on to the world stage when he made the world think of the implications of making a defeated enemy pay for a war. He made us think about the practical problems of reconstruction. He taught us to realize the implications of unrealistic exchange rates. He was eternally fertile in ingenious Keynes schemes for all the many crises of the 1930s. People have said that he was inconsistent. He adapted his ideas to changing circumstances, it is true. But he stuck firmly to certain principles, and if he were with us today I am sure he would still be sticking to them. He hated using unemployment as a weapon of policy; he hated the export of its problems of adjustment by one country to another.

Of all the monuments to Keynes as a man of action, I think that three are outstanding. In each case others greatly contributed. But in each case the others recognized Keynes's predominant part. And in each case the principles I have mentioned received embodiment.

First, he created for this country a new means of shaping the budget and gave a new meaning to fiscal policy which over the next thirty years gave Britain the highest rate of growth in its history.

Second, his contribution to Bretton Woods and all that went before it gave the world for the first time, in the Fund, and the Bank, continuing instruments for international discussion and for the framing of a world policy of mutual help and consultation.

Third, there grew out of his work in the 1930s and his thinking about 'How to Pay for the War' those two essential instruments of British economic policy making, the Central Statistical Office and the Economic Section of the Treasury.

But having said all this I feel that I am leaving out the real Keynes, the Keynes we worshipped and admired.

Great man as he was, he never played the great man. He was never pompous. Eternally young, he was always encouraging the young. Always bubbling with talk, infectious, exciting, it was always fun to be in his company.

And yet in the big things he was caring. He was prepared to kill himself, as in the end he did, to achieve the things that mattered.

I ask you to rise and drink with me to the enduring memory of John Maynard Keynes.

RICHARD BRAITHWAITE

I have been asked to speak tonight because I am the only Fellow of King's College now alive who enjoyed Maynard Keynes's friendship for the last 26 years of his life, during 22 of which I was also his colleague in our egalitarianly democratic Society of Fellows.

But I have no talent for describing people, and you will expect me to say something that has not been said before. So what I will do is to tell you an anecdote about Keynes's practice as Bursar of the College which for me is paradigmatic of the uniqueness of his personality in his dealings with his colleagues in the College.

Up to recently Fellows received part of their annual stipend in the form of a 'Fellowship dividend' which was limited by law to a maximum of £300, a figure at which it remained until this form of remuneration was abolished some 15 years ago. Before that we Fellows, like the equity shareholders in a public company, had to meet annually to declare the dividend for the year. At this meeting held on the last Tuesday in November each year we Fellows had had before us for a few days printed copies of the College's accounts for the past financial year, of the professional accountant's certificate after auditing the accounts and of what most Fellows concentrated their attention upon – a quite elaborate report on the College finances composed by three Fellows appointed each year to be 'Inspectors of Accounts'. (Their function corresponded approximately to that of the Public Accounts Committee of the House of Commons: they made recommendations for the future as well as comments upon the past.) These papers were all before us (some 40 of us in Keynes' time) at the November meeting at which, as First Bursar, he rose formally to propose the amount of the dividend and informally to make what we all called his 'Budget speech'.

This was as considered a performance as Lydia's can-can in the *Boutique*. Maynard started by congratulating the Inspectors of Accounts for doing a reasonably good job, allowing for their being amateurs in accountancy and economics, as they frequently were. He then amiably corrected their misunderstandings of the College accounts and the prognoses based upon these misunderstandings. He proceeded to give his own views both as to the past and to the future. My memory is that, however gloomy the accounts were and the prospects seemed to be, there was always something that could be done about the matter: we need not merely drift with the current financial tides. To give an example to make you smile, we could improve the quality of the sheep on the farms the College owned in Lincolnshire by correcting a deficiency of cadmium in their diet.

But of course the College's financial prospects were intimately linked with national and international policy; and Keynes's speech passed easily from domestic to public affairs. I was elected a Fellow in time to hear him denounce Churchill's returning Britain to the gold standard in language too intemperate to publish in his famous tract. Speaking of Britain's economics led naturally to remarks about world economics, including, so far as I can remember, offering advice to the Federal Reserve Board. And, after every sphere of economic activity from the College's upwards had been brought into his purview, there was an unexpected conclusion. Money and economic matters were ultimately of no importance whatever, as compared with the things of the spirit – the arts and sciences, philosophy, religion – and we ought not to waste much time thinking about them.

These annual 'Budget' performances exemplify what I take to be the essence of Keynes's contribution to the intellectual life of the College – that *theoria* and *praxis* had to be pursued together. And moreover that thinking about them was fun: seriousness of the subject did not require solemnity, still less pomposity, of expression. Keynes loved jokes. Not only did he frequently tease his friends, but he enjoyed being teased himself. I was one of the College Inspectors of Accounts in 1936, just after the publication of the *General Theory*; and I complained that the criterion used in the College accounts for discriminating income from capital-reduction in the receipts from a stone quarry which the College owned did not accord with the definition of Income given in his book. Maynard took my obvious tease poker-faced, and explained to the Inspectors at some length why this definition could not properly be used in the College's quarrying case.

To use journalistic epithets Keynes was, to the Fellows of the College, a *life-enhancer*: his presence among us improved the quality of life. Preparing this speech has compelled me to try to say something of the nature of this enhancement. Here I can only speak for myself. What I absorbed was that good theory and right practice were Siamese twins: neither could live without the other. And that thinking seriously was not *grau* (as Goethe's Mephistopheles pictured it in contrast with the *grün des Lebens goldner Baum*) but was an essential feature, for many of us, of the goldenness of the tree of life. Learning these things from Maynard Keynes was in itself the greatest fun.

JAMES MEADE

Maynard Keynes is without question to be numbered among the really great economists of all time, but he had in addition an extraordinary range of other interests and activities in which he excelled: his connection with this great College; his outstanding work as a public servant in particular during the two Great Wars of this century; his activities on the Stock Exchange not only on his own behalf but, to name only two other parties, on behalf of this College and of an Insurance Company; his patronage of the Arts, Theatre, Ballet, and Painting; his collecting of books; his notable group of close friends; and his full family life crowned by his marriage with Lydia. All these aspects of his life are represented here tonight.

I can claim only to be one of his devoted economic admirers. But I shall not attempt to repeat Austin Robinson's eloquent tribute to Keynes's work as an economist. I shall speak as a representative of that group of men and women of the inter-war years who fell under the influence of Keynes because we thought that the mass unemployment of those years was both stupid and wicked and because we found in Keynes someone who inspired us with a hopeful answer to that problem. I said that we fell under the influence of Keynes; it would be more accurate to say that we fell under the magic spell of Keynes, and I personally am still under that spell 53 years after it was cast upon me and 37 years after the death of the magician. I am going to try to describe what it was like to become spellbound in this way.

In the summer of 1930 I had just been elected to a Fellowship at an Oxford college but was told to go away for a year to learn my subject before I started to teach it. I had the greatest good fortune of being taken into Trinity College here in Cambridge by Dennis Robertson to whose teaching during that year I owe a deep debt of gratitude. At an early stage he told me that there was a young man in King's called Richard Kahn whom I should get to know.

Keynes's *Treatise on Money* had just been published. A small informal group was set up consisting of Richard Kahn, Joan and Austin Robinson,

Piero Sraffa, Charles Gifford, and myself; we met regularly, discussed the *Treatise*, and suggested what we thought would be better ways of tackling the problem; Richard Kahn then took our ideas to Keynes, developed them in discussion with Keynes, and then reported back to us at our next meeting. I think that these activities can be described as the first steps towards the translation of the *Treatise on Money* into the *General Theory*. In all this Richard Kahn played the central role; indeed, it is difficult to say how much of the *General Theory* is due to him. A book by him on *The Making of Keynes's General Theory* is about to be published, in which I suspect that he will underplay his own part.

At that time Keynes worked in London during the week and came to Cambridge for a long week-end. Our group met during the week and our contact with Keynes was through Richard Kahn acting as messenger at the week-end. At a later date, in 1934 I think, my wife and I were staying for the week-end with Austin and Joan Robinson; regularly during our visit people came in and explained that they had just seen Keynes, who had expressed such-and-such an opinion. My wife described Keynes as having played that week-end the role of God in a Miracle Play: he dominated the scene without ever appearing on the stage.

But one did in fact from time to time come into direct contact with God. During my year in Cambridge in 1930–31 Keynes entertained me here at this High Table and took me to Sunday lunch with his parents in Harvey Road. Above all there was his Monday Club which met in his rooms in King's, surrounded by the Duncan Grant nudes on the panels of the walls, and with Maynard Keynes himself lounging in the leisured pose depicted so accurately by Low as if he had nothing else to occupy his mind, intervening in the discussion and summing up at the end with a wit and clever insight that was unmatchable; and I can still hear the unmistakable melodious voice with which he did it.

I came near Keynes again during the Second World War when I was a member of the Economic Section of the Cabinet Secretariat. Keynes became an adviser in the Treasury in the autumn of 1940 until his death in the spring of 1946. His position was unique; he was neither a civil servant nor a minister; he was merely a member of the Chancellor's advisory council (which I believe never met) with a room at his disposal in the Treasury, into which he imported his own secretary, Mrs Stephens, his own typewriter, and his own typing paper. But whatever his formal status, he came once more to dominate the scene; he felt free to interest himself in any economic or financial affair of state; and powerful senior civil servants were seen to blench when they came into their office and saw lying on the top of their in-tray one of the unmistakable minutes typed with Keynes's typewriter by Mrs Stephens on their own brand of paper.

He dealt with War Finance and the Budget, continually fed by Dick Stone with the relevant national income – national expenditure figures. He spent a very great deal of his energy, as he did in the First World War, on the problems of overseas war finance. He was much concerned with plans for post-war reconstruction, both the domestic full employment and also, even more particularly, with post-war international financial institutions, culminating in Bretton Woods and the Anglo-American Loan Agreement.

His wit and the magic of his personality remained unchanged. In one report to the Cabinet he wrote about one prominent United States personality that 'Mr *X* kept his ear so close to the ground that he was unable to hear what an upright man said to him.' I was on an inter-departmental committee with him, set up at an early stage to consider post-war reparations. Keynes, with the reputation of *The Economic Consequences of the Peace* behind him was, of course, in a special position. He waited in silence while the committee went through all the restrictions that were to be imposed on Germany after the war, deciding to add to complete disarmament the requirement that Germany should impose no tariffs on imports; upon which he quietly interjected: 'But surely you are not going to impose on Germany the benefits of Free Trade as well as of Disarmament.'

I was present at one session in Washington in 1943 of negotiation between Harry White and Keynes on what became in the end the International Monetary Fund. Keynes hated to be presented at the early stage of negotiation with a detailed legalistic draft. Such a draft was put before him by the American delegation; he started to read it, but soon looked up and enquired innocently: 'Is there any one present who can translate from Cherokee?' On a subsequent occasion, on presenting a draft to Keynes, Harry White asked: 'And will *that* satisfy Your Highness?' These were not perhaps the normal terms in which formal negotiations were conducted between two countries on a question of the first importance. But when Keynes was taking part, things were different; and everyone, on both sides of the table, had to accept such interventions as part of the fun of the game – and most of us, but perhaps not quite all, were prepared to do so.

As I have said, one was spellbound by this great man and one's admiration became something very near to idolatry. Why was it? I think, looking back, that in my own case there were three reasons.

First, there was the magic of his personality, the versatility of his mind, his wit, his command of the English language, and his extreme cleverness. I shall say no more about all that.

Second, there was his pragmatic wisdom and statesmanship – something quite different from cleverness. Behind the fireworks of his display, he was in fact always seeking a workable solution to a problem. Quite apart from difficulties due to political commitments – and Keynes was fully aware of these – there are in fact in human affairs almost always two sides to every question – in particular much to be said for and much to be said against any particular governmental intervention. The normal wise economist for this reason becomes the dull two-armed economist with his 'On the one hand this . . .' and 'On the other hand that.' But Keynes could never be dull. He coped with this problem by becoming a two-day economist and asserting On the One Day This and On the Next Day That. This tendency to change his mind so readily was often counted against him and could certainly be disconcerting. But it was his way of considering both sides of a question and it was the preparation for finding in the end a sensible, pragmatic, workable compromise solution.

In addition to his cleverness and his pragmatic wisdom there was a third feature in his make-up which on looking back I think was the decisive factor in binding me so closely to him. Austin Robinson has already expressed it by calling Keynes a Do-Gooder, the exact expression which I had planned myself to use. He had, beneath the wit, charm, magic of personality, and cleverness, a passionate desire to devise a better domestic and international society. Indeed he can be said to have killed himself by his untiring work in this cause which he continued unabated in spite of the weak state of his heart. I was dazzled by his wit and cleverness; I was persuaded by his wise statesmanship; but I was finally bowled over by the unsparing devotion and the unceasing and determined activity to build a better world on the part of a great man who knew how to set about it. He was not merely a very great man; he was a very good man also.

INDEX